HUMAN RESOURCE MANAGEMENT IN HOSPITALITY AND TOURISM

HUMAN RESOURCE MANAGEMENT IN HOSPITALITY AND TOURISM

M. C. METTI

ANMOL PUBLICATIONS PVT. LTD.
NEW DELHI - 110 002 (INDIA)

ANMOL PUBLICATIONS PVT. LTD.

H.O.: 4374/4B, Ansari Road, Darya Ganj,
New Delhi-110 002 (India)
Ph.: 23278000, 23261597

B.O.: No. 1015, Ist Main Road, BSK IIIrd Stage
IIIrd Phase, IIIrd Block
Bangalore - 560 085 (India)
Visit us at: www.anmolpublications.com

Human Resource Management in Hospitality and Tourism

ISBN 978-81-261-3233-1

PRINTED IN INDIA

Printed at Mehra Offset Press, Delhi.

Contents

Preface

In today's world of quality-driven, highly competitive organizations, in order to succeed and successfully grow, hospitality organizations need to refocus traditional approaches to "managing people." This refocus is necessitated by what has been referred to as the "paradigm shift" of hospitality human resources management. This paradigm shift is driven forward by forces outside of the hospitality industry, which include new designs for flatter organizations, teamwork, more information sharing, and the concept of empowerment, new training and induction models, and the changed general expectations of employees. However, and most important, it is driven by the concepts of "king customer."

When measured against the valid needs of the entire hospitality industry, success is determined by the employees. Regardless of how well a system of quality improvement, or production, or whatever checks and balances are in place to ensure compliance to rules, policies, or business and service philosophies, it is the responsiveness of the staff—interpreting the rules, serving guests, and producing high-quality product and service—that determines each organization's success.

An outstanding feature of this book is that it is very flexible; educators can pick and choose cases they would like to discuss. Students have an opportunity (if given by the instructor) to peruse the cases and select the ones they feel would be most beneficial to them. Another feature is case studies within the global arena that give students an opportunity to recognize the cultural differences in various countries and how working with individuals in a global setting brings many challenges.

The cases vary in length as well as in the depth of discussion required by students. Depending on course objectives, these cases can be used with students at various educational levels and within courses related to human resources, management, and strategic management or as part of a comprehensive course that relates the functional areas of the industry. The cases lend themselves for use within the industry by managers and human resources personnel.

Author

Chapter 1

Introduction

BASIC HUMAN RESOURCE PLANNING

The objectives of managements, the ways in which enterprises are managed to achieve these objectives and the human resource management (hereinafter referred to as "HRM") and hotel industrial relations (hereinafter referred to as "HIR") initiatives in this regard, are affected by pressures, many of which are exerted by globalization. Changes in HIR practices (rather than in institutions and systems) such as increased collective bargaining at enterprise level, flexibility in relation to forms of employment as well as in relation to working time and job functions have occurred as a result of such factors as heightened competition, rapid changes in products and processes and the increasing importance of skills, quality and productivity.

These factors have also had an impact on HRM policies and practices. In managing change, the key elements include employee involvement in effecting change, greater customer orientation, and ensuring that the skills of employees are appropriate to the production of goods and the provision of services acceptable to the global market. As such, managing people in a way so as to motivate them to be productive is one important objective of HRM. The implications and consequences of globalization include the following:

1. Countries are more economically interdependent than before, particularly in view of foreign direct

investment interlocking economies, as well as increased free trade. The inability of economies to be 'self-sufficient' or 'self-reliant' or 'self-contained' has been accompanied by a breakdown of investment and trade barriers.

2. Governments are increasingly less able to control the flow of capital, information and technology across borders.
3. There has been de-regulation of financial and other markets, and the integration of markets for goods, services and capital such as the European Community.
4. It has led to the de-nationalization of enterprises and the creation of global companies and global webs.
5. Production of goods and services acceptable to the global market, and the convergence, to a great extent, of customer tastes across borders determined by quality.
6. The need to achieve competitiveness and to remain competitive in respect of attracting investment, goods and services. This means, inter alia, the necessity for high quality skills at all levels to attract high value-added activities, as distinct from cheap labour low value-added ones, and improvements in productivity.

Hotel Enterprises driven by market pressures need to include in their goals improved quality and productivity, greater flexibility, continuous innovation, and the ability to change to respond rapidly to market needs and demands. Effective HRM is vital for the attainment of these goals. Improved quality and productivity linked to motivation can be achieved through training, employee involvement and extrinsic and intrinsic rewards.

The growing interest in pay systems geared to performance and skills reflects one aspect of the increasing significance of HRM in realizing management goals and a gradual shift from collectivism to the individualization of pay. In such pay systems a critical attraction is the possibility of achieving these goals without increasing labour costs but at the same time increasing earnings. Realizing management goals and managing change need employee involvement, commitment and training, employee participation, cooperation and team-work - all important HRM initiatives and activities.

The dominant position towards which HRM is moving points to a "change in power relations and highlights the supremacy of management. The management prerogative is rediscovered but in place of command and control the emphasis is on commitment and control as quality, flexibility and competence replace quantity, task and dumb obedience. To put it another way: the managerial agenda is increasingly focused on innovation, quality and cost reduction. Human resource management makes more demands on employees, work is intensified there is less room for managerial slack and for indulgency patterns."

From a purely HRM perspective, one writer has identified the following six factors as accounting for the increasing interest in and resort to HRM practices:

a. Improving the management of people or utilizing human resources better as a means of achieving competitive advantage.

b. The numerous examples of excellence in HRM have created an interest in such models.

c. The traditional role of personnel managers has failed to exploit the potential benefits of effective management of people; neither did personnel management form a central part of management activity.

d. In some countries the decline of trade union influence has opened the way for managements to focus on more individual issues rather than on collectivist ones.

e. The emergence of better educated workforces with higher individual expectations, changes in technology and the need for more flexible jobs have, in turn, created the need to incorporate HRM into central management policy.

f. Many important aspects of HRM such as commitment and motivation emanate from the area of organizational behaviour, and place emphasis on management strategy. This has provided an opportunity to link HRM with organizational behaviour and management strategy.

When identifying some of the trends in HRM and when subsequently analysing how they could contribute to achieving management objectives, it is necessary to voice a note of caution. The fact that one elaborates on an ideal model of HRM does not mean that such models have been widely adopted in the real corporate world. As Thomas A Kochan and Lee Dyer point out, "even today we find that the human resource function within many American corporations remains weak and relatively low in influence relative to other managerial functions such as finance, marketing, and manufacturing despite the outpouring of academic writing on 'strategic human resource management' little progress has been made in developing systematic theory or empirical evidence on the conditions under which human resources are elevated to a position where the firm sees and treats these issues as a source of competitive advantage."

The 'best practice' models are really the exceptions, but their value is that they, in a sense, prove the rule, so to speak. Absence of widespread practice is no argument against such a model, but is rather a reason to advocate it, in the same way that the absence of a harmonious HIR system in a given situation or country is no argument against advocating it.

However, it is possible that the various pressures on enterprises in the 1990s will result in increased resort to effective HRM policies and practices. In the ultimate analysis, HRM and HIR are about how people are treated, and their relevance increases where an enterprise takes a long-term view, rather than a short-term one, of what it wants to achieve.

Two writers, after examining some of the successful hotels observe that "there are a series of things concerned with corporate objectives and culture that seem to matter. Agreement on basic directions for the long-term development of the business, and on how to treat people within the firm, are perhaps the most essential common features of these companies."

The increasingly significant role of HRM in achieving management objectives is reflected in the transformation of the personnel management function. Over the last two decades this function was often marginalized in terms of its importance in management activities and hierarchy. It has evolved from a concentration on employee welfare to one of managing people in a way so as to obtain the best and highest productivity possible from the employee, through methods that provide the employee with both intrinsic and extrinsic rewards.

Therefore today "far from being marginalised, the human resource management function becomes recognized as a central business concern; its performance and delivery are integrated into line management; the aims shift from merely securing compliance to the more ambitious one of winning commitment. The employee resource, therefore, becomes worth investing in, and training and development thus assume a higher profile. These initiatives are associated with, and maybe are even predicated upon, a tendency to shift from a collective orientation to the management of the workforce to an individualistic one. Accordingly management looks for 'flexibility' and seeks to reward differential performance in a differential way. Communication of managerial objectives and aspirations takes on a whole new importance."

What separates or distinguishes HRM from the traditional personnel function is the integration of HRM into strategic management and the pre-occupation of HRM with utilizing the human resource to achieve strategic management objectives. HRM "seeks to eliminate the mediation role and adopts a generally unitarist perspective. It emphasizes strategy and planning rather than problem-solving and mediation, so that employee cooperation is delivered by programmes of corporate culture, remuneration packaging, team building and management development for core employees, while peripheral employees are kept at arms "length."

HRM strategies may be influenced by the decisions taken on strategy (the nature of the business currently and in the future) and by the structure of the enterprise (the manner in which the enterprise is structured or organized to meet its objectives). In an enterprise with effective HRM policies and practices, the decisions on HRM are also strategic decisions influenced by strategy and structure, and by external factors such as trade unions, the labour market situation and the legal system. In reality most firms do not have such a well thought-out sequential model. But what we are considering here is effective HRM, and thus a model where HRM decisions are as strategic as the decisions on the type of business and structure.

At a conceptual level the interpretations of HRM indicate different emphases which lead to concentration on different contents of the discipline. The various distinctions or interpretations indicate that HRM "can be used in a restricted sense so reserving it as a label only for that approach to labour management which treats labour as a valued asset rather than a variable cost and which accordingly counsels investment in the labour resource through training and development and through measures designed to attract and retain a committed workforce.

Alternatively, it is sometimes used in an extended way so as to refer to a whole array of recent managerial initiatives including measures to increase the flexible utilization of the labour resource and other measures which are largely directed at the individual employee. But another distinction can also be drawn. This directs attention to the 'hard' and 'soft' versions of HRM. The 'hard' one emphasizes the quantitative, calculative and business-strategic aspects of managing the headcounts resource in as 'rational' a way as for any other economic factor. By contrast, the 'soft' version traces its roots to the human-relations school; it emphasizes communication, motivation, and leadership."

There are several ways in which HRM has changed earlier attitudes and assumptions of personnel management about managing people. The new model of HRM includes many elements vital to the basic management goal of achieving and maintaining competitiveness.

First, HRM earlier reacted piece-meal to problems as they arose. Effective HRM now increasingly seeks to link HRM issues to the overall strategy of the organization. Organizations with the most effective HRM policies and practices seek to integrate such policies in corporate strategies and to reinforce or change an organization's culture. Integration is needed in two senses -integrating HRM issues into an organization's strategic plans and securing the acceptance and inclusion of a HRM view in the decisions of line managers.

The HRM policies in respect of the various functions (e.g. recruitment, training, etc.) should be internally consistent. They must also be consistent with the business strategies and should reflect the organization's core values. The problem of integrating HRM with business strategy arises, for example, in a diversified enterprise with different products and markets. In such cases there is the difficulty of matching HRM policies with strategies which could vary among different business activities, each of which may call for different HRM policies. For instance, in particular cases "the 'hard' version of human resource management appears more relevant than the 'soft' version of human resource management.

In other words, matching HRM policies to business strategy calls for minimizing labour costs, rather than treating employees as a resource whose value may be enhanced. by increasing their commitment, functional flexibility, and quality." This contradiction is sometimes sought to be resolved through the claim that developing people is possible only where the business is successful. Therefore if reducing the labour force or dispensing with poor performers is dictated by business conditions, resorting to such measures and treating people as a resource are not antithetic. Another reconciliation of this contradiction is sought through management initiatives to change business strategy (e.g. in sectors where reducing costs is a common practice such as in mass production and supermarket retailing) through greater employee involvement, commitment and training.

Second, building strong cultures is a way of promoting particular organizational goals, in that "a 'strong culture' is aimed at uniting employees through a shared set of managerially sanctioned values ('quality', 'service', 'innovation', etc.) that assume an identification of employee and employer interests." However, there can be tension between a strong organizational culture and the need to adapt to changed circumstances and to be flexible, particularly in the highly competitive and rapidly changing environment in which employers have to operate today.

Rapid change demanded by the market is sometimes difficult in an organization with a strong culture. IBM has been cited as a case in point. Its firmly-held beliefs about products and services made it difficult to effect change in time, i.e. when the market required a radical change in product and service (from mainframe, customised systems, salesmen as management consultants to customer-as-end user, seeking quality of product and service) to personal computers (standardized product, cost competition, dealer as customer). Nevertheless in the long term a strong organizational culture is preferable to a weak one:

"Hence it could be said that the relationship between 'strong' cultures, employee commitment, and adaptability contains a series of paradoxes. Strong cultures allow for a rapid response to familiar conditions, but inhibit immediate flexibility in response to the unfamiliar, because of the commitment generated to a (now) inappropriate ideology. 'Weak' cultures, in contrast, when equated with ambiguous ideologies, allow flexibility in response to the unfamiliar, but cannot generate commitment to action. Yet strong cultures, through disconfirmation and eventual ideological shift may prove ultimately more adaptive to change, assuming the emergence of a new strong yet appropriate culture. This may be at the cost of a transitional period when ability to generate commitment to any course of action -new or old - is minimal."

Third, the attitude that people are a variable cost is, in effective HRM, replaced by the view that people are a resource and that as social capital can be developed and can contribute to competitive advantage. Increasingly, it is accepted that competitive advantage is gained through well-educated and trained, motivated and committed employees at all levels. This recognition is now almost universal, and accounts for the plausible argument that training and development are, or will be, the central pillar of HRM.

By the end of the 1980s leading companies in Germany, Japan and the USA were spending up to 3% of turnover on training and development, but in the UK such expenditure amounted to only about 0.15%. The economic performance of some of the East Asian countries (Japan, Korea, Hong Kong and Taiwan) and of some of the South East Asian countries (Singapore and Malaysia) are intimately connected with their high level of investment in education and training. Other countries are now placing human resource development at the centre of their national strategic plans - Indonesia being a recent example. Thus "The existence of policies and practices designed to realize the latent potential of the workforce at all levels becomes the litmus test of an organization's orientation."

Fourth, the view that the interests of employees and management or shareholders are divergent and conflictual - though substantially true in the past - is giving way to the view that this need not necessarily be so. HRM seeks to identify and promote a commonality of interests. Significant examples are training which enhances employment security and higher earning capacity for employees and which at the same time increases the employee's value to the enterprise's goals of better productivity and performance; pay systems which increase earnings without significant labour cost increases, and which at the same time promote higher performance levels; goal-setting through two-way communication which establishes unified goals and objectives and which provides intrinsic rewards to the employee through a participatory process.

Fifth, top-down communication coupled with controlled information flow to keep power within the control of management categories is gradually giving way to a sharing of information and knowledge. This change facilitates the creation of trust and commitment and makes knowledge more productive. Control from the top is being replaced by increasing employee participation and policies which foster commitment and flexibility which help organizations to change when necessary. The ways in which the larger Japanese enterprises have installed participatory schemes and introduced information-sharing and two-way communication systems are instructive in this regard.

In enterprises which tend to have corporate philosophies or missions, and where there are underlying values which shape their corporate culture, HRM becomes a part of the strategy to achieve their objectives. For example, in Matsushita Electric Company "finance, personnel and training are all fully centralised. Personnel and training exist to create 'harmony' In other words the central role of these functions is to help build and maintain the Matsushita culture people are seen as the critical resource." In some types of enterprises such as ones in which continuous technological change takes place, the goal of successfully managing change at short intervals often requires employee cooperation through emphasis on communication and involvement. As this type of unit grows,

"If there is strategic thinking in human resource management these units are likely to wish to develop employee-relations policies based on high individualism paying above market rates to recruit and retain the best labour, careful selection and recruitment systems to ensure high quality and skill potential, emphasis on internal training schemes to develop potential for further growth, payment system designed to reward individual performance and cooperation, performance and appraisal reviews, and strong emphasis on team work and communication... In short, technical and capital investment is matched by human resource investments, at times reaching near the ideals of human resource management."

If, as is often the case, (the UK is a good example), enterprises are dominated by financial issues, HRM will not be a part of the central strategy of such enterprises.

HRM as a means of achieving management objectives - at least in enterprises which have recognized, or have been compelled to recognize, the utilization of the human resource in achieving competitive edge - becomes clear from an examination of four important goals of effective HRM. HRM is closely linked to motivation, leadership and work behaviour. An enterprise's policies and practices in these areas have an impact on whether HRM contributes to achieving management goals.

The first goal of HRM is integration, which in itself has four aspects. Although "a comprehensive corporate strategy is essential to continuing business success... in many cases, human resource planning is not an integral part of strategic planning, but rather flows from it", so that giving effect to strategic plans becomes more difficult. This is especially so in today's context when the success of the process of adapting to change requires an increasing degree of individual and group involvement, so that human resources need to be integrated into strategic plans. As has been aptly stated in regard to managing change:

"Corporate entrepreneurs - single-minded individuals that they are - still get their projects done by crafting coalitions and building teams of devoted employees who feel a heightened sense of joint involvement and contribution to decisions. The integrative, participative vehicles surrounding innovators - open communication, interdependent responsibilities, frequent team efforts- keep them close to the power sources they need to operate, ensuring access to information, resources and the support needed for implementation. Involving grass roots employees on participative teams with control over their own outcomes helps the organization to get and use more ideas to improve performance and increase future skills. Whether called 'task forces', 'quality circles', 'problem-solving groups', or 'shared-responsibility teams', such vehicles for greater participation at all levels are an important part of an innovating company. Masters of change are also masters of the use of participation."

Human resource policies should also be internally consistent in the sense that policies in each area of human resources (e.g. selection, motivation, rewards) should further common strategic objectives. Further, successful integration depends on line managers accepting and practising the appropriate HRM policies. Moreover, employees should be integrated (as in the case of the best practice in Japanese companies) so that there is as little divergence of interests between those of the enterprise and the employee.

The second is the goal of commitment, which involves identification of the type of commitment sought e.g. attitudinal, behavioural. Commitment could be to the organization, to the job, to career advancement. Commitment could be seen as acceptance of enterprise values and goals, and could be reflected in behaviour which seeks to further these goals. Thus:

"The theoretical proposition is therefore that organizational commitment, combined with job related behavioural commitment will result in high employee satisfaction, high performance, longer tenure and willingness to accept change."

Among measures to achieve commitment are setting objectives through a two-way communication process which requires consultation and involvement; performance appraisal systems based on agreed goals and performance measures; intrinsic and extrinsic rewards.

The third is the goal of flexibility and adaptability, which in essence means the ability to manage change and innovation and to respond rapidly to market demands and changes. This requires a HRM policy which is conducive to change at all levels of the organization, a structure which is not bureaucratic, rigid and hierarchical, with an absence of rigid job demarcations and with functional flexibility (flexible skills and willingness to move from one task to another). Promoting these is possible only "if employees at all levels display high organizational commitment, high trust and high levels of intrinsic motivation." Measures to achieve flexibility would include training, work organization, multi-skilling and removal of narrow job classifications.

The fourth goal of HRM is the goal of quality. This assumes the existence of policies and practices to recruit, develop and retain skilled and adaptable staff, and the formulation of agreed performance goals and performance measures. To these goals could be added two broader goals - building a unified organizational culture and achieving competitive advantage through the productive use of human resources.

In considering the relationship between HRM and HIR, two central concerns are: in what way does HRM pose a challenge to HIR and how can conflicts between the two, if any, be reconciled so that they can complement each other? This section concerns itself with the first of these two issues. In considering the issue, it is necessary to identify the broad goals of each discipline. The goals of HRM have already been identified in the previous section. It remains to consider some of the basic objectives of HIR, which could be said to include the following:

1. The efficient production of goods and services and, at the same time, determination of adequate terms and conditions of employment, in the interests of the

employer, employees and society as a whole, through a consensus achieved through negotiation.

2. The establishment of mechanisms for communication, consultation and cooperation in order to resolve workplace issues at enterprise and industry level, and to achieve through a tripartite process, consensus on labour policy at national level.
3. Avoidance and settlement of disputes and differences between employers, employees and their representatives, where possible through negotiation and dispute settlement mechanisms.
4. To provide social protection where needed e.g. in the areas of social security, safety and health, child labour, etc.
5. Establishment of stable and harmonious relations between employers and employees and their organizations, and between them and the State.

HIR is essentially pluralistic in outlook, in that it covers not only the relations between employer and employee (the individual relations) but also the relations between employers and unions and between them and the State (collective relations). HIR theory, practice and institutions traditionally focus more on the collective aspect of relations. This is evident from the central place occupied by labour law, freedom of association, collective bargaining, the right to strike, employee involvement practices which involve unions, trade unionism and so on.

HRM deals with the management of human resources, rather than with the management of collective relations. There is of course a certain measure of overlap. Individual grievance handling falls within the ambit of both disciplines, but dispute settlement of collective issues more properly falls within the scope of HIR. Policies and practices relating to recruitment, selection, appraisal, training and motivation form a part of HRM.

Team-building, communication and cooperation, though primarily HRM initiatives, have a collectivist aspect. Thus joint consultative mechanisms are as much HIR initiatives, which may (as in Japan) supplement collective bargaining. But HIR has not, in regard to team-building for instance, developed any techniques or theories about how to achieve it; in fact, it is not a focus of attention because it implies a potential loyalty to the enterprise through the team and is seen as conflicting with loyalty to the union. HIR has a large component of rules which govern the employment relationship.

These rules may be prescribed by the State through laws, by courts or tribunals, or through a bipartite process such as collective bargaining. HRM differs in this respect from industrial relations in the sense that it does not deal with such procedures and rules, but with the best way to use the human resource through, for example, proper selection and recruitment, induction, appraisal, training and development, motivation, leadership and intrinsic and extrinsic rewards. Thus "at its most basic HRM represents a set of managerial initiatives." Four processes central to a HRM system - selection, appraisal, rewards and development - leave only limited room for HIR as a central element in the human resource system. "Based on theoretical work in the field of organizational behaviour it is proposed that HRM comprises a set of policies designed to maximise organizational integration, employee commitment, flexibility and quality of work. Within this model, collective industrial relations have, at best, only a minor role."

A discernible trend in management is a greater individualisation of the employer-employee relationship, implying less emphasis on collective, and more emphasis on individual relations. This is reflected, for instance, in monetary and non-monetary reward systems. In HIR the central monetary reward is wages and salaries, one of its central themes (given effect to by collective bargaining) being internal equity and distributive justice and, often, standardisation across industry.

HRM increasingly places emphasis on monetary rewards linked to performance and skills through the development of performance and skills-based pay systems, some of which seek to individualise monetary rewards (e.g. individual bonuses, stock options, etc.). HRM strategies to secure individual commitment through communication, consultation and participatory schemes underline the individualisation thrust, or at least effect, of HRM strategies.

On the other hand, it is also legitimate to argue that HRM does not focus exclusively on the individual and, as such, does not promote only individual employment relations. Though much of HRM is directed at the individual, "at the same time there is a parallel emphasis on team work, whether in the form of quality circles or functional flexibility, and above all, on the individual's commitment to the organization, represented not just as the sum of the individuals in it, but rather as an organic entity with an interest in survival.

The potential conflict between emphasizing the importance of the individual on the one hand, and the desirability of cooperative team work and employee commitment to the organization, on the other, is glossed over through the general assumption of unitarist values..: HRM stresses the development of a strong corporate culture -not only does it give direction to an organization, but it mediates the tension between individualism and collectivism, as individuals socialised into a strong culture are subject to unobtrusive collective controls on attitudes and behaviour."

Some of the tensions between HIR and HRM arise from the unitarist outlook of HRM (which sees a commonality of interests between managements and employees) and the pluralist outlook of HIR (which assumes the potential for conflict in the employment relationship flowing from different interests). "It is often said that HRM is the visual embodiment of the unitarist frame of reference both in the sense of the legitimation of managerial authority and in the imagery of the firm as a team with committed employees working with managers for the benefit of the firm."

How to balance these conflicting interests and to avoid or to minimize conflicts (e.g. through promotion of negotiation systems such as collective bargaining, joint consultation, dispute settlement mechanisms within the enterprise and at national level in the form of conciliation, arbitration and labour courts) in order to achieve a harmonious HIR system is one central task of HIR. The individualization of HRM, reflected in its techniques which focus on direct employer-employee links rather than with employee representatives, constitutes one important difference between HIR and HRM. It has been observed that:

"The empirical evidence also indicates that the driving force behind the introduction of HRM appears to have little to do with industrial relations; rather it is the pursuit of competitive advantage in the market place through provision of high-quality goods and services, through competitive pricing linked to high productivity and through the capacity swiftly to innovate and manage change in response to changes in the market place or to breakthroughs in research and development. Its underlying values, reflected in HRM policies and practices, would appear to be essentially unitarist and individualistic in contrast to the more pluralist and collective values of traditional industrial relations."

How does HRM more specifically challenge HIR and trade unions, though HRM is not per se anti-union and its central themes are not necessarily inconsistent with unionism? First, HRM does not focus, as does HIR, on collective bargaining, which is a central institution in HIR. However, collective bargaining should not be understood only in the narrow sense of negotiation of terms and conditions of employment leading to a formal agreement.

It should be viewed as a process, and as including all mechanisms introduced to arrive at a consensus on matters affecting the two social partners, even if they do not result in formalised agreements. If viewed in this way, it reduces the conflict between HRM and HIR within this area. A second area in which HRM is said to pose a challenge to unions is on the issue of flexibility- critical in HRM but traditionally absent as a factor in HIR where a degree of standardisation for purposes of internal equity has been an objective of unions and of HIR. Here the scene is undergoing considerable change.

There is today a major thrust towards achieving flexibility in the labour market on matters such as functions, working time, pay and types of contracts. Unions are being compelled to 'participate' in these changes as an alternative to being marginalized. The trend towards greater decentralization of collective bargaining has compelled viewing issues more from a workplace perspective.

It has provided an opportunity for unions in countries with a high rate of unionization to be involved in issues other than wages and related ones, such as technology introduction, new work processes and organization, It involves, on the one hand, the willingness of employers to deal with unions on such matters (which they have to be willing to do in high union-density enterprises), and on the other the willingness of unions to cooperate on legitimate measures to achieve competitiveness -especially where the employees themselves are willing to do so -and to adapt to the realities of the workplace.

A third - and perhaps the principal challenge - emanates from employee loyalty and commitment, which are central objectives of HRM. The issue here is whether dual allegiance is possible i.e. commitment to the goals and values of the organization, and to contribute to its success on the one hand, and commitment to the trade union on the other. It is at this point that HIR becomes a critical factor. In principle there should be no antithesis, because trade unionism need not (and should not) be conflictual in approach and attitude. Much of the empirical evidence drawn from the USA indicates that in a workplace with a cooperative HIR system dual loyalty is possible, but that it is not possible in one where a cooperative climate is absent or minimal. In some of the larger unionised corporations in Japan, this conflict of loyalty is less felt.

Traditional HIR and trade unionism can be challenged in other ways - that is, other than through anti-union activity. Downsizing the labour force as a HRM initiative to achieve competitiveness and offering monetary incentives to employees to improve productivity could create HIR tensions, especially if the union has not been involved in the process. A similar result may occur when an employer, without seeking to dismantle existing HIR practices, establishes other mechanisms and practices such as direct communication and consultation systems, small group activities, employee share option schemes and so on without involving the union.

The unitarist approach of HRM and the pluralist tradition of HIR, though regarded by some as incompatible, are not regarded in the same light by others. There are three issues involved here. The first is whether the pursuit of HRM policies such as employee involvement and commitment, two-way communication and small group activities, and the integration of HRM policies in corporate objectives and strategies pose a challenge to central HIR institutions such as collective bargaining and to unionism. The second is whether such HRM policies are pursued consciously as a union avoidance strategy. The third is whether HRM and HIR are necessarily incompatible or whether there is scope for their co-existence.

David E. Guest points out that HRM, which is an American concept, "finds its fullest expression in a number of well-known and successful American companies." He points out that research indicates that the established model of HRM is often found in a non-union company. Referring to the research done by one writer, he states:

"He notes that in almost all the companies he looked at the HRM policies came first, often encouraged by the values of a powerful CEO, preceding any considered non-unionism. In many cases, remaining non-union has subsequently become a policy goal. On the basis of the companies he studied, this has a number of cost implications. Personnel policies must be sufficiently good and sufficiently integrated and reinforced by line management practice to avoid giving grounds for union organising. Foulkes found that most of the companies he studied paid above average rates. They also provided mechanisms for individual expression of grievances and were likely to monitor reactions to personnel policies through the communication system and the use of attitude surveys. All of these practices are to be found in a hotel which provides the best known model of HRM but which is also what Bassett refers to as the 'ultimate non-union company'."

This does not mean that HRM is anti-union or that unions have no role to play in HRM, but rather that effective HRM policies and practices are sometimes either used as a union avoidance strategy or else it can have that effect. Three very influential scholars have put forward the view that there is a role for union involvement in HRM, and point to hotels which have involved unions in the move towards HRM, and by so doing unions have facilitated this move. Such an involvement, if it is to take place, would require, in many countries, a substantial change of attitude on the part of both management and unions. David E. Guest remarks however:

"If a new set of practices can be introduced, it is not clear what role is left for the union. The most likely one is that of policing management practices and dealing with grievances which seem almost inevitable with repetitive production line work and persisting pressures to increase productivity. By implication, management is not practising effective HRM and the door is left open for the unions to play a role."

At the annual meeting of European employers' organizations, held in Bordeaux in 1993 the compatibility of new trends in HRM with the traditional HIR systems was considered. The following summary is indicative of the growing attitude of employers in many industrialized market economies:

"The key to competitiveness is quality. And quality depends more on the commitment of individuals than on their acquired technical skills; more on the way these individuals behave and their team spirit than on the passive execution of orders received. Regulations - be they internal to the enterprise or imposed by the legislator - plague innovation and have a negative effect on motivation. Good human resource management lies in the behaviour of each employee within an enterprise. It applies to individual men and women. The classic approach to industrial relations is entirely different, with its peculiarity being collective bargaining - which, by definition, does not consider the individual but the mass.

The status of a worker is defined by a few general criteria, such as his professional category and possibly his seniority and his age. Remuneration, for example, is calculated on the basis of a few simple elements, which do not take into consideration personal behaviour and individual performance. Work provided is considered purely from the quantitative angle. The future of collective bargaining, therefore, depends on the extent to which it can take into account the demands for individualization which modern methods of human resources management imply. This should not of course lead to arbitrariness. Legislation and regulation imposed by the State should also leave a sufficient margin of flexibility to allow for adaptation."

The foregoing analysis has presented human resource management as unitarist and individualistic in focus. It follows from this that the trade unions are unnecessary or at best marginal. Therefore neither the model presented here, nor the American frameworks (of several writers) see industrial relations, as conventionally conceived, as a central human resource activity a company practising human resource management will normally pay above the average rate and will have excellent communication and grievance systems. Implicit in such policies is a model of unions as providing a collective 'voice' for sources of grievance and discontent and promoting worker interests.

There is no recognition of any broader concept of pluralism within society giving rise to solidaristic collective orientations. Walton identifies a number of American cases, notably in the automobile industry, where unions have been involved in moves to increase commitment. At the same time he acknowledges that the role of the union is likely to become somewhat marginal and ambiguous.

The issue considered here is whether the apparent incompatibility between HIR and HRM can be reconciled. There are several writers who have expressed strong criticisms of HRM as being exploitative. But a reconciliation can be explored only on the assumption that ultimately both HRM and HIR have as one of their objectives fairness and equity, that both parties are prepared to recognize the need for enterprise and employee growth, that these are necessarily inter-linked, and that though their interests are to some extent divergent, there are increasingly areas of common interest for mutual survival.

For example, in many countries employers and employees are perceived as two interest groups with generally opposing interests and as belonging to different classes. In the past the relevance of employees to enterprise and national competitiveness was less significant, but the level of employees' education and skills has never been as crucial as it is today. Now we see - and by the turn of the century it will be all the more apparent - a convergence of interests between employers and employees in the latter's level of education and skills.

Before exploring the possibility of reconciling the seeming conflict between HRM and HIR, it is instructive to note some of the positions of trade unions. In his analysis of trade union views in the USA, Canada and Britain, P.B. Beaumont points out that unions have sometimes expressed views about particular elements of HRM such as quality circles, rather than of HRM as a whole. Further, the avowed policy positions of unions at national level do not necessarily reflect what actually happens at enterprise level. In Canada unions have expressed considerable opposition to HRM initiatives, so much so that in the early 1980s anti-quality of work life resolutions were passed by some unions in two states. According to a conclusion based on interviews of 17 high level union officials in Canada:

"Union leaders are convinced that management attempts towards employee involvement, and demands for greater flexibility in work arrangements are nothing but a 'misguided desire for a union free environment'. They are of the view that management is more interested in speed up, more productivity than in the worker input. Labour leaders strongly believe in the adversarial system of labour relations citing the fundamentally different roles of union and management at the workplace. Participation in management decision-making initiatives, according to them, are largely cost driven, motivated by management's desire to abdicate its responsibility by transferring to the union the role of disciplining workers, setting one worker against the other."

In the USA union attitudes have been mixed and more flexible, and the difference between Canada and the USA in this respect has been explained on the basis of higher unionisation rates in Canada. In the USA the AFL CIO did not propound an official-policy, and in some cases such as the United Auto Workers' Union, cooperation at local union level was encouraged. In the case of communication workers, support for involvement was provided by the international president. On the other hand, the ideology motivating those who oppose initiatives such as team work and related pay structures is that participation arrangements would enlarge the non-union sector.

In regard to Britain, it has been observed that the "view that HRM is in essence the development of a set of policies, practices and arrangements designed essentially to 'individualise' industrial relations, and thus circumvent the unions and weaken individual membership commitment and loyalty to the union, is one that is probably widely accepted throughout the British union movement. However, where individual unions may well disagree is on whether they see all individual components of HRM as equally threatening in this way, and on how to appropriately respond to employer initiatives along these lines."

The British Trade Union Congress has shown conditional support for some components of HRM such as the generally contentious functional flexibility. It has supported ESOPS, but not linking a substantial part of income to organizational performance.

The pronouncements of the TUC lead to the conclusion that "the TUC:

1. View HRM developments in total as having the potential to 'individualise' industrial relations, but
2. Recognizes the inevitability of certain environmental pressures on employers encouraging some moves along these lines and
3. Feels that individual unions should basically judge their value and worth on a situation by situation basis, although
4. Certain safeguards and quid pro quos should be ensured and obtained in situations where such moves actually take place." Other unions have reflected attitudes ranging from support for HRM initiatives to opposition to them.

If the apparent incompatibility between HRM and HIR can be reconciled so that both could operate as parallel systems (as collective and individual focused systems), it would require the satisfaction of several conditions. The two can co-exist if unions and managements are prepared and able to carve out a role for HRM, and they are able to agree on narrowing the gap between HRM and HIR. This requires changes in the thinking of unions and managements. Some of the attitudes of unions noted earlier which are opposed to HRM initiatives, as distinct from those which are prepared to treat particular components on their merits, could push employers further towards noninvolvement of unions in HRM initiatives. The result of unions keeping HRM at arms' length is reflected in the statement of a Manager at Austin Rover (UK):

"The unions were invited to the party but they didn't seem to want to come. So, the party went ahead without them."

Unions would need to consider the possible scenario that in the years to come the likelihood is that managements will look increasingly to HRM to enhance enterprise competitiveness. This is particularly so as enterprises come to depend on people - on their skills and productivity - as one critical factor in this regard. HRM is being increasingly taught as a part of management education, and this would perhaps increase resort to HRM by future managers. Besides, declarations of policy at national or central level may not necessarily affect what employees and unions may in fact be prepared to do at local level.

Unions could opt to be involved in consultation mechanisms at workplace level at which new HRM initiatives are discussed. This implies that unions need to concentrate more on enterprise level problems and issues. It also implies massive training programmes for unions in HRM issues, if they are to be in a position to respond to and participate in HRM initiatives. The attitude of unions on productivity issues is likely to condition the willingness of employers to involve them in HRM initiatives. Perhaps most of all, unions which are able to take a long-term perspective on issues are most likely to be involved in or participate in change. For example the German unions and works councils "have a structure of incentives, including employment security, effective representation, and participation, continuing retraining in broad skills, which gives them a long-term perspective in plant bargaining."

Obtaining union cooperation would partly depend on management attitudes. If managements believe - as some appear to do - that effective HRM can be popularised by regarding individual enterprise action in isolation from the external labour market, then effective HRM may in the foreseeable future remain isolated islands of excellence, rather than common practice throughout the economy. Perhaps it is this somewhat isolationist attitude which accounts for effective HRM in many countries still remaining the preserve of high technology enterprises, despite its growing popularity.

If management strategy is union avoidance, then HIR and HRM will be incompatible. The possibility of HRM and HIR having a parallel existence is more likely in large enterprises where direct communication with individuals is more difficult. In this connection it may be instructive for managements to consider whether a union-free environment is necessary for effective HRM. Contrary to popular belief, in some countries such as the UK, HRM has been found to be seriously practised in unionised workplaces, rather than in non-unionised ones. Some lessons can perhaps also be drawn from the USA, which has a low unionisation rate and where much of the practice of HRM and research has taken place. It has been found that in the 1970s in the USA several companies "began to adopt some of the practices of the non-union companies. Managements, much as they have done in the UK, targeted individuals and the trade unions were kept at arms' length. They soon found, however, that they were not getting the maximum: the 'cold war' relations with trade unions were undermining their efforts. In the 1980s therefore there has, at least in the USA, been a considerable about-turn. Attempts have been made to integrate individual and collective policies. In particular there has been a trend towards the greater involvement of trade unions in the process of change."

Further, Japanese practices in their large enterprises have reflected a successful blend of collectivist HIR and HRM, made possible to some extent by their enterprise union system which has facilitated union involvement in HRM initiatives through mechanisms such as their joint consultation system. As significant is the case of Britain, with its long tradition of HIR and trade unionism. The evidence indicates that in some instances established HIR and new HRM approaches have run parallel, indicating the practical feasibility of a dual arrangement. It must be stated, however, that there is also evidence that managements pursuing new initiatives tended to neglect union relations. The overall situation in Britain appears to be that "unions and industrial relations have to be demonstrated as relatively secondary and incidental to meeting market priorities, and secondary also to the newly discovered alternative ways of managing the labour (human) resource."

Second, there would have to be a loosening of the demarcation between HRM and HIR, and changes in HIR thinking to narrow the gap between the two. Two-way communication, training and motivation would be examples of HRM functions. But a major problem is in the areas of flexibility (functional, working time, types of contracts, workforce size), job design and pay systems, where traditional HIR and HRM are most likely to conflict. If, for example, reward systems geared to performance and skills proliferate, as they are likely to, it will have an impact on pay determination through collective bargaining. Unions may have to recognize that collective bargaining may need to be redesigned to cover a lesser quantum of pay increases than in the past, and that they should seek to be involved in the flexible and skill-based elements of pay.

This would involve a greater emphasis on enterprise level negotiation. HIR will be the chief means of maintaining industrial peace, and would concentrate on the means to avoid and settle conflicts and disputes. Some countries may, for instance, opt for legal machinery such as labour court, arbitration and conciliation processes which are external to the enterprise and in which there is a role for all the tripartite constituents. But the relevance of unions would also have to be in the area of conflict avoidance, and not only in the area of conflict resolution. HIR would have to adapt to changed circumstances, and accept that hitherto sacrosanct mechanisms like collective bargaining would have to similarly adapt. "Either unions and collective bargaining adapt to the changed environments, where markets take precedence over hierarchies and managerial power is enhanced as regulation and protectionism recede, or their future is increasingly questioned."

In essence HIR may have to accept that in the future its relevance will be more at macro level e.g. in formulating overall HIR policy through tripartite processes, delimiting the boundaries of action for the two other parties and providing a measure of social protection where needed through labour law and judicial or semi-judicial bodies, and providing the necessary framework for the two other parties to function e.g. freedom of association. When HIR practitioners and even unions engage in initiatives to improve workplace HIR, ironically they are engaging in an essentially HRM function. If HIR moves towards a much greater concentration at enterprise level and promotes harmonious relations at that level, it is likely to reduce the gap between HIR and HRM and lessen the tension between the two. In that eventuality, unions would have to seek an adaptive role.

Third, HIR will have to open its doors to other disciplines. HRM has been responsible for compelling HIR to recognize the contributions made by other fields of study - industrial sociology, organizational behaviour and psychology - and not only by economics and law, which "were the two major social science disciplines in the development of HIR and (which) has led to a traditional emphasis on national level analysis of the role of union, employers and government, as well as giving special attention to collective bargaining as a system of adjusting influence and power." Since HRM deals in large measure with how people are managed within an enterprise and involves an analysis of its effects on employees, HRM has to be accommodated within the ambit of HIR study and analysis.

The future of HIR may well depend on the capacity to develop more collaborative relations and to move away from adversarial ones. To some extent such a development could be influenced by HRM itself which, if effectively practised, should reduce hierarchical and authoritarian management and result in the setting up of consultative procedures. Implicit in the workplace HIR surveys in Britain is the recognition that the subject matter of industrial relations has to move beyond the exclusive preoccupation with the collective aspects of the employment relationship that has dominated policy as well as teaching and research for the past thirty years. The individual aspects of the employment relationship can no longer be treated simply as part of the context. The obvious justification for giving these individual aspects greater prominence is that the union-free sector is becoming numerically more and more important. But this is not the only consideration. In the union sector it is the interplay between 'collectivism' and 'individualism' that emerges as increasingly important. Some might say that it was ever thus, and that it was only the myopia of industrial relations specialists that stopped us from recognizing the obvious. Be that as it may, there is no longer any justification for not accepting that industrial relations is about the employment relationship as a whole.

Further, HIR has often been seen (like personnel management) as a non-strategic operational function. The notion that it represents collective relations between an employer and employees and the union, conducted mainly through collective bargaining, reduces the collaborative processes of communication, discussion and participation, and emphasizes bargaining.

The implication of HIR is that it involves unions rather than employees. The signs are that - in industrialized countries at least - HIR is assuming more strategic proportions. This is reflected in trends such as the move towards increased enterprise and plant level bargaining. This is a strategic change which enables HIR bargaining to focus more on workplace needs and issues, and to also promote more direct participation of employees in bargaining. The trend towards flexibility in place of standardisation is also a strategic move in the sense that it is designed to increase competitiveness and the ability to respond rapidly to change.

Specific conditions in countries outside the West could affect the possibility of reconciling HIR and HRM in those countries. For instance, in countries with union multiplicity and rivalry employees would need to organize themselves in such a way as to reduce the number of competing unions in a workplace. The desire often expressed by employers in such countries for one union in one workplace is an outcome of the problems flowing from multiplicity, which include the difficulty of reaching durable and implementable agreements. In such situations employers are unlikely to consult or involve unions in HRM strategies.

In many Asian countries unionisation is so low that there is no pressure for union involvement in HRM. Especially in those Asian cultures which are conflict-avoidance oriented and where relationships are determined by authority and status, HIR is likely to be seen as conflict-generating, and HRM as more likely to achieve integration. In this connection foreign investors have also sought union-free environments. With increasing foreign direct investment, it is not impossible that HRM, rather than HIR, will sometimes be the preferred option of some managements.

In the final analysis, it would be unrealistic for unions or anyone else to expect managements to abandon or reduce their resort to effective HRM when the latter is one means of achieving management objectives geared to better enterprise management. The pre-occupation with HRM on the part of employers is not confined to industrialized countries. The Asian emphasis is reflected in the fact that programmes on HRM are far more likely to attract management participation than HIR, in the same way that HIR programmes would attract trade unions.

Though perhaps the main challenge to unions comes from management initiatives to secure employee commitment, the question which needs to be asked is: what is intrinsically wrong or immoral in an employer seeking to secure such loyalty, so long as the employees themselves stand to gain from it? Here again the Japanese example demonstrates the possibility of dual commitment. As noted earlier, effective HRM is not widespread. If more managements succeed in practising effective HRM, on present trends it is not impossible that HIR will come to be relegated to a secondary role. This possibility is enhanced by the fact that traditionally HIR has never been a part of strategic planning, nor has it been seen as a means of achieving management objectives. On the other hand, HRM is increasingly seen as having a strategic role and as a means of achieving management objectives. The convergence of other factors such as declining union rates (if this trend continues) could also combine to push HIR and unions to the fringes.

Chapter 2

The Hospitality and Tourism Industry

For people who think this is the industry for them, strongly suggest that they really think about their personality and be sure they can thrive (and survive) in the atmosphere. It truly is different from anything else. It is critical that they work for a hotel while they are still in school, preferably in a few different hotels, and departments, so they can get a feel for it and know where they would be the happiest and most successful. The growth in the services sector of the worldwide economy has been phenomenal in the last 25 years. In the United States, services currently account for more than 75 percent of the gross domestic product (GDP), which is a popular measure of an economy's productivity.

Similarly, on an international scale, services continue to account for an ever-increasing percentage of economic activity. Most new jobs are created in the service sector, and the growth in the hospitality and tourism industry is a major contributor. Until the mid-1980s, the emphasis within the marketing community was on products. Now services have surpassed products and have taken on a more important role in marketing.

Services, such as those offered by providers in the hospitality and tourism industry, have developed marketing strategies and practices that are unique. It has been established that the strategies, tactics, and practices that have been used successfully for product marketers do not always work successfully for those who market services. With the distinct differences between products and services in mind, the field of services marketing has evolved.

Services Defined

Unlike products, which are tangible, services are usually intangible. A service is not a physical good; rather, it is the performance of an act or a deed. This performance often requires consumers to be present during the production or delivery of the service. Service industries, including hospitality and tourism, are actually selling consumers an experience. Services have been defined to "include all economic activities whose output is not a physical product or construction, is generally consumed at the time it is produced, and provides added value in forms (such as convenience, amusement, timeliness, comfort or health) that are essentially intangible concerns of its first purchaser."

Service employees such as front desk agents, housekeepers, hostesses, wait staff, car rental agents, flight attendants, and travel agents are responsible for creating positive experiences for customers. These frontline employees are critical to the success of service firms and play boundary-spanning roles because of their direct contact with customers.

These roles are important because customers' perceptions of service firms are formed as a result of their dealings with the boundary-spanning employees. Several reasons underlie the remarkable growth in services. Two leading services marketing experts, Christopher Lovelock and Lauren Wright, cite numerous reasons for this growth:2

Changing patterns of government regulation: The reduction in government regulation has spurred the growth of services. In recent years, there has been a very noticeable shift toward the government taking a much less active role in the regulation of business activities. The most noteworthy of these shifts have been in the airline, trucking, telecommunication, and electrical generation and distribution industries. All of these industries have seen significant changes, as the barriers to entry have been removed and regulations governing such marketing elements as price have also been relaxed or entirely removed.

Relaxation of professional association restrictions on marketing: A new element of competition has been introduced into professions such as law and medicine as more of the practitioners in these areas advertise their services. Bans or restrictions on promotion have been largely removed. Within the hospitality and tourism industry, standards have also changed. We have seen an increase in advertising focusing on direct comparisons, or attacks, on competitors' products and services. This type of advertising strategy creates, or sustains, the perception of superiority in the mind of the consumer in favour of the brand being advertised.

Privatization of some public and nonprofit services: The term privatization was first used in Great Britain when the government adopted the policy of returning national industries from government to private ownership. This transformation has resulted in a greater emphasis on cost containment and a clearer focus on customers' needs. Later, in Central and Eastern Europe, following the fall of communism, we witnessed a continuing transformation from planned or government-run economies to market-driven economies fueled by private companies. Many of these countries' governments have released the control of airlines and travel agencies to private firms.

Technological innovation: Technology continues to alter the way firms do business and interact with consumers. In all types of businesses, consumers take a more active role in the service delivery process. For example, airlines, in an effort to reduce labor costs and increase speed of service to customers, have aggressively promoted self-check-in, both at the ticket counter and through their Web sites prior to arrival at the airport. Customers print boarding passes, receipts, and other documents without intervention by an airline employee. Express checkout for hotel guests has been in place for many years, but hotel chains continue to experiment with ways to enhance the service, thereby reducing labor costs and/or increasing the customers' perceived value.

In other settings, touch-screen computers collect feedback from guests, in much the same manner that comment cards have been used previously. The ease with which a company can maintain and access a database has permitted the development of sophisticated reservation systems and has led to more sophisticated frequent traveler programs. The use of more sophisticated reservations and property management systems has allowed hospitality and tourism firms to improve the level of service provided to guests. Guest history data serve as another example of how a hospitality organization can use technology to gain a competitive advantage. If a hotel guest requests a specific type of pillow, staff can record this preference within the individual's guest history file. When this guest checks into another hotel operated by the chain, the items that were previously requested can be waiting, without the guest even having to request them.

Growth in service chains and franchise networks: Much of the growth in service firms, including the hospitality industry, has been the direct result of franchising efforts by some of the major companies. Franchising represents a contractual arrangement whereby one firm (the franchisor) licenses a number of other firms (the franchisees) to use the franchisor's name and business practices. Notable lodging organizations such as Choice Hotels International and Marriott International, as well as food service firms such as McDonald's, Burger King, Taco Bell, and Wendy's, have all used franchising as a major vehicle for growth. The continued growth of the hospitality industry by means of franchising has put additional stress on independent owners and operators. In fact, each year the percentage of hospitality and tourism operations that are independently operated decreases.

Internationalization and globalization: Increasing shareholder value often remains directly associated with increasing company sales and profits, and globalization is one means of achieving this. As more and more of the prime locations are developed domestically, companies look internationally for expansion opportunities. This has been particularly true for fast-food franchisors: a significant proportion of their expansion during the last few years has occurred outside of their traditional domestic markets.

Pressures to improve productivity: In many industries within the service economy, competition stays very intense. This factor, when combined with the pressure from investors for higher returns on capital, has resulted in pressure to increase productivity and reduce costs. In many cases, managers seek to reduce labor costs by running leaner operations or using technology to replace humans for some tasks An example of this was when Delta Airlines encouraged passengers to check in via the Internet, thereby reducing the number of passengers who wanted to check in at the airport. They offered an incentive of 1,000 extra frequent-flyer miles to any passenger who used this service. While increasing productivity and profits remains a highly desirable goal, it must not be done at the expense of long term customer satisfaction. Without long-term satisfaction, future profitability may exist in jeopardy.

The service quality movement: With the advent of consumerism, the public's perception is that service quality has declined. In response, successful firms are using the customer's perception of quality to set performance standards, rather than relying solely on operationally defined standards for service quality. They often conduct extensive research to determine the key elements that impact the customer's perception of service quality. When Ritz-Carlton won the Malcolm Baldrige National Quality Award, this was tangible evidence that paying careful attention to customers' service expectations can have a dramatic impact on the firm.

Expansion of leasing and rental businesses: The expansion of businesses that lease equipment and personnel to firms has been a contributing factor in the growth of the service sector. More and more firms are looking to outsource some elements of their operation, and they often start with elements that are not part of the firm's core product or business. For example, most hotels that host meetings and conventions have outsourced the servicing of the audiovisual needs of groups to a company that specializes in that type of business. The company in turn leases the audiovisual equipment to groups that are holding meetings in the hotel. The company is able to provide more up-to-date and specialized equipment to groups than the hotel might if it provided the service itself. The hotel does not have to maintain an inventory of equipment, and therefore capital costs are reduced.

Manufacturers as service providers: Some of the firms that traditionally manufactured and distributed tangible products have found it profitable to provide services as well. For example, most automobile manufacturers have consumer credit agencies to facilitate the leasing and purchasing of automobiles. In the hospitality industry, PepsiCo decided to enter the restaurant industry and distribute its products through acquisitions such as Taco Bell and KFC, but the company later reconsidered this strategy and sold these brands to Yum! Brands, Inc. In the computer industry, firms such as IBM and Hewlett-Packard provide services in addition to hardware and software. In most cases, the profit margins on services are higher than on products, contributing significantly to the bottom line of the firm.

Pressures on public and nonprofit organizations to find new income sources: All organizations are under pressure to increase sales, which often becomes difficult within the traditional products that a firm sells. There are many reasons for this, but increasing competition and mature industries are often contributing factors. In an effort to find new sources of income, firms often seek new services that will generate new net sales, without cannibalizing sales of existing products. For example, a limousine company might expand its city tour business in addition to the other services offered.

Hiring and promotion of innovative managers: In the past, managers in the service industries often spent their entire careers within a single industry, or perhaps even with the same firm. This situation no longer reintroduction to services marketing mains the same, especially at the corporate level of management. Firms often hire individuals from other industries to provide a fresh perspective and fresh ideas. The results can become dramatic. One such individual is Steven Bollenback, president and CEO of Hilton Hotels. Prior to his very positive impact on Hilton Hotels, he had engineered innovative financing at both Marriott International and Trump Hotels and Resorts.

THE NATURE OF SERVICES

Along with the growth in services, an appreciation for the ways in which services are different from products has developed. The traditional ways of marketing tangible products are not equally effective in services marketing. In many industries, marketing involves tangible manufactured products, such as automobiles, washing machines, and clothing, whereas service industries focus on intangible products such as travel and foodservice. However, before we can explore how services get successfully marketed, we need to examine the ways services differ from products. Lovelock and Wright have identified nine key differences.

- *No ownership by customers:* A customer does not take ownership when purchasing a service. There is no transfer of assets.

Service products as intangible performers: The value of owning a high performance car or the latest computer lies in the physical characteristics of the product and to some extent the brand image it conveys. The value of purchasing services lies in the nature of the performance. For example, if you decide to celebrate a birthday or anniversary by dining at an expensive restaurant, the value lies in the way in which the service actors perform. When servers come to the table and present all the entrees simultaneously, the choreographed presentation appears in the same manner as a choreographed play or performance.

Greater involvement of customers in the production process: Because consumers tend to be present when receiving service within a hospitality operation, they remain involved in the service production. In many instances, they are directly involved through the element of self-service. Examples of this can be seen in fast-food restaurants as well as in hotels that provide automated check-in and checkout by means of either a machine or a video connection through the television. Airlines have greatly expanded self-service within their operations as a means of reducing labor costs. In any case, the customer's level of satisfaction depends on the nature of the interaction with the service provider, the nature of the physical facilities in which the service gets provided, and the nature of the interaction with other guests present in the facility at the time the service is provided.

People as part of the product. People or firms that purchase services come in contact with other consumers as well as the service employees. For example, a hotel guest waits in line at the front desk or the concierge desk with other guests. In addition, the guests share facilities such as the pool, the restaurant, and the fitness center. Therefore, service firms must also manage consumer interactions to the best of their abilities to ensure customer satisfaction. For example, a hotel's sales office would not want to book group business with a non drinking religious group at the same time as a reunion of military veterans. The two groups are significantly different in behaviour, and the expectation is that they would not mix well within the facilities at the same time. Similarly, restaurants separate smokers and nonsmokers, and they should try to separate other patrons that show some potential for conflict.

Greater variability in operational inputs and outputs: In a manufacturing setting, the operational production can be controlled very carefully. For example, staff carefully manage inventory and precisely calculate production times. Services, however, are delivered in real time, with many variables not being fully under the control of managers. For example, if a guest has been promised an early check-in but all of the guests from the preceding night are late in checking out, it becomes more difficult for the hotel to honour the arriving guest's request. A service setting remains a more difficult site in which to control quality and offer a consistent service experience. Service firms try to minimize the amount of variability between service encounters, but much of the final product stays situational. There are many uncontrollable aspects of the delivery process, such as weather, the number of consumers present, the attitudes of the consumers, and the attitudes of the employees. Therefore, it becomes impossible to consistently control the quality for services in the same manner as the quality of manufactured products.

Harder for consumers to evaluate: Consumers can receive considerable information regarding the purchase of products; however, they often do not obtain it for services. Prior to buying a product, a consumer can research the product attributes and performance and use this information when making a purchase decision, especially an important one.

No inventories for services: Due to the intangible nature of services, they cannot be inventoried for future use. Therefore, a lost sale can never be recaptured. When a seat remains empty on a flight, a hotel room stays vacant, or a table stays unoccupied in a restaurant, the potential revenue for these services at that point in time becomes lost forever. In other words, services are perishable, much like produce in a supermarket or items in a bakery. It remains critical for hospitality and tourism firms to manage supply and demand in an attempt to minimize unused capacity. For example, restaurants offer early-bird specials and airlines offer deeply discounted fares in an attempt to shift demand from peak periods to non peak periods, thereby increasing revenue and profits.

Importance of time: Hospitality services are generally produced and consumed simultaneously, unlike tangible products, which are manufactured, inventoried, and then sold at a later date. Customers must be present to receive the service. There are real limits to the amount of time that customers are willing to wait to receive service. Service firms study the phenomenon of service queues, or the maximum amount of time a customer will wait for a service before it has a significant (negative) impact on his or her perception of service quality. Airline companies offer curbside check-in for the most time-conscious passengers, and restaurants have devised practices such as providing guests with pagers and expanding the bar area in order to reduce the negative effect that results from waiting for service.

Different distribution channels: The distribution channel for services is usually more direct than the traditional channel (i.e., manufacturer-wholesaler retailer- consumer) used by many product firms. The simultaneous production and consumption normally associated with service delivery limits the use of intermediaries. The service firm usually comprises both the manufacturer and the retailer, with no need for a wholesaler to inventory its products. Consumers are present to consume the meals prepared in a restaurant, to take advantage of the amenities in a hotel, and to travel between cities by plane.

Search, Experience, and Credence Qualities

Consumer behaviour is covered in greater depth, but a brief introduction to the subject as it relates to services becomes useful at this point. When consumers make purchase decisions, they move through a series of steps that explain the thought process leading up to and following the purchase of a product or service. Prior to making a purchase decision, consumers look for information about the product or service. Search qualities are attributes that the consumer can investigate prior to making a purchase.

When purchasing hospitality and tourism services, consumers rely heavily on word of mouth and on promotional elements such as advertising and publicity. Since services are intangible, search qualities can be difficult to evaluate. However, advances in technology and the increase in consumer advocacy groups have resulted in more information being available to consumers prior to purchase. The second set of qualities consumers use to evaluate services are experience qualities.

These refer to the attributes that can be evaluated only after the purchase and consumption of a service. The intangible nature of services forces consumers to rely heavily on experience qualities in the final evaluation of services. Therefore, a high risk remains associated with the purchase of services. For example, consumers who want to purchase an automobile will test-drive the car and review and consult the consumer performance data that are available on that model. Conversely, consumers who rent cars cannot evaluate their purchases until after they have committed their payment. Few consumers will take the time or make the effort to test-drive potential rental cars prior to making a decision at the time of rental. Similarly, consumers are taking a risk when they choose a restaurant because they cannot sample meals before they are purchased.

Finally, credence qualities are those attributes that are difficult to evaluate even after the service is consumed. Even though you arrive safely at your destination after a flight, you cannot evaluate the pilot's work in any real depth. In many cases, you know a service was not performed correctly only when an obvious mistake exists. For example, bacteria often appear on food served in restaurants, but the public becomes aware of it only when major ramifications such as food poisoning or deaths get publicized.

Purchase decisions related to services are more difficult to make because of the lack of search qualities and the difficulty in evaluating credence qualities. Consumers tend to rely on their own past experiences and those of others when making purchase decisions. Therefore, service firms must obtain as much feedback from consumers as possible. If consumers do not return, the firm may not know why, and the consumers will probably tell others about their experience. Service firms should know if consumers are not satisfied so that appropriate actions can be taken to improve the quality of service and increase repeat business.

Service Quality

Firms use two basic strategies to compete: become a low-cost provider of a particular service and focus on price competition, or focus on quality and try to differentiate your service from those offered by your competitors. Firms that can project high-quality images can charge higher prices. Service quality is a perception resulting from attitudes formed by customers' long-term, overall evaluations of performance.4 Maintaining high quality service in the hospitality and tourism industry remains difficult because of the variability in service delivery mentioned earlier in this chapter. Service quality is affected by all of the individuals who have contact with customers. If one employee provides below-standard service or fails to satisfy the customer, a negative experience could result. Therefore, it is important to understand the entire process of service delivery that leads to consumer perceptions of quality.

The Service Quality Process

The service quality process is the product of the expectations and perceptions of a firm's management, its employees, and the customers it serves. Whenever there are differences in expectations or perceptions between the people involved in the delivery and the consumption of services, a potential for a gap in service quality exists. Firms should diagnose any service quality gaps because there is a direct relationship between service quality and customer satisfaction. Simply stated, when customers are satisfied, they are much more likely to purchase from the service provider again. Over time, if they remain satisfied, they become loyal customers.

The service gap is the final gap that exists when there is a difference between customers' expectations of a service and their perceptions of the actual service once it is consumed. When this difference occurs, it is the result of one or more gaps that occur earlier in the service quality process. The first potential gap is referred to as the knowledge gap, which occurs when management's perception of what consumers expect is different from the consumers' actual expectations. This gap may lead to other gaps in the service quality service quality process, and it is usually the result of a failure in the firm's research programme or organizational structure. Firms need to obtain feedback from customers and employees that can be used to design services that will appeal to customers.

If the current service offering is not satisfying customers, then the firm should know from its customer surveys or because its employees are willing, and able, to provide valuable information that they obtain from customers, either voluntarily or involuntarily. The second potential gap is referred to as the standards gap, which refers to the discrepancy that can occur between management's perception of what customers expect and how the service delivery process is designed to meet those expectations. Management establishes the specifications to provide the desired service at the desired level of quality.

Therefore, even if management remains accurate in its perception of customer expectations, a gap could still exist in service because the delivery process does not accomplish the goals of the firm. For example, management may have correctly determined the amount of time that customers are willing to wait to check in to a hotel, but they may not schedule enough front desk clerks to meet the customers' expectations. This could result from a lack of commitment on the part of management or the result of management trying to reduce the firm's operating costs. One of the techniques used by management is to develop a service blueprint— a flow chart that details the delivery process, including the points of contact with customers. This will help to uncover any shortcomings in the delivery process that may lead to a gap in service quality. Management should document each step in the process to identify areas for improvement.

The third potential gap is referred to as the delivery gap, which occurs when there is a difference between the service delivery specifications and the actual service delivery. Management may have correctly assessed customer expectations and developed specifications that will meet these expectations, but employees may not deliver the service properly. For example, a restaurant may specify that wait staff should approach customers within two minutes of seating. However, the wait staff may stand around discussing their plans for later in the evening and ignoring the specifications. Firms must find ways to create an atmosphere for employees that ensures their willingness to perform the job tasks as desired by management. Employee selection and training are critical in this process, as are the rewards and recognition provided for good performance. The fourth potential gap is referred to as the communications gap, which occurs when there is a difference between the service delivered and the service quality promised through the firm's external communications with customers. Many firms have a tendency to promise more than they can deliver in an attempt to persuade customers.

For instance, advertisements for hospitality and tourism firms lead customers to believe that in the event of a problem or mishap the firms will do whatever they can to satisfy customers. Making promises to consumers that cannot be delivered is a big mistake that service providers often make. It results in service performance levels that are below consumer expectations, leading to dissatisfaction. Each individual consumer makes purchase decisions and has established, based on past experiences, a set of expectations for the performance of a product or service.

Anyone who travels on a regular basis can provide stories related to experiences with airlines, hotels, and restaurants. Ironically, firms that advertise 100 percent satisfaction guarantees are banking on the fact that most customers will not complain or force the issue. In other cases, firms simply neglect to inform customers about procedures or policies that would affect their expectations. For example, a good waitress will make sure that customers know that a dish is spicy or that a certain entree will take longer to properly prepare, so that customers can make informed decisions and are less likely to become dissatisfied, because the actual performance will more closely match consumer expectations.

If any of the first four gaps occur, then the service gap will occur because the actual service will not meet the customer's expectations. Comment cards and basic surveys will often uncover a service gap, but they may lack the detail needed to evaluate the other potential gaps. Therefore, firms should have a mechanism in place to obtain feedback from customers and employees that can be used to examine the entire service quality process. If services do not meet customers' expectations of quality, then the customers become dissatisfied and will likely not return. Also, they will convey these negative experiences to their friends and colleagues.

Managing Service Quality

To provide high-quality service, all members of the staff, from the highest to the lowest level on the organizational chart, must view the guest as the highest priority. Delivering high-quality service is based on an attitude of serving customers. For example, the mission statement of The Greenbrier, a well-known resort, states, "We are ladies and gentlemen serving ladies and gentlemen." Developing an attitude that places the customer as the highest priority for the business remains critical. Without satisfied customers and repeat patron- age, the business will not succeed in the long term.

To develop a service quality orientation, customers should be perceived in the following way:

- Each customer is the most important person in any business.
- Customers are not dependent on us, but we are dependent on them.
- Customers do not interrupt our work. They are the purpose for it.
- Customers do us a favour when they call. We are not doing them favours by providing them services.
- Customers are part of our business, not outsiders.

- Customers are human beings like us, with the same feelings and emotions.
- Customers bring us their wants, and it is our job to fulfill them.
- Customers deserve the most courteous and attentive service we can provide.
- Customers are the lifeblood of every business.

Firms that use a customer orientation become more successful at providing products and services that meet customers' needs and expectations. In contrast, firms that assume they know what is best for the customer are more likely to fail. This is further illustrated by those firms that successfully engage in relationship and internal marketing.

RELATIONSHIP MARKETING

All progressive companies devote marketing resources to attract and retain new customers. Relationship marketing is based on the proposition that it is less expensive to keep the customers you already have than to acquire new customers. It is shortsighted to think that merely attracting new customers will keep the business headed in a successful direction. Rather, an equal amount of attention and resources should be devoted to keeping the customer base that already exists. In times of slow market growth and increasing competition, it will be less expensive to maintain an existing customer base than to seek new customers.

Relationship marketing involves attracting, developing, and retaining customer relationships. This long-term view toward the customer must be seen as being equal in importance to attracting new customers. Many firms make the mistake of focusing on new customers at the expense of existing customers, and the level of service quality diminishes. For example, hotel sales managers are expected to develop new accounts with corporate and association groups.

Sometimes they spend so much time trying to get these new accounts that they neglect some of their existing accounts.

This lack of attention may cost the hotel the group's future business because they took the customer for granted. Service firms should build relationships and maintain them.

A relationship marketing approach is highly desirable upon meeting the following conditions:

- A customer has an ongoing or periodic desire for the service.
- The service customer controls the selection of the service organization.
- Alternative service providers make it easy for customers to switch.

All three of these conditions are present in the hospitality and tourism industry. Many firms offer special prices and additional services to highly desirable customers in an attempt to build long-term relationships. These practices are most commonly used with business accounts and frequent users. For example, hotels provide contract rates for corporations that supply a high volume of annual business. Airlines receive one of the lowest rates possible in hotels near airports because they have flight crews who need guest rooms on a daily basis. Also, airlines build relationships with frequent flyers by providing them with additional services such as preboarding, free upgrades, and airport clubs where they can rest or conduct business away from crowded lounges at departure gates.

INTERNAL MARKETING

In addition to focusing efforts on consumers, firms can achieve higher levels of service quality by marketing to their employees. Internal marketing encompasses all activities used by a firm in an effort to improve the marketing effectiveness of its employees. Efforts should be made to communicate with all employees, especially those in boundary spanning roles who come in contact with customers. The ability to deliver consistent, high-quality service depends on the organization's ability to recruit, train, retain, and motivate dedicated service personnel. First, service firms need to select and hire employees who are willing and able to provide high-quality service. There are many people in the job market, and firms need to create attractive positions that appeal to highly motivated individuals.

A range of potential service exists that an employee can provide from the minimum necessary to retain the position and not be penalized to the maximum possible service. This variability in the level of possible service is referred to as discretionary effort. For example, if an airline passenger leaves a carry-on item on a flight, the airline's personnel have some discretion as to the level of service they will provide. They can take their time and forward the item to the traveller's next destination, or they can try to deliver it to the traveler before he or she boards the next plane or leaves the airport. Second, service firms should provide employees with adequate training so they possess the skills that are required in performing their job tasks.

In addition, the firm should communicate with employees so they are aware of changes within the organization as well as upcoming events. If service personnel are well trained and they understand what management expects, the environment is right for success. Firms can use both internal communications, such as newsletters and e-mail, and external communications, such as advertising and public relations, to convey their expectations to employees.

An advertisement can be used to create and manage consumer perceptions and expectations, but at the same time, the ad can be used to educate employees as well. One of the major airlines aired a commercial on television that showed an athletic employee running through the airport to catch a traveler who left his briefcase at the check-in counter.

This commercial served two purposes:

1. It let customers know that the airline provided high-quality service, and
2. It gave employees an idea of the firm's service expectations.

Finally, firms need to provide employees with rewards and recognition when they perform at a high level of discretionary effort. This motivates service providers to continue performing at high levels and to remain loyal to the firm. Retaining good employees is important in providing high-quality service, and it reduces the costs associated with turnover. It takes a great deal of time and effort to hire and train good employees. Firms can use extrinsic rewards such as salary increases and bonuses or intrinsic rewards such as recognition and job satisfaction to motivate employees. Many firms recognize "employees of the month" by honouring them with plaques displayed where customers can see them or allowing them to use special parking spaces close to the building.

CUSTOMER SATISFACTION

Most firms understand the importance of customer satisfaction and will provide basic training to their employees. The more sophisticated firms actually have instruments that they use to measure customer satisfaction and establish benchmarks for future comparisons. Benchmarking is a process whereby a firm establishes a level of performance by comparing current performance against past performance, or by comparing current performance against the performance of other companies or an entire industry.

Data are used to create benchmarks, which then become the standard against which current and customer satisfaction future performance is evaluated. Unfortunately, many firms still only pay lip service to customer satisfaction and the complaints received from customers.

The following information was collected through the efforts of the Technical Assistance Research Programme in the 1980s, but it remains accurate today:

- The average business does not hear from 96 percent of its unhappy customers.
- For every complaint received, 26 other customers have the same problem.

- The average person with a problem tells 9 or 10 people, and 13 percent will tell more than 20.
- Customers who have their complaints resolved to their satisfaction tell an average of 5 people about the experience.
- Complainers are more likely to do business with you again than non complainers who have a problem: 54–70 percent if resolved, and 95 percent if resolved quickly. These statistics support the contention that a dissatisfied customer tells people about a bad experience more often than a satisfied customer tells people about a good experience. However, firms should take note that it is beneficial to have customers voice their complaints so that they can be resolved and increase the likelihood that the customers will return.

Improving Customer Service and Customer Satisfaction

Improving customer service should be a top priority of all managers working in the hospitality and tourism industry. Customer satisfaction occurs when a firm's service, as perceived by customers, meets or exceeds expectations. Firms that can consistently meet or exceed customer expectations will develop good reputations and often good quality images. When we travel, we encounter service providers in hotels and restaurants who provide exceptional service. This type and consistency of service does not happen by accident; it begins with a commitment by management to make it that way. Conversely, when the opposite occurs, the finger should be pointed at management as well.

1. *Define your standards of quality service with measurable indicators:* Before you can evaluate the level of service provided by employees within your organization, you must establish the standards by which they will be judged. These standards, or benchmarks, should be observable and measurable. For example, it might be reasonable to expect front desk agents to answer

the telephone within four rings or room service to deliver meals within 30 minutes of when the order was received. Once these standards are developed, they must be communicated to all personnel. It remains crucial that standards be clearly defined before any plans are developed to improve the level of service. Martin suggests two major dimensions to define quality service: the procedural dimension and the convivial dimension. The procedural dimension includes incremental flow of service, timeliness, accommodating consumer needs, anticipating consumer needs before they occur or are requested by the consumer, communicating in a clear and concise manner, customer satisfaction. obtaining consumer feedback, and coordinating through proper supervision. The convivial dimension includes displaying a positive attitude and body language, using the guest's name as a means of delivering personal attention, attending to the guest on a personal basis, providing guidance to guests who are indecisive, and solving problems that arise.

2. *Assess your current situation*: As in any continuous improvement programme, before you move forward, you must determine your current position. This can be done by objectively assessing the level of service currently provided within the organization; this involves conducting an audit of the services provided by service personnel within the organization. As a result of the audit, the strengths and weaknesses of the firm can be determined; this will provide a means of building on the aspects of service that are positive and improving the areas that are deficient. Audits can be conducted using mystery shoppers, or corporations may use staff members to audit the performance of units within the company.
3. *Develop effective service improvement strategies:* This must be accomplished through well-planned and

thorough training of service providers. Attention must be paid to identifying objectives for the training and providing specific instructions and clear descriptions of the expected outcome (s) of the training.

4. *Initiate your solutions carefully:* As with any plan, implementation is the most critical stage. You should proceed with caution, taking steps incrementally rather than all at once. You should build on small successes, rather than trying to accomplish too much too soon.
5. *Provide feedback, recognition, and rewards:* Positive feedback must be provided if the change in behaviour continues. A reward structure must be provided that will maintain the level of interest and enthusiasm among the service providers throughout their careers. This represents a major challenge for management, but one that is well worth the effort. Finally, management must continually evaluate the performance of its employees and make the appropriate changes. Over time, customers' expectations of service firms change, and competitive firms may increase the level of service that is considered the standard in an industry. Therefore, firms must constantly reassess their strategies and redefine their service standards. Service performance and customer satisfaction should be measured and evaluated using benchmarks established during previous periods. Also, direct comparisons with the performance of firms considered industry leaders are an excellent way to establish goals for future improvement.

Service Failures, Customer Complaints, and Recovery Strategies

Service failures occur at critical incidents, or "moments of truth," in the service encounter, when customers interact with a firm's employees. It is important to provide service personnel with the authority and the recovery tools necessary to correct service failures as they occur. This section will discuss the types of service failures, common consumer complaints, and recovery strategies that can be used to repair the service failures.

SERVICE FAILURES

The timeliness and form of response by service providers to service failures will have a direct impact on customer satisfaction and quality perceptions.

Service failures are assigned to one of three major categories:

1. Responses to service delivery system failures,
2. Responses to customer needs and requests, and
3. Unprompted and unsolicited employee actions.

The first category, system failures, refers to failures in the core service offering of the firm. These failures are the result of normally available services being unavailable, unreasonably slow service, or some other core service failure that will differ by industry. For example, a hotel's pool may have a leak and be closed, a customer may have to wait a long time for the shuttle to an airport car rental agency, or an airline might mishandle a passenger's luggage.

The second category, customer needs failures, are based on employee responses to customer needs or special requests. These failures come in the form of special needs, customer preferences, customer errors, and disruptive others (i.e., disputes between customers). For example, a hotel guest may want to have a pet in the room, a customer may want to be switched to an aisle seat on an airplane, a customer at an event may lose his ticket, or a customer in a restaurant may be smoking in a nonsmoking section.

The third category, unsolicited employee actions, refers to the actions, both good and bad, of employees that are not expected by customers.

These actions can be related to the level of attention an employee gives to customers, to unusual actions that can be performed by employees, to an action's reinforcement of a customer's cultural norms, or to an employee's actions under adverse conditions. For example, a hostess in a restaurant could anticipate the needs of a family with a small child, a hotel front desk clerk could give a free upgrade to a guest who waited in line too long, a flight attendant could ignore passengers with children, or a cruise ship employee could help to evacuate passengers during a crisis. customer satisfaction

Customer Complaint Behaviour

As mentioned earlier in this chapter, certain undesired outcomes are associated with dissatisfied customers. Two of the most common are to engage in negative word of mouth and to change service providers. A third, less common reaction is to engage in some form of retaliation. This retaliation can range from a negative word-of-mouth campaign to causing physical damage or launching a major protest. The way a firm approaches and handles complaints will determine its long-term performance. Some firms show a dislike for customers who complain, while other firms create an atmosphere that encourages customers to voice their concerns.

For example, Bertucci's Brick Oven Pizzerias, headquartered in Massachusetts, offers customers a tollfree number that they can call to register a complaint. One of the primary reasons for doing this is to provide dissatisfied customers with an outlet to have their concerns heard and to take immediate steps to resolve the complaint. By doing so, the firm hopes to reduce negative word of mouth and to retain customers. Most customers complain in an attempt to reverse an undesirable state.

Other more complicated reasons for complaining are to release pressure, to regain some form of control over a situation, or to get the sympathy of others. Whatever the reason, the outcome is that customers are not completely satisfied, and it is in the firm's best interest to know when this occurs. There are many other dissatisfied customers who do not complain because they don't know what to do or they don't think it will do any good.

Recovery Strategies

When customers complain, firms are presented with the opportunity to recover from service failures. Recovery strategies, and actions occur when a firm's reaction to a service failure results in customer satisfaction and goodwill. In fact, customers who are involved in successful service recoveries often demonstrate higher levels of satisfaction than customers who do not report service failures or complain. The following list describes popular service recovery strategies:

Cost/benefit analysis: Service firms should compare the costs of losing customers and obtaining new customers with the benefits of keeping existing customers. Most firms place a high value on retaining customers. However, some guests take advantage of satisfaction guarantees and complain on every occasion. Many hotel chains, such as Doubletree, maintain a database on complaints and will flag chronic complainers.

Actively encourage complaints: It is better to know when customers are not satisfied so that action can be taken to rectify the situation. It is important to note that while unhappy customers may not complain to service firms, they will often complain to their family and friends. Hospitality and tourism firms use comment cards and toll-free numbers to encourage customers to provide feedback. Also, service personnel are trained to ask customers whether everything was satisfactory.

Anticipate the need for recovery: Service firms should "blueprint" the service delivery process and determine the moments of truth, or critical incidents, where customers interact with employees. The process can be designed to avoid failures, but recovery plans should be established for use in the event that a failure occurs.

Respond quickly: The timelier the response in the event of a service failure, the more likely that recovery efforts will be successful. Once a customer leaves a service establishment, the likelihood of a successful recovery falls dramatically. Based on this principle, firms such as Marriott International provide service hotlines at each hotel to help resolve problems quickly. Managers and associates know that the speed with which they respond is often as critical as what the final resolution becomes.

Train employees: Employees should be informed of the critical incidents and provided with potential strategies for recovery. For example, some hotel training programmes use videotaped scenarios of service failures to show employees potential problems and the appropriate solutions.

Empower the front line: In many cases, a successful recovery will hinge on a frontline employee's ability to take timely action and make a decision. Firms should empower employees to handle service failures at the time they occur, within certain limits.

For example, Ritz-Carlton allows its employees to spend up to $1,000 to take care of dissatisfied customers. One of the classic examples of a service failure involved Northwest Airlines during a major winter storm at the Detroit airport. Unfortunately, due to the heavy snow, many outbound flights were canceled, and no gates were available for unloading passengers from the inbound flights. This traffic jam left many passengers stranded as the airplanes sat on the taxiways for as long as eight hours. Northwest's inability to provide the passengers with information or a solution resulted in hundreds of unhappy passengers and a class action lawsuit. Having delayed flights and a shortage of gates is not a new phenomenon at airports in climates such as Detroit's, and Northwest Airlines should have had a viable service recovery programme in place that could have lessened the severity of the problem.

Techniques to Assess Customer Satisfaction

One of the critical components of a firm's commitment to customer satisfaction is feedback that provides an assessment of the firm's performance. Then benchmarks can be established and future progress can be evaluated. Also, these measures can be used to reward service personnel in a way that stays consistent with a firm's customer satisfaction goals. The following section describes the most common techniques used by firms to assess customer satisfaction.

SPOKEN COMMENTS AND COMPLAINTS

Listening to consumer comments and complaints remains the most straightforward way to evaluate customer satisfaction. Service firms should set up formal systems that encourage customer and employee feedback regarding service experiences. Management should not overlook the value of the information obtained by boundary-spanning personnel through their normai contact with customers. One of the most recent approaches is providing toll-free numbers so that customers can call to voice complaints.

Surveys and Comment Cards

Many hospitality and tourism firms leave comment cards in guest rooms, on tables in restaurants, and at other points of contact so that they can obtain feedback. One of the problems associated with this method is the lack of representation. The response rate is small, and it tends to be biased toward those who are most upset and chronic complainers. Larger operations will conduct surveys through the corporate offices by either telephone or mail. Surveys will normally be more representative than comment cards and provide more detailed information. These types of surveys also provide for a more representative sample of customers.

Number of Repeat Customers

Service firms can gauge customer satisfaction by keeping track of repeat business. Higher levels of satisfaction would be associated with higher percentages of repeat customers. This models an unobtrusive method of assessing customer satisfaction, but it does not provide much detail.

Trends in Sales and Market Share

Another way to evaluate customer satisfaction without direct contact with customers is to examine the firm's internal sales records. Comparisons can be made on a month-to-month basis and with the same period of the previous year. Higher levels of satisfaction would be associated with increases in sales. However, firms should be careful with this method because there are many possible explanations for increases in sales. For example, the firm may have launched a new advertising campaign, a competitor may be renovating or going out of business, or the firm may have decreased its prices. In addition to examining sales records, firms should also look at market share. This measure considers sales in relation to the competition, which is a more accurate assessment of improved market performance. However, there could also be other explanations for changes in market share besides customer satisfaction.

Shopping Reports

Another approach used by hospitality and tourism firms involves having someone consume a service just like any other customer. The "secret shopper" can be an employee of the firm, an outside person chosen by the firm, or an employee of an outside firm that specializes in this service assessment activity. These shoppers are normally equipped with detailed evaluation forms based on company guidelines that can be used to record the desired information. It is often recommended that someone outside the firm be used in an attempt to maintain some level of objectivity. It is important to have a particular operation evaluated by more than one shopper on several occasions throughout the desired period. Doing so will result in a more representative sample of service experiences.

SERVICE TRENDS AFFECTING THE HOSPITALITY AND TOURISM INDUSTRY

Identifying trends within any business is one of the keys to success. Being in a position to identify what is occurring and what is likely to occur in the future remains very important. As discussed earlier, when studying trends in a broad sense, one should examine five major areas: the competitive environment, the economic environment, the political and legal environment, the social environment, and the technological environment. Several issues and trends are critical to understanding hospitality and tourism marketing. They help put into proper perspective what occurs within the competitive marketplace. Three trends that are having an impact on the hospitality industry and will continue to do so are shrinking customer loyalty, increasing customer sophistication, and increasing emphasis on the needs of individual customers.

SHRINKING CUSTOMER LOYALTY

Advertising and promotion for the hospitality and tourism industry's product-service mix have traditionally focused on the product, the services service trends affecting the hospitality and tourism industry provided, and the physical plant or atmosphere in which the customer enjoys the product-service mix. Today, many hospitality and tourism firms focus their promotions on price; that is, heavy price competition exists along with a good deal of discounting. Unfortunately, price discounting exists as a short-term strategy that seldom builds brand loyalty. Consumers often shop around for the best deal and are loyal only to organizations that give them a consistently superior one.

Recognizing this, companies have sought ways to increase brand loyalty, especially among heavy users of the product service mix. The best examples of this approach are the frequent flyer programmes promoted by the airlines and the frequent traveler programmes promoted by the lodging companies. These loyalty programmes are commonplace in the lodging industry; all of the major chains use loyalty programmes to encourage and reward frequent guests. The strategy behind loyalty programmes is to hook the customer with points which can be redeemed for products or services. The more frequently the customer stays at a hotel operated by the company, the more points are earned. The basic concepts common to all of these programmes are:

- Identify individuals who frequently purchase your product-service mix.
- Recognize the contribution those individuals make to the success of your company.
- Reward those individuals with awards and incentives that will increase their loyalty to your company and its brands.

Tie-ins with other companies providing travel-related services are also frequently used. For example, airlines, hotels, and car rental companies frequently offer bonus points within their programmes if the traveler uses the services offered by one of the companies participating in the tie-in. Both the airlines and the hotel companies are constantly making minor alterations to their programmes.

Increasing Consumer Sophistication

The budget segment of the lodging industry has undergone significant growth in the last several years. This growth has been fueled by the consumer demand for affordable accommodations that provide good value. In fact, consumers focus more on value and less on quality or price alone. Consumers have become more sophisticated and understand the concept of value at any price level. Hotels have responded that offer good quality service at an affordable price. Each of these brands features nicely appointed guest rooms, limited or no public meeting space, limited or no food service provided on the hotel site, and a complimentary continental breakfast for guests. These limited- service brands incur lower development and operating expenses and thereby can provide guests with a lower price and good value, something that all consumers are seeking.

Hotels in the upscale segment are also trying to increase the consumer's perception of value. They continually provide a broad assortment of amenities, such as health clubs on the property, business centers, rooms that provide more work space for business travelers, and personalized concierge service. These properties are striving to become "one-stop" destinations, providing a complete product-service mix that includes many food and beverage outlets, in-house office services, a wide variety of meeting room configurations, and other services, such as recreation, that will appeal to potential guests.

Within the fast-food service segment, companies often "bundle" their products in an attempt to increase sales and provide a better value for their customers. For example, they combine a sandwich, a large order of french fries, and a large soft drink at a price lower than what the items would cost if purchased separately. Similarly, tour operators and travel agents attempt to provide customers with more value by "bundling" the various components of travel (e.g., airline ticket, hotel room, car rental, and tickets for tourist at service trends affecting the hospitality and tourism industry tractions) at a price lower than the sum of the individual components. This approach is known as product bundling.

Increased Emphasis on the Needs of Individual Customers

The markets within both hospitality and tourism segments have been segmented for a long time. In the past 5 to 15 years, this trend has become even more pronounced. Mass marketing has become a thing of the past as more firms extend their product lines to meet the specific needs of smaller segments of travelers and diners. This phenomenon has become most apparent in the lodging industry. During the last decade, most of the major lodging chains developed several new brands or types of lodging properties to appeal to market segments that they were not currently serving. In addition, many hotel chains have merged with or acquired other hotel chains that focus on different market segments. Improvements in technology have given firms the ability to maintain large databases that detail consumer purchasing behaviour and preferences.

This information can be used to direct marketing efforts toward individual customers or market segments. Instead of relying on the mass media for promotions, a marketer can target past customers through direct mail and e-mail with special promotions and incentives that have a higher probability of being successful. There is more customization of products and promotions and less wasted coverage with media campaigns.

It began by defining services and explaining the characteristics that separate tangible products and services. Services are intangible and cannot be inventoried. This requires changes in the distribution process, and it makes it difficult to maintain consistent quality. It also requires more involvement on the part of customers, who actually become part of the product. The intangible nature of services results in more of an emphasis on experience qualities that are evaluated after a product becomes consumed, and less on search qualities that can be evaluated prior to purchase.

The concept of service quality remains important because consumers form perceptions of a firm based on its ability to provide a consistent level of service. This chapter introduced the service quality process and the potential gaps that could occur throughout the process. These gaps in service will decrease the level of service quality and lead to a decrease in customer satisfaction. Firms learn to manage service operations and improve quality through employee selection and training.

Once a firm focuses on the needs of consumers, it can build customer loyalty through relationship marketing. The overall performance of the firm can be improved through internal marketing efforts that attempt to communicate with employees and provide them with an environment for success. Customer satisfaction exists as the ultimate goal for a firm because it leads to brand loyalty and repeat purchases. Firms must meet or exceed customer expectations on a consistent basis in order to satisfy them. This chapter discussed ways to improve customer service and increase customer satisfaction. There are critical incidents, or moments of truth, when customers interact with employees and service failures can occur. Firms should encourage customers to voice their complaints so that the firms can anticipate and avoid possible failures. Also, firms can prepare service recovery strategies and train their employees to use them.

A firm's progress concerning customer satisfaction can be assessed using the techniques provided in this chapter, and benchmarks can be set for future comparisons. Finally, the chapter discussed some of the current trends in the hospitality and tourism industry that affect service operations. First, there is shrinking customer loyalty. Customers have many alternatives for fulfilling their needs, and it is easy to compare these alternatives using all of the information that is available.

The stronger the competition, the more incentives customers are given to switch service providers. Second, consumers are becoming more sophisticated. Consumers have access to a proliferation of information about products and services. This information allows them to focus on overall value, rather than price or quality alone. Also, consumer advocacy organizations provide helpful tips for getting bargains and avoiding firms with poor reputations. Finally, there is an increased emphasis on the individual needs of customers. Improved technology has made database marketing possible, allowing more precise targeting of markets and less wasted coverage with promotions. Firms are able to service more market segments by introducing new brands or forming relationships with other firms (e.g., strategic alliances, mergers, and acquisitions).

CASE STUDY

Service Quality at the Excelsior Hotel

Kristen Adams had recently transferred to the Excelsior Hotel to improve the level of customer service. She had been with the company for five years and had been quite successful in improving the level of customer satisfaction at the two previous hotels to which she had been assigned. Kristen knew that the Excelsior was going to be a real challenge. The mix of business was 60 percent individual transient guests and 40 percent group business. Of this group business, about one-third was motor coach tour groups.

On her first day on the job, she witnessed quite a sight. There was a line of about 20 guests waiting to check in when two motor coaches arrived and more than 80 additional guests and guides walked into the lobby to check in. Needless to say, the two front desk agents had a look of terror in their eyes as they worked diligently to process the registrations for those waiting to check in. Some 40 minutes later, everyone had been checked in, but the general manager said to Kristen, "I'm glad that you are here; we need to work out a better system. Let's meet for lunch tomorrow to discuss your initial ideas."

Kristen had just picked up a pen to start brainstorming ideas to present to the general manager when a guest approached her desk. "Hello, my name is Bill Foster, and I stayed at your hotel last night with my family. We really did not have a good experience, and I want to tell you about it. I want to make sure that this does not happen again, to me or anyone else." Mr. Foster then proceeded to tell Kristen his account of the events. "I was traveling with my wife and our son, who is four years old. Our connecting flight was delayed, so we did not arrive at our final destination until 10 p.m. The Excelsior had an advertised check-in facility at the airport, and I assumed that I would be able to secure my room while waiting for the luggage.

When I approached the employee at the hotel's airport facility, I was told that check-in service was not available at that time of the day. I found this to be surprising, since this was the very type of situation in which an airport facility would be beneficial. "Next, my family took a shuttle van from the airport to the hotel, where we were given directions to the front desk. Two front desk clerks were on duty when the passengers from the airport shuttle arrived a little before 11 p.m. However, one of the front desk clerks was apparently going off duty at 11, and she proceeded to close her drawer at that exact moment. This left a line of approximately 10 or 12 guests to be checked in by one clerk. Needless case study to say, it took some time to process all of the guests, and we had to wait 20 or 30 minutes for our turn. We were assigned to a room, but at this point we had a few bags and my son was fast asleep and had to be carried. When I asked for assistance with our luggage, I was told that no one was available at that time of night. The hotel was large, having over 1,000 rooms, and the rooms were spread out among several adjacent buildings.

Our room was two buildings away from the lobby area. My wife and I struggled to carry the luggage and our son to the room. We arrived there about 11:30 and attempted to enter the room. The key unlocked the door, but the door would not open. After a couple of attempts, we heard a woman's voice in the room. Obviously, the room had been double-booked and the woman woken from her sleep. I used the house phone to call the front desk and explain the predicament. The front desk manager offered a quick apology and said that she would send someone with a key to a nearby room. About ten minutes later, a housekeeper happened to be going through the hallway, and she let my family into the room that I had been given over the phone. However, the housekeeper had no idea what was going on and took my word. After we had been in the room for ten minutes, the phone rang and I spoke with the front desk manager. She acted as though she had sent the housekeeper to open the room, but she still needed to send someone with the room keys. She apologized one last time and told me to call the front desk if I had any other problems."

Chapter 3

Changes in Asian HRM

Some Asian economies continued to open up, restructuring financial sectors and receiving foreign direct investment (FDI). The years since our earlier collection have witnessed tremendous and massive economic, social and political change in Asia. There was, primus inter pares, the Asian financial crisis which swept though the region in 1997 and 1998, impacting on many countries, albeit in different ways, ferocity and length. It most certainly had an effect in a range of areas, including the style and approach of human resource management (HRM) and how human resources (HR) are dealt with.

More recent are current economic and political changes that have taken place in Asia, not least China's membership of the World Trade Organization (WTO), with impacts both on China and many other economies. All these developments mean that much of what we know about Asia is outdated and may well be irrelevant. This is particularly the case with HRM, and it is this area that will form the basis of this collection.

This contribution focuses on the importance of the volume and the need to update our knowledge and understanding of Asian HRM. We present a model that can be used for a comparative analysis of HRM, and one that allows the various levels of change to be assessed. This is followed by an overview of the collection's contents, with the common focus being on the changes that have occurred since 1997.

FOCUS AND IMPORTANCE

The focus of this collection is on change and continuity in Asian HRM and how HR are dealt with. This is both within and between Asian economies. The specific aim is to explore and analyse what has happened to HRM in a number of Asian countries since the mid-1990s. A good way to approach this task was to revisit our earlier work and to ask all the contributors to build on our 1997 collection entitled HRM in the Asia Pacific Region: Convergence Questioned (Rowley, 1997). This would allow for some precision to be built into the present study and would provide a useful framework for all the authors. Thus, this new collection replicates all the countries analysed earlier, and as far as possible its structure and coverage, in order to give it a framework and base comparison for 'changes' and/or 'continuities' in HRM.

Undertaking this task is important for at least two reasons. First, as mentioned above, the macro level changes that have taken place in this region necessitate such a volume. In particular, globalization, perceived by some as the harbinger of universal HRM and the need for convergence of HR practices to 'one best way', retains profound resonance in a range of areas. There remains a continuing fascination in the management literature and practice for the search for this 'holy grail' of universal (often under the rubric of 'international' or 'global') management, allowing difficult and complex HRM practice to be put on some sort of 'automatic pilot' and so reduce management problems.

Furthermore, within some countries particular HRM practices, such as lifetime employment and seniority based pay in Japan and Korea, have moved from 'saint' to 'sinner' in explanations of success. Why is this? Can there be such an easy sea change of practices often presented as former causes of economic success and deeply rooted in cultures (personal, organizational and national) and institutions. Also, there has been a varied range of developments across economies, with rebirth (Korea), continuing stagnation (Japan), emergence (China), assimilation (Hong Kong) and competition, to both developed (Singapore, Taiwan) and developing (Thailand, Philippines) ones. The following brief overviews of changes since our previous collection indicates this.

In China rapid economic growth has continued at a faster rate than most of the rest of Asia. While the impact of the Asian crisis was less, there were nevertheless some ripples and increasing unemployment. Japan remains moribund with its general downturn in economic activity, unemployment and low consumer demand reinforced by the collapse of overseas demand for its goods. South Korea (henceforth Korea) faced a likely nemesis when the former shining lights and star performers of the economy, the chaebols, collapsed. The economy has, however, strongly bounced back, albeit that the new government is promising closer control and reforms of business. In the Philippines both the crisis and political problems damaged the economy, ending the optimism of the earlier period.

Thailand was one of the originators of the crisis when its currency went into free fall, the property bubble burst, unemployment increased, FDI collapsed and the IMF bail came with 'strings'. By 2002 some economic stability had returned albeit in the context of a loss of FDI to China. The earlier prosperity, praise and concern about the post-transfer sovereignty of 'one country two systems' in Hong Kong was replaced as the crisis hit the currency, stock market and property prices.

With a continuous deflationary spiral and the consumer price index falling for more than 50 consecutive months (Economist, 2003), the earlier decamping of local manufacturing capacity was joined by waves of FDI into China post-WTO, by-passing Hong Kong as its monopoly 'gateway'. Singapore was affected by the crisis, with reduced external demand, although the economy had recovered by 1999.

Taiwan initially benefited from the crisis as a 'safe haven' for FDI and continued non-Asian demand for its products. By 1998 the economy had declined, bankruptcies and unemployment rose, whilst by 2002 the economy had recovered, FDI and employment had not.

A second reason why this symposium is important is because we contribute to a number of theoretical debates, not least the resilient key ideas around convergence (universalism) and divergence (contingency) and aspects of cultural and institutional approaches. They remain important as some of the more naïve literature and commentators, such as in the area of international HRM, have ignored or underplayed this. While an improvement on the earlier narrow study of expatriate management, much more is needed. Indeed, such myopia often reduces the subject to the study of multinational companies (MNC) operations void of the complexity involved and detail required.

We can develop such theoretical aspects further by adding another dimension which concerns the ideas of disaggregating different levels within national HRM systems (Rowley and Benson, 2002). Commonly these are the three levels of architecture, policy and practice, to distinguish developments, which may be different, or even contradictory, even within a particular HRM system. This sort of framework provides greater nuance and a more calibrated and sensitive analytical device.

Aids to Comparisons and Benefits

To assist in the comparisons (temporal, geographical and dimensional) of the selected countries we utilize several analytical devices. First, we again consider the developments in comparison to the HRM dimensions . This provides an integrating mechanism for this symposium. We have, however, reduced the earlier twelve dimensions to ten, with some internal reconfiguration and recompositions. The ten dimensions are listed.

ASSESSMENT OF HRM CHANGES AND CONTINUITIES

Dimension	Presence	Change
1.	Rules: adherence to	
2.	Behaviour: common values and norms	
3.	Key managers: personnel/specialists versus line/general	
4.	Personnel selection	
5.	Payment systems	
6.	Work conditions: harmonized	
7.	Contracts: individual versus standardized	
8.	In-house training	
9.	Right to hire and fire	
10.	Strategic role for personnel manager	

Key: (Practice)

present

% present to some degree

not present

(Degree of change in past 4 years)

+ + major change

+ change

0 none

Second, we have used many of the original authors where possible (although new authors do bring fresh insights and perspectives on the original works) to cover the same mixed set of economies. These are the developed, large economies of Japan and Korea, the developed, smaller economies of Hong Kong, Taiwan and Singapore, the developing, medium size economies of Thailand and the Philippines and the developing, large sized economy of China.

A third way we encouraged comparison was to be internally rigorous. Thus, as far as possible we have the same structure and format for each of the contributions. This had five main sections with several sub-sections to each.

They are as follows.

- Introduction
- Contextual Factors and Issues

- Political and historical
- Economic
- Labour markets
- 1997 Asian financial crisis and reactions
- Current economic situation

Changes in HRM

- Major changes taking place
- Table outline of these changes
- Possible changes in the immediate future
- Discussion
- Why changes have occurred
- Convergence or divergence
- Key issues for HRM
- Implications for theory development
- Conclusion

Not only did this forced common format and framework help forge each contribution in a similar shape to add consistency of coverage and ease of analysis, but a by-product was that it allows quick direct comparisons between individual aspects of the economies covered-speedy cross-comparisons, for example, of political and historical backgrounds, labour markets, and so on, are rendered easier.

HRM Going : Continuity or Convergence

A wide range of relevant work has emerged post-1997. Some of this Asian-related literature can be divided into three types: countries/ themes, convergence and divergence. The first group can be single or multi-country. Keeley (2001) in International HRM in Japanese Firms: Their Greatest Challenge, examines the integration of local managers into the management process of overseas subsidiaries and parent Japanese MNCs. Kwon and O'Donnell (2001) in The Chabeol and Labour in Korea: The Development of Management Strategy in Hyundai, present a fascinating, detailed and historically grounded account of the forces shaping labour and the organization of work.

Bamber and Lansbury (1998) in their latest edition of International and Comparative Employment Relations, cover issues and countries relevant to our collection. Bamber et al. (2000) in their Employment Relations in the Asia Pacific: Changing Approaches, also include relevant countries.

Kidd et al. (2001) in their Advances in HRM in Asia, adopt a thematic approach. This includes indigenous firms, for example, venture business culture and also knowledge workers in R&D in Japan, HR development in Korean chaebols, Chinese family businesses in Hong Kong and Thailand, and business culture, career planning and development of managers, and training in Thailand. Western firms in China are also covered, including HR strategy, HR development of European MNCs, joint ventures and culture. Other volumes include Debrah and Smith's (2001) Work and Employment in a Globalized Era: An Asia Pacific Focus, covering, inter alia, the Japanese service sector and Chinese job search. Felstead and Jewson (1999) in Global Trends in Flexible Labour, touch on a number of Asian experiences. Leisink (1999) in Globalization and Labour Relations, covers labour markets and employee relations. Hutchinson and Brown (2001) in Organising Labour in Globalising Asia, includes the Philippines garment industry, Chinese joint ventures, and Thai health and safety. Hollinshead and Leat (2003), with their new edition of HRM: An International and Comparative Perspective, provide a mix of themes and countries. Jackson (2002) in International HRM: A Cross-Cultural Approach, uses a range of models, such as 'The Motivation Organization' (the Japanese model) and The Joint Venture Organization' (the Chinese model).

Second, there are those pieces that can be placed broadly within the universal and convergence school. A Special Issue of the American journal Human Resource Management in 2002 was on 'best practices' in nine countries: US, Canada, Mexico, Australia, Japan, Korea, China, Taiwan, Indonesia, plus one region: Latin America, composed of Costa Rica, Guatemala, Panama, Nicaragua, Venezuela. This analysis of HRM is in terms of areas including selection, pay and appraisals. The results are somewhat ambivalent. For instance, Drost et al. (2002:67), on training, state that 'While the results do not indicate any universal practices across all countries studied, they do indicate significant similarities in practices within country clusters' where common practices were influenced by cultural values and industry trends. Therefore, 'While we could find no universal or common practices we found significant similarities in practices within country clusters' due to culture and industry trends.

Yet for many of the others in this volume, this similarity was seemingly less prevalent. Huo et al. (2002:42) note more divergence than convergence in practices, although this was in the process of converging on ways of recruitment even though selection criteria remained driven by a country's prevalent cultural values. They concluded '...inching toward global convergence, we expect national cultures to continue affecting the hiring practices used...' therefore, cross-national differences will continue to exist. Such divergence was even more obvious in other papers, such as Milliman et al. (2002), on performance appraisals, who state that practices varied significantly between countries, influenced by various contextual factors. Bowen et al. (2002), on strategic HRM, note significant differences in HRM status across countries. In conclusion, for Von Glinow et al. (2002: 123), this project's findings revealed that there were international HRM 'best practices', but somewhat damningly for this school of thought (and actually more worryingly for the neutrality and open-mindedness of the research itself) was their caveat: 'However, they are not as universal as we had hoped.'

Third, from the 'other side' is work confirming the continuity of management differences across countries. Beeson (2002) in Reconfiguring East Asia: Regional Institutions and Organisations after the Crisis, notes that apparently universal institutions, including legal systems, while sharing many common features superficially similar to those elsewhere, may operate in very different and distinctive ways. Whitley (1999:3) in Divergent Capitalisms: The Social Structuring and Change of Business Systems, argues that: 'Convergence to a single most effective type of market economy is no more likely in the twenty-first century than it was in the highly internationalized economy of the late nineteenth century.' Differences in systems of economic organization and control are explained in terms of the specific features of institutional environments.

This is important as it usefully highlights that 'economic relationships and activities are socially constructed and institutionally variable, such that the ways competitive processes operate, and the nature both of the actors engaged in them and of their outcomes, vary significantly between societal contexts'. Thus, Venter in Common Careers, Different Experiences: Women Managers in Hong Kong and Britain, using both qualitative and quantitative data, argues that culturally different conceptions of equality and family are key variables underpinning the different work experiences of women managers in Hong Kong and Britain. Therefore, the impact of industrialization was mitigated by cultural constraints and rejected the convergence thesis.

A comprehensive example is the two-volume, 21 country collection by Zanko and Zanko and Ngui, The Handbook of HRM Policies and Practices in Asia-Pacific Economies. All the countries in our volume are contained, inter alia, in their collection. They also develop the interesting and important idea of 'regionalism', and its impact on HRM, within an Asian context. It concludes that across the 21 countries in APEC '...there are many ways of managing human resources for success. There was no evidence of a universalist 'one best way' of HRM being followed'.

Similarly, of relevance is Cousins, who compared non-standard employment in Europe (Germany, Spain, Sweden, UK) and found that despite similar pressures and direction of change 'these forces for change are mediated through the social, political and institutional structures within each country'. Also, there were clear differences between the extent to which such employment was precarious or stableA useful collection combining countries and themes is our earlier ten country collection titled Globalization and Labour in the Asia Pacific Region. Warner is a useful piece on Asia, and Warner and Joynt Managing Across Cultures: Issues and Perspectives, is a collection with a theoretical background, area studies and cross-cultural issues. Warner's Culture and Management in Asia also covers similar areas.

Divergent Convergence : Levels of Change

An aspect of this analysis new to this collection is the idea of levels of change in HRM, had been simplified for use here. Three levels of HRM change can be analysed: architecture, policies and practices. One way of operationalizing these levels is to adopt Storey's model of HRM. The first level, system architecture (or deep structure), can be measured by differences in 'Beliefs and Assumptions'. That is, it is HR that gives a competitive edge, that the aim is not merely compliance but employee commitment, and that employees should be carefully selected and developed.

Levels	Elements	Dimensions
1. Architecture	Beliefs and Assumptions	Rules: adherence to Behaviour: còmmon values and norms
2. Policy	Strategic Qualities and Managerial Roles	Strategic role for personnel manager Key managers: personnel/ specialists versus line/general
3. Practice	Key Levers	Personnel selection Payment systems Work conditions: harmonized Contracts: individual versus standard In-house training Right to hire and fire

The second level refers to policy choices and mix of policies. These policy options can be measured by 'Strategic Qualities and Managerial Roles', namely that HR decisions are of strategic importance, that HR policies should be integrated into business strategy and that line managers play the critical role in HRM. Finally, the third level refers to the actual HRM practices in the enterprise. These are referred to as the 'Key Levers' and consist of integrated action on selection, training, reward and job redesign that allows for devolved responsibility and empowerment. Of course, these three levels and their corresponding dimensions represent an idealized version of HRM that will not be present even in all Western enterprises. The value of this approach, however, lies in having a common reference point by which to measure changes in HRM.

This framework for analysis leads us to extend the key question of whether change has taken place to include where and at what levels have changes occurred, and whether this change has led to a degree of convergence? These questions are addressed in the contributions that make up this symposium.

OVERVIEWS OF COVERAGE

China

In the past five years, there have been changes in many walks of life, notwithstanding those in the economy and especially in the area of HRM. Once the government embarked on its 'Four Modernizations' and 'Open Door' strategies, the path was decisively mapped out, but the implications for HR only became clearer as the 1980s unfolded. The main impetus for the shifts relate to the changes in the historical, political and macro-economic environments. The main factor has been the unbundling of the economy and its factor-markets that involved the continuing fall in the state sector's share of economic activity and the growth of the non-state sector. This has been accompanied by a change in the outlook of managers and entrepreneurs, as well as in workers' attitudes to reform (some of it voluntary and some of it imposed by circumstance). This contribution explores the relationship between greater marketization and the pragmatic, step-wise adoption of HRM norms and practices, arguing that the faster the former proceeds, the more widespread the diffusion of the latter.

Hong Kong

Enterprise-level HRM practices were developed in the context of an open, competitive, market economy, a colonial regime disinclined to interfere in business decisions or the labour market, and a trade union movement with minimal economic and political clout. The types of employment systems that emerged within this environment, and how changes in the economy and polity impacted on these systems from the late 1970s to the mid-1990s, are outlined. A review of survey evidence on the ways that HRM practices in the private sector have since shifted in response to the Asian crisis and the change of sovereignty is also presented.

Japan

It was reported in 1997 that HRM was best characterized by continuity with some changes to assessment and pay practices. Since then the context of HRM has undergone significant change in four respects. First, very low levels of growth with unemployment rising and firms continuing to shed labour have continued. Second, the labour market is ageing and reduced recruitment of young graduates is occurring. Third, although only indirectly affected by the Asian crisis, the decline in the demand for capital goods from Asia, coupled with a series of financial scandals and a decrease in public spending, contributed to Japan's economic woes. Finally, employers are strongly advocating that HRM reform be undertaken that would see the system move away from uniform employment conditions. What impact these changes have had on HRM is the focus of this piece.

Korea

The operating context of HRM has undergone radical shifts since 1997. These include government change, South-

North Korean summit talks, labour market turbulence, corporate bankruptcies, restructuring and downsizing (and even co-hosting, with Japan, the football World Cup). Economic development ground to an abrupt halt and went into reversal when the dark shadow of the Asian crisis was cast over Korea. Yet, the economy confounded the merchants of doom and gloom, and quickly and strongly recovered from 1999. All these factors have undoubtedly influenced the practice of HRM. Therefore, the focus of this piece is to compare the current situation with the past and to delineate the amount and type of such change vis-à-vis continuity in HRM.

Philippines

The purpose of this piece is three-fold: to build on the 1997 study, to demonstrate differences in HRM practices in the import substitution industrialization (ISI) and export-oriented industrialization (EOI) sectors and to highlight changes, if any, since the mid-1990s. This contribution agrees with the earlier position that suggested there was a trend towards the adoption of more sophisticated and more Western HRM practices. However, it also contends that the overall findings may be of limited value as the earlier study focused more on a small number of Philippine-owned ISI sector firms. To better capture the diversity between sectors this study draws a comparison between HRM practices in the ISI and EOI sectors. These two sectors have been very different in terms of their history, design and operating rationale.

Singapore

This contribution traces the development of HRM from the mid-1990s with particular reference to the impact of the Asian crisis. In particular, it explores the changes in HRM since 1997. National HRM concerns and strategies to maximize human capital as Singapore transforms itself into an innovation and knowledge economy are highlighted. The issue of convergence versus divergence in the management of HR is also considered. Current and future HRM challenges that are most likely to impact on the country's competitiveness and economic performance are also explored.

Taiwan

The changes in the macro-economic environment, due to the Asian crisis, have been an important stimulus to organizational and HRM changes in Taiwanese enterprises. This contribution tackles these responses by looking at individual firms, using a case study approach. The pattern of organizational responses introduced in these companies has exhibited a variety of different characteristics. Most have implemented strategies towards enhancing the competitiveness of individual firms. The situation has changed since 1997, marked by differences between a period of economic boom and recession. Consequently, as key economic and labour market conditions have changed so have HRM practices evolved.

Thailand

The Asian crisis, which severely impacted on the economy, and its aftermath, was the product of a number of forces, but management practices in Thailand played a major role. The period since has seen efforts at innovation and reform in the managerial arena, including changes in HRM policies and practices. To date, these shifts are still incomplete, particularly in locally owned companies. Companies surveyed in the post-crisis period tend to exhibit approaches to HRM more consistent with flexible, high-performance work systems (HPWS) than with more traditional approaches. Although subsidiaries of MNCs are generally ahead of locally owned companies in this respect, data presented in this contribution show that Thai companies (at least larger, globally active ones) are seemingly more a HPWS methods, though adapted in many ways to the Asia

There have been tumultuous changes in the operating cont in Asia and its HR practices and policies since our earlier This issue continues to attract much management and debate, especially under the rubric of 'globalization'. Indeed, of former 'traditional' HRM systems and models have been and different practices introduced. It is the impact of this the inter-play with the existing systems that interests us resulted in convergence towards some sort of 'stereotypical' or perhaps Asian, model of HRM given the common overarc of 'Asian' and geographical proximity? In what areas a levels? It is this theme that informs the following pieces turn shed light on HRM practices.

IMPLICATIONS FOR THEORY AND PRACTICE

The specific aim was to explore changes since 1997. In this period many Asian countries experienced the direct effects of the Asian financial crisis. There was also a substantial economic downturn in the US, which impacted on Asian exports, low levels of growth, as in Japan, dramatic changes in direction and increases in foreign direct investment (FDI), particularly in China, and a range of social and political changes. As a consequence, much of what has been written about Asia in that period is outmoded and may well be irrelevant.

To provide a unified approach to investigating change in the Asian region we built on the earlier collection by Rowley (1997) which explored the question of whether the changes taking place in Asian HRM were leading to a convergence towards what may be termed the 'Western HRM' model. By extending this work and exploring the same economies, this has allowed us to make more balanced judgements and to explore change in the context of its implications for theory development and HRM practices.

For theory, the key issues were why such changes are occurring and was this leading to the application of a similar model of HRM throughout the region. In other words, are we now witnessing a period of convergence of practices or are key national differences maintaining or leading to distinct HRM systems? For practitioners, both in Asia and elsewhere, this raises a multitude of questions concerning 'best practice', the relevance of national cultures and the ability to transfer and successfully transplant human resource (HR) practices.

As discussed earlier, the volume includes a variety of Asian countries that represent the divide between developed and developing countries and also the differences in size. These are important criteria when exploring HRM change in country settings. In addition, we adopted a model of change that explores change at the levels of architecture, policy and practice. This meant that superficial change at the practice level was not equated equally with changes in the architecture that underpins a system. To answer the questions raised above, this piece is divided into three parts. The next section provides a summary and analysis of the individual contributions. Following this a comparative analysis is provided which will locate both the level of change and the key components of that change. The contribution concludes by discussing the implications for theory and practice.

OVERVIEW OF CHANGES

China

The key issues for HRM in China have been related to the elimination of the 'iron rice bowl' and the transition to market-driven employment practices, not just in large firms but also across the wide range of businesses now to be found. The weight of tradition and inertia has been a drag on such a process but the change is now more noticeable, particularly as the state sector withers away. Recruitment is more dependent on the market rather than on allocation by the labour bureaux and selection is increasingly based on merit. Reward systems remain complex but are more performance driven. Motivation of employees is now based on material rewards rather than a pledge of job security and benefits in kind. Training is more systematic, at least in larger firms, even if development is less de rigueur. In short, the 'long march' from personnel management to full-blown HRM is under way, with some changes to the basic architecture of the system.

Hong Kong

A number of significant changes have occurred in the management of HR in Hong Kong in the past five years. First, employment security has declined as firms across all sectors cut the number of employees. Second, pay freezes and/or pay reductions have become widespread and fringe benefits have been cut while the use of discretionary performance bonuses has spread. Third, employees are expected to work harder, upgrade their skills and become functionally more flexible. Fourth, employment relations have been affected by the political transition as well as the Asian crisis.

This was most clearly illustrated by the post-handover government repealing a collective bargaining bill that had been passed in the final days of the colonial regime. Public sector HRM practices are undergoing substantial modification as a consequence of public sector changes and more recently civil service reforms. The hiving-off of government functions to the private sector, the introduction of a voluntary retirement scheme, a management-initiated retirement scheme for directorate-level officials and the hiring of new staff on contracts without guarantees of moving to permanent terms, are examples of changes that have occurred and that represent partial HRM policy and architectural changes.

Japan

Important changes have occurred in Japanese HRM. First, wage settlements are becoming more disparate and are linked to the nature of employment. In this period real wages also fell. Second, there has been a gradual shift towards a merit-based appraisal system for wages and promotion in Japanese companies. Third, there has been a clear departure from age and tenure as key criteria for wages and promotion. Whilst this has been a trend for the past two decades, the process has accelerated over the past five years.

Finally, there has been a general restructuring of HRM with the speed of change substantially increasing. What may have been considered unique practices five years ago have now become more widely established. Nevertheless, HRM reform is still ostensibly at the level of practice and experimentation. There is little indication that the change is systematic or has occurred at the policy or architectural level.

Korea

The core ideology of the traditional Korean HRM system has changed from 'organization first', 'collective equality' and 'community oriented' towards 'individual respect', 'individual equity' and 'market principle'. The main underlying assumptions of traditional HRM-lifetime employment and seniority-based remuneration-have weakened vis-à-vis flexible employment. Outsourcing, performance pay and redeployment policies have become more popular.

Recruitment has changed more towards recruitment on demand and selection based on speciality and creativity. Reinforcing competencies is now achieved by more performance-based promotion, while the retaining of such competencies is aided by the development of flatter structures, team-based design, and the development of professionals. Finally, competencies are seen as replaceable and this has led to increased job mobility and flexible employment. Such changes have created the climate for a rapid recovery from the effects of the Asian crisis and have begun to penetrate both the policy and architectural levels of the HRM system.

Philippines

The adoption of HRM practices has, until recently, been distinguishable by sector. Export-oriented firms have faced global competitive pressure and have adopted HRM practices different from the domestic firms. Recently these domestic firms have adopted HRM practices that have been more characteristic of those in the export-oriented sector. Such practices have included the increased use of subcontracting, labour contracting and retrenchments, Many of these changes have occurred over the past five years and this suggests that the Asian crisis played a significant role. The realities of falling trade and investment barriers, the privatization of state-owned firms and the deregulation faced by domestic firms, are all a result of the numerous structural adjustment programmes sponsored by the international financial institutions. Yet, as most of the changes in the domestic sector have taken place in the past few years, the degree of change has been relatively small and represents change at the level of practice. Nevertheless, given that many of these changes are due to the systematic removal of regulatory protection it is quite likely that, over time, these changes will represent fundamental policy and architectural shifts. In this case further convergence is likely.

Singapore

The HRM system is in a state of transition and will continue its evolution to one that pays much less attention to lifelong jobs. In the face of severe competition, organizations will continue to restructure and introduce new work processes. More companies are using performance-based pay and promoting employees on merit. While the strategic role of HR professionals is likely to become more crucial, they will need to identify those added values that they can create and develop measures to evaluate their own performance. Similarly, individual employees will have to be more active in charting their own future.

In a restructured economy, executives and managers, professionals, and ordinary workers will need to continually improve their knowledge and skills to stay employable. More firms will relocate their labour-intensive activities to nearby countries while at the same time Singapore will encourage higher valued-added companies to locate in Singapore. These companies will demand a highly skilled and flexible workforce and thus will put more pressure on the adoption of HRM practices. It is therefore likely that the changes identified above will become institutionalized at the policy and architectural levels.

Taiwan

Taiwan has moved substantially towards adopting International HRM standards. Much of the pressure for this change has stemmed from changes in the economic environment; from a period of economic boom conditions to one of prolonged recession. This has led to higher unemployment and a fall in demand for migrant labour. As a consequence, HRM policy has shifted to one emphasizing flexibility at both national and enterprise levels in order to develop the required skills, the training of laid-off workers for re-employment and the refocusing of long-term HR strategic plans.

At the same time FDI and multinational companies (MNC) have had a profound impact on HRM and the move to international HR practices. In response to the increased competition and global conditions, firms, irrespective of their size or sector, have began to adopt 'western' HRM practices. This trend will continue in the foreseeable future and it is likely that these changes will influence, in the long-term, the policy and architecture of the HRM system.

Thailand

The last five years have witnessed innovation and reform in the managerial arena, including changes in HRM policies and practices. These changes are best characterized by the adoption of HRM practices and their subsequent adaptation to the particular Thai context. Nevertheless, it is clear that increasingly companies are exhibiting HRM approaches that are more consistent with flexible, high performance work systems than with the traditional approaches. Rule adherence is somewhat relaxed and common values and norms exist. These approaches, however, are more engendered by Thai culture.

HR managers are widespread in Thai companies and the increasing professionalization of these managers is enhancing their role. On the other hand personnel selection still involves a focus on 'job fit' rather than 'organizational fit'. Job evaluation methods are widespread, at least in the larger and more sophisticated companies and some movement has occurred towards performance-based pay. Continuous training is now increasingly emphasized. In contrast there has been little promotion of collective bargaining in the private sector. It is too early to say how far such changes have gone beyond the practice level and if they have penetrated the policy and architectural level.

COMPARATIVE ANALYSIS OF NATURE AND LEVEL OF CHANGE

The above analysis of HRM changes in the eight case study countries points to convergence of at least some HRM practices at the level of practice. How widespread are these changes and do they represent changes at the HRM policy and architectural levels? These dimensions represent three levels of change: system architecture as measured by the beliefs and assumptions underpinning the system, policy choices as measured by strategic qualities and managerial roles, and HRM practices as measured by the key levers.

It is clear that all the countries represented in this study have made substantial moves towards the HRM model in terms of the first level, practice or key levers. Merit-based selection, performance-based pay, employment contracts, harmonized work conditions and continuous in-house training have increasingly become the norm. These are more developed in some countries than others and the pace of change over the past five years has varied considerably. At the level of practice it can therefore be concluded that a more 'Western' HRM model has emerged, albeit in some cases with some unique characteristics.

At the second level of change, policy choices or strategic qualities and managerial roles, less change has been found. With the exception of Japan, few of the other countries have implemented, in full, the HRM model, although all, with the exception of the Philippines, have made some progress in this direction. A more strategic role for personnel managers is emerging and line managers are taking a more active interest in HR issues.

At the third level, system architecture or beliefs and assumptions, most studies in this collection have reported mixed progress over the past five years. While common values and norms seem to be guiding HRM, at least to some extent, it remains unclear as to how far these remain based on traditional customs and practices. Almost with out exception, however, adherence to a set of standardized rules still set the parameters for HRM in the eight case study countries. That is, there is little evidence that a 'can do' outlook or an impatience with rules attitude has been adopted, although some movement in this direction has been detected in all but one of the countries.

Levels/Dimensions	China	Japan	Korea	Thailand	Hong	Philippines	Singapore	Taiwan
SystemArchitecture								
Rules: adherence to	(+)	(+)	(+)	%(++)	%(+)	(0)	%(+)	(+)
Behaviour: common values and norms	(+)	(+)	(+)	(0)	%(+)	(0)	(+)	(+)
Strategic Qualities and Managerial Roles								
Key managers: personnel/specialists v. line/general	(0)	(+)	%(+)	%(+)	%(+)	(0)	(++)	(0)
Strategic role for personnel manager	%(+)	(0)	%(+)	%(+)	(0)	%(+)	%(+)	%(+)
Key Levers								
Personnel selection	(+)	(+)	(+)	(0)	(+)	(0)	(++)	(+)
Payment systems	(+)	%(+)	%(++)	%(++)	%(+)	%(+)	(++)	(+)
Work conditions: harmonized	%(+) (++)	(+) %(+)	(0) %(+)	%(++) %(+)	(0) (0)	%(0) (+)	%(+) (+)	(0) %(+)
Contracts:individual v. standardized	(+)	(+)	(0)	%(++)	%(0)	(+)	%(+)	(0)
In-house training	(++)	(0)	%(+)	(0)	(0)	(0)	(+)	(+)
Right to hire and fire								

(Degree of change towards HRM model in 5 years)

Key: (Practice) present; % present to some degree; not present — + + major change; + change; 0 none

Based on these findings, it can be concluded that practices associated with the HRM model have been widely adopted in companies operating in the economies of the eight case studies. Yet such practices have not yet been internalized in policy choices or system architecture. This leaves the HRM systems in these countries unstable and that the best way to characterize the reform is widespread experimentation with the various component practices of the HRM model. Further, the way the same practice is viewed and implemented can vary, as in the case of non-standard employment in terms of the extent to which it is precarious or stable.

The lack of significant change at the policy and architectural levels also suggests that business structures and some unique cultural attributes remain important constraints on convergence. Notwithstanding the above it is also clear that some reforms in this direction are occurring at these two higher levels which suggest that in the next five to ten years the adoption of the HRM model may have consolidated. On the other hand, this consolidation may develop with each national system forming a unique set of characteristics that represent varying cultural and institutional influences.

Implications

In attempting to understand the changes identified in Asian HRM, this collection addressed four questions. First, why have such changes have occurred? The initial changes were fuelled by globalization and the impact of the Asian crisis which forced firms to become more competitive and efficient. HRM in this context was seen as the appropriate way to improve labour productivity and achieve international 'best practice'. The impact of these factors was not, however, uniform and they were supplemented in particular countries by other more unique factors.

In Japan the depressed state of the economy, the ageing workforce, the changing attitudes of younger workers, and a more general loss of faith in the traditional model of Japanese HRM were instrumental in the push for HRM reform. On the other hand, the breakdown of the traditional divide between the public and private sectors in Hong Kong after the handover to China in 1997 were important contextual factors driving change. Other factors included the impact of MNCs (Taiwan and Thailand), the change in the attitudes of managers and workers (China), the removal of regulatory protection (Philippines), strategic choices of management (Korea), and the need to broaden the country's economic base (Singapore).

The second question addressed was whether these changes represented a convergence towards the Western HRM model. All country studies in this collection point to a range of practices that suggest some convergence is taking place. The adoption of the HRM model appears strongest at the level of practice and far weaker at the policy or architectural levels. Yet, even at the HR practice level there is some evidence that embedded custom and practices are constraining convergence. In addition, other factors, such as the stage of economic development and the configuration of technology and management styles, can restrain the onward push of globalization and the convergence to the 'one best way' of managing people internationally. It is therefore concluded that while convergence of practice has occurred it is too simplistic to argue that HRM system convergence is taking place. It would be better to characterize the changes as a transitional stage where the final outcome is difficult to predict and may differ substantially from the HRM model. What is less in dispute is that experimentation with western HRM practices will continue, and in all likelihood will be modified to suit the unique needs of each system.

The third question considered was what are the implications of these changes for HRM. At a practical level a number of issues has arisen from the case studies. These include the issues of improved labour productivity and flexibility, the development of new ways to retain valued employees, the removal of the growing tensions that arise from the adoption of an HRM approach and how to address the paradoxes arising out of the implementation of HRM. The change to HRM practices raises the more important question of how change to policy and architecture will take place. Two scenarios are possible. If change continues in a gradual and continuous fashion, then practice developments will put pressure on reform at higher levels.

HRM will then involve considerable experimentation at the policy and architectural levels. It is not immediately clear as to how these changes will occur and what types of policy and systems will be put in place. A large degree of uncertainty will exist and temporary structures will arise to fill the vacuum caused by managerial experimentation. This transitional stage may extend for many years with little indication as to the final outcome. On the other hand, if more radical reform is undertaken and extended to all levels of HRM, then it is likely that, in the transitional period, HR practices will also be affected and make HR more uncertain and difficult to manage. Workers will be alienated in this process and companies will not be able to appeal to the wider norms and values of society to gain the necessary commitment.

The final question concerned implications for the development of HRM theory. The case studies raised a number of issues that will need to be incorporated into any broad theory of HRM. In particular, hybrid systems (Hong Kong, Taiwan) multiple approaches (Philippines), external and internal HRM (China), the superficial and paradoxical nature of change (Korea) and the unitary underpinnings of the HRM approach (Japan), will all need to be considered. This means any generalized model of HRM must be based on context rather than on prescriptive outcomes, able to incorporate a multiplicity of approaches and to recognize the dynamic and inherently unstable nature of HRM.

New models of HRM must also accommodate the various levels at which any system operates and develop clearer linkages between these levels. Does change at one level imply increasing pressure for change at other levels or can HRM adapt to accommodate singular events? Equally important is the need to have less focus on convergence as a measure of HRM adoption and the need to place more attention on how systems develop and change to accommodate various cultural, institutional and macro-economic forces.

This volume set out to explore the changes in HRM in eight Asian countries since 1997. Such a task was considered important given that many have argued that globalization will lead to the convergence of national systems of HRM. While the earlier volume (Rowley, 1997) concluded that the case studies provided some support for convergence, there was considerable diversity of practice. Some five years later that diversity at the practice level has considerably reduced and a more uniform set of HRM practices has appeared.

Yet, much of this development has been limited to the practical aspects of HRM where considerable experimentation and development has taken place, albeit often with 'Asian characteristics'. The case studies provided little evidence to suggest that much of the reform had been converted to policy or institutionalized into the basic architecture of the HRM systems of the eight economies. Indeed, at this level there existed considerable diversity both within and between countries. While this has implications for HRM practice in each country it also has implications for the further development and refinement of HRM theory.

Chapter 4

Causing Change in Human Resource Management

The world of work in which human resource management (HRM) operates has changed dramatically in the last half century. Not surprisingly, therefore, the HRM concepts and practices being created and carried out today are also increasingly different from those of the past. Planners and practitioners who understand this and who also have a way to anticipate the coming changes and needed HRM practices of the future will provide their organizations with a strategic competitive advantage.

It is our view that virtually all the changes we see in HRM concepts and practices are in response to changing social, economic, and business environments. We therefore need to understand these influences on our work setting because many of those factors that have affected us in the recent past will continue to do so in the future, though perhaps in different ways. By examining these forces, we will be better able to understand what challenges we need to cope with today and those that are likely tomorrow.

In this chapter, we look at the major forces affecting the world of work. We will also lay out a framework to help examine them. Although much of what we present can be seen as a description of past events, the framework will also be useful as a blueprint for periodically doing an environmental "scan" of the forces that are likely to have an impact in the future.

THE FIVE DELTA FORCES

We believe that the significant environmental forces influencing HRM policy and practice fall into five sets:

- Demographics refers to those aspects of the quantity and quality of the workforce itself that are determined by birth rates, participation by women and minorities, immigration, migration, and education.
- Economics covers issues like the basis of the national economy, productivity and labor rates, inflation, and the increasing importance of competition and participation in a global economy.
- Legal and regulatory issues include civil rights legislation and laws covering safety and health, plant closings, and so on, as well as government deregulation in some industries.
- Technology involves the obvious and the subtle shifts caused by new products such as computers, fax machines, cellular phones, fiber optics, robots, space satellites, and various drugs and medicines.
- Attitudes and values refer to subjects as varied as the psychological contracts formed with employers, notions about careers and commitment, feelings about extending employer benefits to cover unmarried partners, and so on.

These five forces can easily be remembered by the acronym DELTA. This seems appropriate because the symbol for the Greek letter delta is used in mathematics to represent change. This five part framework, will help us to grasp the relevant issues. But at the same time, we must recognize that many of these forces are complex and often all are operating at the same time. It may be useful to examine each of them now.

Demographics

The flow of people, recorded in a society's vital social statistics, are major if sometimes invisible forces in our work lives. Trends in the birthrate make interesting social history, but they are also important to human resource planners because nearly all the workers who will enter the workforce during the next two decades have already been born. Birth statistics tell us how many people there will be to employ. For example, Americans born during the low birthrate years of the 1930s formed a relatively small cohort.

Yet they entered the workforce during the 1950s and 1960s, a long period of unparalleled growth and expansion in the post–World War II economy. Being much in demand, these workers stepped onto an escalator to career growth and prosperity that often seemed to exceed their individual work achievements. Similarly, we can see important if not always recognized demographic influences on the career patterns of other well-known age cohort groups.

The Baby Boom

Beginning in 1946, returning veterans of World War II started their families in earnest. The extraordinary surge in the population, called the baby boom, saw the number of newborns jump from 2.9 million in 1945 to 3.8 million a year later. This high birthrate continued until about 1964. The baby boomers started joining the workforce in the mid–1960s, providing an ample supply and in fact creating much competition for the available openings. Selection of the best available candidates from the many applicants became an important issue.

As the baby boomers have aged, their interests and needs have naturally changed. In the year 2000, they will range in age from about thirty-six to fifty-four, with cares and thoughts now on mid career issues, medical benefits, retirement planning, and fears about Social Security.

Increased Participation of Diverse Workers

The shortage of entry-level workers during the early 1990s was foretold by the low birthrate of the 1970s. Starting in 1964, when oral contraceptives became widely available, the birthrate declined significantly and it dropped still more sharply in 1970, when abortion became legal. Thus, the effects of a new technology—contraceptive drugs—and the Supreme Court's legal decision on abortion combined to reduce the birthrate during that decade to an even lower one than in the era of the Great Depression.

The result, called the baby bust, means that the children born during the 1970s form another relatively small cohort, again much in demand, as they enter the workforce some two decades later. Combined with a healthy economy in the late 1990s, this situation puts a premium on effective recruitment. In addition, this relative shortage of workers has coincided with and fostered the increased participation in the workforce of certain segments of the population: women, minorities, and immigrants. As a result, the diversity of the American workforce has reached a level unparalleled in our history.

Women

One of the most fundamental shifts in work patterns over the last few decades has been the increased participation of women, a trend documented by rather startling statistics. The number of women in America who are in paid employment surged from eighteen million in 1950 to sixty-five million in 1998, based on data from the U.S. Department of Labor and the Census Bureau. Similarly, the proportion of all women who work has increased over that time from 34 percent to 60 percent, so that women as a percentage of the total workforce have gone from 30 percent to 47 percent of all workers.

Equally remarkable is the range of occupations that women now work in. No longer restricted to traditionally female jobs such as secretary, nurse, and teacher, they have entered all fields in great numbers. Women are found among the professional ranks of accountants, programmers, engineers, lawyers, physicians, managers, and executives and are visible in some traditionally blue-collar jobs, such as police officer and mail carrier. This pattern is also seen in the educational achievements of women who moved from a small portion of academic degrees earned to now make up about half of all college and professional school graduates. The long and short of it is that women are distributed widely throughout the workforce and are there to stay. Rather than taking low-involvement jobs until they marry and then becoming full-time homemakers in an Ozzieand-Harriet scenario, women have become permanent members of the workforce at all levels.

As a result, there are many more two-paycheck or dual-career families. This in turn has created enormous pressures for flexibility in work arrangements to cope with family needs. It has also led to more employee reluctance to relocate for job advancement and to the need for better child-care arrangements. As a result, even before the states and the federal government created the Family and Medical Leave Act (FMLA), many firms had introduced various child-care support programmes, made geographic relocation less of a requirement for career mobility, provided spousal relocation aid, eased rules barring nepotism, and introduced more flexible work schedule arrangements.

Minorities

Ethnic and racial minorities of all backgrounds have also increasingly joined the workforce during the last few decades. In large part, this has come about as traditional discrimination barriers were lowered in response to legislation such as Title VII of the Civil Rights Act of 1964, which forbids discrimination in employment on the basis of sex, race, religion, colour, or national origin. HRM has been required to respond proactively to avoid breaking the law in all conditions of employment. This includes recruitment and selection, work assignments, training, appraisal, pay, and promotion. Social enlightenment—that is, a greater acceptance of nonwhites as employees—may have also played a role. And, of course, employers' needs for more people to do the available work has lowered barriers.

Immigrants

Historically, America has been a land of immigrants. This is still so. But it is a surprise to many citizens to learn that during the 1980s more immigrants entered the United States than in any other decade since 1900. In the past, most immigrants to the United States came from Europe. In the last two decades a much higher proportion than previously have come from Asia and Latin America. At the end of the 1990s, this trend is continuing.

The enormously increased diversity of the workforce first made headlines with the publication of Johnston and Packer's Workforce 2000 (1987). Their report made it abundantly clear that the native born white men who largely made up the workforce would be increasingly replaced by women, minorities, and immigrants. Although the study was often exaggerated or misquoted, the general thrust of its predictions is proving true. Employers are faced with diversity in their workforce that is obvious in the workers' appearance but also shows up in their varying work experiences and assumptions. HRM needs to take and has taken the leadership role in many firms in order to promote effective communications and work relationships that may be challenged by this worker diversity.

Economics

Companies today operate in an intensely competitive global economy. For most firms, it has been a huge transition to realize this and operate accordingly. In the years right after World War II, the U.S. economy produced about three-fourths of all the world's goods and services; today it produces less than one-quarter of them. America's economic dominance then, set against the war weary manufacturing base in Europe and Asia, gave American companies a great advantage in satisfying the enormous consumer demands put on hold during the hostilities. Automobiles, houses, refrigerators, and other such goods could be easily sold, despite qualms about their cost or quality.

For most American companies, this was a highly stable period with relatively little competition. Combined with the command and-control organizational style that had proven so successful during the war, it led to large bureaucratic organizations mining economies of scale and able to engage in long-range planning. Judith Bardwick (1991) sees this affluence, along with the limited supply of workers born in the 1930s, as leading to a mindset of entitlement among management and employees rather than to a more competitive notion of earning one's success. This, she notes, is an inappropriate mindset for today's changed circumstances.

Global Forces

By the 1970s European and Japanese plants had been rebuilt, and many new and highly competitive products came in from overseas. Automobiles and television sets were among the most obvious new entrants, and they were soon joined by other well-made and innovative products. The globalization of commerce had begun in earnest. For many American firms that had grown "fat, dumb, and happy, " the good times would no longer keep on rolling. Serious competition set in, with market shares being threatened and eroding, and for the first time massive layoffs and cutbacks were seen in industries that had rarely been touched before.

These tradition-breaking layoffs altered the "psychological contract" for many workers. Thousands and thousands of workers were affected, mostly in large companies, during the late 1980s and throughout the 1990s. These shocking downsizings were sometimes euphemistically called "rightsizing, " although the effect on the traditional perception of job security was still disastrous.

However, not always visible behind the glare of bad-news headlines, an equal number of jobs (if not more) were being created in small and medium-sized companies. All this came about as a result of the increased efforts of companies to respond quickly to competitive pressures. At the same time, the desire to upgrade product and service quality led to HRM being among the leading proponents of Total Quality Management and related initiatives.

Among the effects of this general shift in employment patterns was a much greater willingness to hire people who were already experienced and had the critical and often different skills needed rather than to hire staff right out of college and train them over a longer period of time. Naturally, assumptions about career growth and development were also changing.

Also a result of globalization—at least in part—has been the truly extraordinary pace of mergers and acquisitions over the last two decades. There has been a much greater willingness than in the past to merge related firms and gain market advantages quickly or to acquire desirable organizations and their skills, markets, and products. The need to undertake organizational culture audits and understand how to bring new organizations together rapidly and effectively as result of these trends created important new demands on HRM.

Cost of Labour

The increased global competitiveness is partly responsible for American labor becoming more competitively priced over the last quarter of a century, mainly through stagnation of their wages. In fact, the average American worker earns less today, when adjusted for inflation, than in 1973. The average weekly earnings of non supervisory workers went down 19 percent by 1995, or almost 1 percent per year. Buying power has actually decreased. Curiously, the average earnings of the typical American family have gone up slightly over that time, about 1 percent in total adjusted for inflation, a trend that is really a reflection of having more two-earner families nowadays than in the past.

One result of these wage trends has been truly extraordinary. Because labor costs are lower here than in their own countries, both Japanese and German auto companies have moved major plants to the United States, giving them a competitive edge in the American market.

But the globalization of commerce has been working in two directions. Just as foreign competitors came to the United States, American firms were expanding overseas. Today, many companies have changed from colonialist international firms expanding overseas from a domestic base, to multinational firms cloning new versions of themselves in other countries or truly global firms where products are made by global teams for global customers. For example, through the use of computer and telecommunications technology, design teams in Ford Motor's European, American, and Asian locations can work around-the-clock on the same project, electronically handing off an ongoing project to colleagues in another continent as the earth rotates.

With increased interaction between staff from different countries, cultural differences have come into play more than ever. The diversity of assumptions and values in different nations has required more training of people on international assignment. It has also raised questions about the applicability of American-based management philosophies in other countries.

Service Economy

In the meantime, the base of the American economy has shifted from manufacturing to service. From 1950 to 1995, the goods producing sector shrank from 41 percent to 21 percent of the total, while the service-producing sector of the economy grew to 79 percent of all jobs. This shift has greatly reduced the proportion of jobs that require low-skill workers and increased the need and opportunities for highly literate and well-trained, technologically sophisticated people. One further effect of the drop in the share of workers employed in manufacturing industries like autos and steel has been the reduction in the proportion and power of unionized workers.

Geographic Influences

A movement related to the long-term drop-off in manufacturing in the United States was the relocation of industry and workers from the "rust belts" of the Northeast and Midwest to the "sun belts" in the West and South. These patterns changed the availability of various skills and the employment rates in different areas. For example, California's

Silicon Valley has become a mecca for people in the computer industry.

As a result, companies trying to grow or establish new locations have had to be aware of these shifts in worker accessibility. In fact, companies have had to pay attention in recent years as various states in the Midwest and Northeast changed their taxation and education policies in order to retain and attract workers who might be at risk of loss to the sun belt states.

Legal and Regulatory Issues

Both the daily practice of HRM and its strategic importance are influenced strongly by the nation's laws. Nowhere is this clearer than with the Civil Rights Act of 1964. Over time this law, like many others, has been amended by Congress, extended by the case law arising from court rulings, and expanded by the president's executive orders and the Equal Employment Opportunity Commission's guidelines.

Legislation

Antidiscrimination laws were once said to apply to groups traditionally considered as minorities, but with the extension of related laws to protect women, workers over age forty, Vietnam-era veterans, and the disabled, now a majority of workers are protected. Thus, in practice, attention to fairness and nondiscrimination in all aspects of employment is required as "a way of life" for all employees in an organization. As these laws open up violators to large financial penalties, the stakes are quite high, and in most firms it is HRM that has taken on the responsibility to ensure compliance. As a sign of HRM's success, many of the actions taken to avoid discrimination, once seen as novel, have become a way of life. This has also been true in the past for other laws. HRM practices regarding child labor, minimum wages, and payment for overtime, considered revolutionary when the Fair Labor Standards Act was first passed in 1938, are standard today.

Many other laws approved in recent decades have profoundly affected the role and function of HRM. These include safety and health practices, funding for retirement and related medical plans, and extension of medical benefits to employees and families of those who leave employment. As a result, HRM has acquired new responsibilities for formulating new practices, educating employees, and keeping extensive records. For example, the increased availability of tax-deferred savings plans (such as 401k's) has given HRM the opportunity to create plans that complement or replace older pension schemes. The government mandate for firms to provide access to health maintenance organizations (HMOs) has been another new responsibility.

Other legislation, such as that requiring early warning of major plant closings, has forced HRM into greater involvement with business planning that may affect employees. Laws and court cases concerning a variety of other issues, such as employee privacy, genetic screening, and illnesses such as AIDS, have had similar effects.

Deregulation

The deregulation of the 1970s in such industries as the airlines and trucking gave rise to many new, low-cost entrants to these businesses. Because many of the new firms were nonunionized and offered lower wages, competition increased greatly while at the same time high wage rates could no longer be as easily passed on to consumers. Two-tier wage systems therefore arose, with new hires being paid a lot less than their predecessors.

Even in unionized companies new work patterns had to be devised to enhance competitiveness. The successful example of Southwest Airlines is generally well known. That company's changed work practices encouraged workers to pitch in wherever needed, so that gate agents and even pilots might move baggage if that were desirable. The breakup of AT&T into multiple companies gave rise to many new firms in the telecommunications industry, and vastly expanded competition. In the near future we will see similarly deregulated competition breaking out among the electric utilities. Here, too, we can expect that HRM will play a key part in trying to gain competitiveness as legal and regulatory requirements change.

In recent years, some deregulation has changed entire industries. For example, the financial services area has been drastically altered, with a blurring of traditional lines between banking, stock brokerage, and insurance activities. This has caused some firms to expand into new product lines and also allowed many mergers of previously unrelated companies. HRM has become heavily involved in combining work activities into new jobs and work groups, with all the related issues such as selection, training, and performance management. In addition, the integration of differing HRM systems among the combined organizations has become a challenge for the affected firms.

Technology

Advances in electronic technology have changed how we work in ways that were scarcely imaginable just twenty years ago. The increased power and lowered cost of computing have made computer chips ubiquitous, increasing our capability for moving masses of information more swiftly, accurately, and cheaply than ever before.

For example, to maximize profit airlines can practice "yield management, " based on models of likely sales on a particular flight in different price categories. Combining historical and projected data, they can monitor real-time inputs to price the remaining seats in a way to attract more travelers at the highest prices and fill their seats. Also in an attempt to enhance efficiency, airlines can combine data about the number of passengers and the weight of their luggage on a specific flight as the passengers are boarding, match this information with the temperature and wind conditions applying to that flight, and determine how much fuel is required and even whether any passengers need to be shifted to other seats to balance the plane better. All this is done before the plane's doors are closed for takeoff. It has important implications for staffing, job demands, and training requirements.

Creation of New Jobs

The PC industry itself has become a huge new part of our economy. It is an industry where the type of selling has changed from one of a relatively low volume of high-priced computers to a high volume of low-priced PCs that are sometimes similar enough to other companies' products as to be interchangeable commodities. The industry now often uses entirely new distribution channels, such as retail stores and telephone sales, rather than employing dark-suited sales representatives to call on major companies. To help in these efforts, HRM has had to look at very different types of employees working in different ways. Among them may be articulate but invisible teleworkers who take orders in remote telephone call centers and have working hours that are adjusted to peaks and valleys in call volume from across the nation.

The use of computers has had an impact on every element of how we work, from data preparation, analysis, and presentation to the determination of who sees what data and when. The effect has been to make many things easier and quicker to do, and to provide people with much more (and more useful) data than ever before. This has expanded the need for people in some jobs, such as programmers and systems managers, at the same time it has minimized the jobs of others. For instance, with so much correspondence now being done through e-mail, where addressees respond through their own keyboards, the number of secretaries has been declining.

Organizational Architecture

Some pundits note that computers have changed the structure of organizations themselves. Nadler and his associates have observed that information gathering and disseminating used to be among the critical tasks of middle managers in most organizations. With computer-based networks doing much of this work, the need for middle managers has declined. Moreover, computers allow organizations to be designed with entirely different structures.

Just as the emergence of structural steel, elevators, and better plumbing permitted twentieth-century buildings to be redesigned in totally new ways, computers and other devices for communicating more widely and quickly permit new and rapidly changing forms of organizational structure to be considered. Flatter, more complex, and even short-term or ad hoc virtual organizations are real and frequent occurrences.

The availability of vastly improved technology has also changed powerful imperatives guiding business. In prior years, cost and quality were the common mantras. With the pressure of competition and the availability of novel technology, an important new consideration is cycle time—the amount of time it takes to create and produce a product or service. In order to meet or exceed your competitors' offerings, you must create new ones in less time than ever. If the cycle time to make a Japanese car is thirty-six months, an American manufacturer's forty-eight-month cycle time means it can never catch up with its competitor.

This has led to entirely new ways of looking at how business operations are conducted. Often called reengineering, this is a way of looking at the process by which work gets done and not just accepting the traditional collection of jobs assembled to do the work. HRM has become one of the key players in reexamining and revising how work gets done. Jobs formerly done by various people have been combined and recombined. Departments as well as jobs have undergone dramatic transformations. The result has been radical change in the makeup of many jobs. Instead of job analyses defining what a worker does, work process analyses are the tools that define work activities. It has also led to many more cross-functional teams, cutting across narrow specialties, to focus on optimum ways to create the total product or service.

Flexibility

The availability of faxes, e-mail, laptop computers, cellular telephones, voice mail, and overnight delivery services has enabled people to work easily from remote locations. The traditional "road warrior" now has more weapons to be effective, to stay in touch with colleagues and vital databases. With this equipment, people can also enter into new work relationships, such as telecommuting from home or satellite locations, and gain more flexibility in work schedules. Under pressure from employees for more flexibility to help them balance work and family obligations, innovative HRM staff in many companies have worked out and continue to explore new ways for people to work.

Attitudes and Values

One subtly occurring change in values has been the gradual recognition that competition has given customers a real choice of what products and services they can buy. The recognition of this new consumerism, with its higher expectations and ability to make better informed choices, has often been translated into a concern for and emphasis on customer satisfaction. Again, HRM has taken a lead role in many firms in educating workers about the importance of customer satisfaction.

Attitudes Toward Work

Attitudes have also changed remarkably about the nature and length of the relationship between companies and their employees. Long-term employment security is no longer promised or implied, and this has changed the degree of mutual commitment that employees and organizations feel toward one another. The consequences are paradoxical for many companies. On the one hand, they want to be freer to shed employees who are not needed; on the other hand, they want to encourage needed employees to stay as long as possible. But employees who know they have no longterm security are often busy looking for better opportunities.

Instead of a long-term relationship or even a "marriage, " both employees and companies can wind up in a "dating game" as they look for short-term selfish advantage. As an HRM strategy in tight labor markets or when employees with rare skills are involved, some firms have committed themselves for specific contracted periods or offered stock options and incentive-based schemes to hang on to desired individuals.

Nevertheless, at least one organizational survey consortium reports that employee attitudes on job security have become much less favourable in all companies over the last decade, even as other attitudes have remained relatively constant Corporation, private communication with the authors, January 1998). As several commentators have noted and as the chapters by Noer and others in this volume note, the psychological contract has changed. One noticeable effect of this change is in college recruiting, where companies no longer promise long-term careers and actually use "signing bonuses" to get the most talented graduates to join them. In other words, short-term payoffs are being used to make up for long-term inducements.

Nonwork Obligations

Most companies now see family responsibilities as a more acceptable counterpoint to work obligations. Many employees desire flexible work schedules and supervisor support for emergencies and use these criteria to select employers when there is a choice. Some books have become best-sellers because they rate and describe "the best places to work".

Underlying realities that have helped give voice to such concerns include changes in marriage patterns. Divorce rates have gone up substantially during recent decades, leaving many women dependent on their own efforts for economic well-being and creating many more single parents than in the past. (In addition, unmarried women are more likely to keep their children, eschewing abortion or adoption.) For single parents, work is an economic necessity but it also competes with family for time and energy.

In a related phenomenon, age at first marriage has increased by almost a year per decade for the last half century, so that it is now about twenty-four for women and twenty-six for men. With this shift, many couples now live together without benefit of the clergy's blessing. Their concerns include many mutual career decisions, which may affect accepting a job or relocating. In recent years, this concern has sometimes emerged as a desire for company benefits to be extended to domestic partners. This has been especially noted when homosexual partners, who do not have the option of legal marriage, want such coverage. The open expression of such living arrangements and sexual orientations by workers represents another major shift in attitudes and values.

Outdated Assumptions

This review of the environmental forces affecting industry and HRM indicates that many of the assumptions made in the past about people in the work setting are no longer valid. If the assumptions are no longer valid, then the concepts and practices based on them may also be invalid. As we indicated in our opening discussion, many of these assumptions arose in the 1950s, and it is these beliefs that need to be reexamined and reevaluated.

The following are outdated assumptions about the operating environment in most organizations today:

- The competitive environment is stable, with control over new product introduction and no undue pressure for innovation or short development and manufacturing cycle times.
- Jobs are well defined and slow to change, with clear relationships to other such jobs on the career ladder.
- Employment relationships are long-term ("womb to tomb").
- The psychological contract exchanges long-term security and gradual advancement for employee loyalty and sacrifice.
- Workforces are relatively homogeneous, largely white and male.
- Most families are one-paycheck, leading to a "family" orientation, so workers have total dedication to company for overtime, relocation, and so on.

- Organizations are made up of functional "silos" with long time horizons for employee development and there is relatively little need for inter group cooperation across different functional specialties.

Today's Assumptions

The changes in the environment we have noted, which most companies operate in today, have required a new set of assumptions that are more appropriate for the times and that generate new HRM concepts and practices. These new assumptions may be subdivided according to their application to organizations and to individuals.

Organizations today contrast in several respects with those of the past.

The shifts are evident in corporate forms and dynamics:

- More than ever, organizations are likely to be fluid, continually changing, and have many new relationships, from joint ventures, alliances, and partnerships to use of vendors and subcontractors.
- Embattled organizations are continually under pressure to increase outputs, improve cycle time, enhance competitiveness.
- A focus on short-term achievements is an imperative. Corporate acquisitions may often be seen as a better bet than undertaking long-term product development.
- Important skills and talent are to be hired as needed rather than developed internally over a long period. Conversely, unneeded employees should be quickly converted or disposed of.

Individuals have been greatly affected by the signals employers send them. Many of these new attitudes are brutally and acerbically depicted in Scott Adams's comic strip series Dilbert. The popularity of the syndicated comic strip and several books about Dilbert testify to the fact that many employees have a less than benign view of their employers.

It seems fair to say that many workers now operate (or should operate) with the following assumptions:

- Expect few long-term commitments from employers.
- Accept that career development is mostly your own responsibility.
- It is a good idea to keep a "parachute" handy (through an upto-date resume and a network of contacts).
- When it comes to job skills and experiences, there is a need for continuous development.
- In general, a certain amount of distrust and suspicion about employers is probably wise.
- Expect and seek quicker advancement when you merit it and don't depend on mere length of service or employer beneficence.

HRM concepts and practices arise from a complex set of forces that form the operating environment for the organizations HRM serves. When the environment is stable, many of the changes are determined by the organization itself, often in a desire to give itself a competitive advantage in attracting, retaining, and motivating employees. Sometimes the concepts and practices arise out of the company founder's personal philosophy and preferences. But the environment has not been very stable during the last two decades.

Many of the operating assumptions on which HRM operates have been severely but gradually challenged in the last two decades in a series of inexorable changes. As a story popular in some management circles puts it, a frog dropped into a pot of boiling water will instantly jump out. But if the frog is placed in a pot of cool water that is gradually brought to a boil, the frog will simply grow warmer and doze off until it is too late. It is the suddenness of change that makes it vivid for people as well.

Many of the shifts noted in this chapter have taken place gradually and in different spheres, and they may not have been given sufficient notice at the time of their occurrence. But when we look back over the last twenty-five years, it is obvious that many principles that were simply taken for granted are no longer true. This is as dangerous for us as the slowly warming pot is for the frog. To be effective, it is necessary for HRM concepts and practices to be lined up with assumptions that are based on the reality of our environments.

For organizations to assess their environments accurately it is useful periodically to go through a disciplined scan of their current and expected environments. In fact, many large firms and some consortia conduct environmental scans on a regular basis. This certainly seems like a healthy practice. We believe that a useful framework for doing environmental scans is one that looks at the DELTA forces around us, that is, the demographics, economics, legal and regulatory issues, technology, and attitudes and values. These are the forces that have greatly affected us in the past and seem the right places to look to for future change.

MOTIVATION AND COMMITMENT BETWEEN EMPLOYERS AND EMPLOYEES

Most knowledgeable observers in the field of human resource management (HRM) would agree that its major development as a profession came during the half century or so between the end of World War II and the early 1990s. As organizations employing as many as hundreds of thousands became dominant influences in the world of work and as questions about selection, training, work motivation, and compensation practices became more challenging in a growing, dynamic society, the need for professionally trained, skilled personnel became great.

Also, despite occasional downturns in the economy, the professional growth of HRM took place against a general culture of prosperity, a belief that such good patterns would continue and even improve, and an assumption that work organizations should and would share in such growth.

Important too as HRM developed during this era was that the policies and practices developed and implemented were based in large part on the assumption that a desire for personal growth was the most important motivational characteristic of the workforce, along with the belief that more of everything (particularly economic outcomes) is better. Korman (forthcoming) has referred to this pattern as self-enhancing motivation and has cited as illustrative of this type of motivation such actions as making choices that match and fulfill one's personal needs, engaging in activities that foster self-growth, attempting to attain high levels of work performance, and working for goals that legitimately enhance oneself in one's own eyes and those of others.

Given the cultural context and the assumption of the dominance of this type of motivational pattern, it was a relatively short step for HRM professionals during this era to develop a perspective that reflected them. Characteristic programmes of this type included job enrichment, career management and career development, self-appraisals and peer performance appraisals, and income incentives of various kinds.

Less significant as an influence on HRM during this era but still of some importance were programmes based on what Korman (forthcoming) has called self-protective motivation, defined as the desire to defend oneself from perceived threatening environmental and personal forces that might affect one's sense of identity. Korman suggests that it is this motivational force that underlies the need for personal and job security. Despite its importance, however, this need was generally viewed as less important than employee needs for growth, development, and achievement during the years of prosperity. There were several reasons for this difference in emphasis. One factor, certainly, was the prosperity and the continued expectations of same. It was not a climate that generated a sense of anxiety, whether warranted or not.

Second, the strength and membership of labor unions—organizations that have traditionally made job security a keystone of their efforts—were declining. With the assumption of continued prosperity and the weakness of labor unions, human resource (HR) managers and their allied professionals, such as industrial-organizational psychologists, worried less about providing job security than about providing the opportunity for growth, development, and achievement.

Third, theorists on motivation in work organizations generally had a low level of interest in such concepts as anxiety, even though important research findings were beginning to be reported on the significance of such related variables as fear of failure in performance settings. Instead, theories were popular if they saw people as growth-oriented, desiring meaningful work achievement, and interested in attaining both intrinsic and extrinsic goals.

Nevertheless, despite these influences, there was some concern even during these years about providing a greater sense of security for employees. Prominent among those expressing such interest was Frederick Herzberg, an important management writer who saw in the reduction of anxiety that came with job security a significant approach to reducing job dissatisfaction. In addition, although their membership continued to decrease, labor unions and their emphasis on job security did not totally disappear from the work scene. Far from it. Unions remained strong in some areas, particularly the federal, state, and local civil services, and their presence did much to ensure that job security remained on the table as an employee concern, at least in some instances.

There were, then, these two patterns of HR practice. One, the more influential, assumed that the more important motivational patterns were desires for growth, development, achievement, and self-enhancement. The second, less significant as an influence, assumed desires for job security and self-protection. Both were recognized, and both influenced HRM practices. Less recognized was that the disparity in influence of these patterns of practice encouraged another important underlying assumption. This assumption was that HRM policies and practices could be developed in a manner that would enable the attainment of two goals.

The first of these goals was to help organizations obtain their objectives. The second was that HRM could help employees meet their most important needs because the employees' desire to attain positive outcomes (both intrinsic and extrinsic), that is, self-enhancement, and their willingness to work for them were congruent with organizational needs for effective performance. Furthermore, this congruence could be maintained and encouraged because of the continuing expected affluence. In contrast, rarely if ever discussed was that these practices and policies and the assumed congruence between employer and employee depended on these assumptions of continued prosperity and that other approaches would become necessary if the situation changed.

The New World of Work

Now that time has come. A new and different world of work has begun to emerge, one that exists alongside the traditional work setting and that may eventually come to supplant it. It is a world characterized by at least three major trends that have implications for HRM.

- First, downsizing is now a frequent key component of managerial decision making, with all the potential short- and long-term anxiety-inducing effects on employee motivation that we would expect.
- Second, the work-family conflict is an endemic part of the lives of both employers and employees.
- Third, we live in a world marked by the extensive use of temporary workers, part-time employees, and outsourcing.

Workforce Reduction

Downsizing has become so much a part of the world of work during the past decade that it is a term familiar to almost all who work or who wish to. Downsizing is a phenomenon that continues to this day. Some of the more recent downsizings announced in 1997 are Eastman Kodak (10,000), Fruit of the Loom (7,700), and Levi Strauss (6,400). Perhaps even more dramatic are the declines in some of the biggest companies. AT&T has shrunk in part as a function of court ordered divesting but also through downsizing, from 313,000 employees in 1993 to 128,000 in 1998. IBM has gone from about 410,000 employees in recent years to approximately 225,000. Downsizing is a fact of the world of work that influences the lives, attitudes, and emotions of millions. That other jobs are continually being created—and they are—may not significantly affect those concerned about their long- and short-term job prospects.

Work-Family Conflict

Also part of this new world of work is conflict with the family, an inevitable fact of life as our society is increasingly characterized by women in the workforce, dual-career couples, and single-parent families. The increasing presence of women in the workforce contributes to this conflict, a conflict that is among the most serious facing American families and work organizations as we approach the new millennium. It is a problem, both actual and potential, that is becoming increasingly widespread. It is also one of the characteristics of the new world of work that has had and continues to have a major impact on the motivational and attitudinal characteristics of people in the workforce, both men and women.

Noncore Workers

We now also have a work setting marked increasingly by outsourcing agreements between companies, relocation of companies from high- to low-wage areas, globalization, a desire for individuals to develop multiskill capability rather than job specialization, and explosive growth in the use of temporary and contingent employees.

Feelings of ambiguity and conflict have resulted from these changes. On the one hand, there are now new ways for individuals to seek self-enhancement in the world of work, paths that have important implications for the practices and policies HRM may adopt. But on the other hand, the resulting anxiety from these changes has led to a high level of self-protective motivation. The outcome has been a world of work where the two different motivations are assuming equal significance. In other words, it is a world in which the desire and need for security has become as relevant as the need for achievement, growth, and development. It is therefore a world in which both motivational patterns will need to be addressed by HRM, but in different ways than they have been previously.

The remainder of this chapter focuses on meeting these challenges through a two-phase process. Phase 1 proposes new conceptual and attitudinal assumptions for HRM as a field. Phase 2 outlines the types of specific programmes that follow from Phase 1 and reflect the changes in the world of work already discussed.

Phase 1: The New Assumptions

HRM needs new and different assumptions on which to base policy and practice. One necessary change, I believe, is to assume no longer that there is a congruence of interests between employees and employers. Sometimes there may be, but sometimes there may not be. Second, we need to assume that the key interpersonal and intergroup relationships in a particular work setting are as likely to be among individuals from different organizations with different investments as they are to be among individuals within the same organization. The following paragraphs elaborate on these recommendations in greater detail.

Because self-enhancement was assumed to be the dominant work motivation during the years of the growth of the field, it is not surprising that HR professionals operated on the belief that it was both possible and desirable to design and implement policies and practices that could and would integrate the goals of both employees and organizations. In fact, one of the major books of this era, and one which served as a sort of conceptual guideline for many, was titled Integrating the Individual with the Organization.

In a similar vein and serving as further illustration of this assumption of congruence between employer and employee was the growth of job enrichment as a management tool, fueled by the belief that individuals would respond to the challenge of enriched jobs. According to this perspective, the enriched job provided a mechanism for self-enhancement and, in satisfying such desires, the individual would be more highly performance motivated and contribute more to the attainment of organizational goals.

Now, however, we need to change this assumption. More specifically, we need to view the individual and the organization as separate entities who will be able to integrate their efforts and cooperate with one another under certain conditions but not under others. Furthermore, determining what those conditions might be will be an important objective for HRM professionals in the coming years.

A second assumption about people and organizations during the years of growth and prosperity was that the interpersonal and inter group relationships HRM needed most to be concerned with were those that took place within the organization, that is, intra organizational relationships. In other words, the focus was on the relationships between people in different jobs, in different functions, and at different hierarchical levels, but all within the same organization. Although it was recognized that individuals often met with salespeople, suppliers, and others, such meetings with "outsiders" were generally limited to specifically designated occupational groups. Now, however, more attention will have to be paid to relationships between those with primary allegiance to a particular organization and those who may work in that organization but not have primary allegiance to it.

Today, individuals work full-time in an organization to which they have primary loyalty while next to them or with them are individuals on temporary assignments, part-time workers, and people working in joint venture settings and in outsourcing situations. The result may therefore be individuals working together whose allegiances and concerns may involve differences that are highly important to us. Relationships, views, and expectations among those who are all part of one group—or who view themselves as part of the same company or as "insiders"—are different from the types of relationships and communication patterns that develop among those who view themselves as belonging to different groups. For example, Korman (1988) has proposed that in situations in which we find insiders and outsiders, the former are more likely to discriminate and act in a prejudicial manner toward the latter.

The result may be unnecessary conflict and sometimes even "tribalistic" patterns, where each group cares only about itself and not about the other or joint goals. Although cases of severe conflict may be extreme—because there are usually some reasons for these different groups and individuals to at least try to work together— the potential for conflict between groups and individuals exists in this new work setting and there will be a need to take account of such possibilities in developing future HRM programmes. These new assumptions, which I believe to be more appropriate for the emerging work setting, suggest the need for new HRM approaches, techniques, policies, and practices that will allow satisfaction of both the self-enhancing and the self-protective motivational processes.

Phase 2: Some Programme Suggestions

Programmes consistent with the new assumptions need to be developed for HRM as it confronts this new world of work. The remainder of the chapter outlines four such programmes, with each discussed in greater detail in the following sections.

- Effective self-career management programmes based on the desire for self-enhancement
- Labour pool associations designed to meet needs for both self enhancement and self-protection
- Performance incentive programmes that are not based on organizational commitment, including financial rewards providing direct income as well as health, welfare, and pension benefits
- Insider-outsider training programmes

Programmes for Self-Career Management

Self-career management programmes are designed primarily for those individuals who view themselves as relatively independent professionals or "businesses, " rather than as organizationally dependent job holders. These are individuals who can and do make their own decisions about their careers, know their capabilities, and understand where they can find the types of work opportunities where they can "sell" themselves as a business or service. Self-career management is a different way of looking at oneself and one's work capabilities.

It is a mechanism for declaring oneself independent of an organizational control system but at the same time being willing to negotiate mutual terms of acceptability concerning work contributions to that system. Self-career management—thus defined as the giving up of relatively permanent organizational relationships in favour of more self-controlled career decision making—has become increasingly recommended to and by HRM professionals as a possible approach to dealing with challenges presented by the emerging world of work, a world still dominated in great degree by the use of downsizing as a management strategy despite continuing questions about its outcomes.

Clearly, there are reasons for such positive evaluation. Self career management recognizes the tentative nature of a specific employment relationship while also emphasizing the need for employee skills and meaningful contributions and the opportunity to fulfill the desire for self-enhancement that is so important in the work setting. In addition, for the appropriate individual and the appropriate situation, self-career management also provides an approach to meeting the need for self-protection, because this can be negotiated by the individual involved. The key, however, is in the word appropriate. Self-career management is appropriate when the individual has or can develop both meaningful self-knowledge and the types of skills and abilities that are in demand. In addition, self-career management is appropriate when the individual has knowledge of the job market and the freedom to respond to the opportunities available.

A variety of techniques reflect self-career management when it is defined in this manner. Perhaps the most important and first question that needs an answer (for which the HRM professional must provide input) is whether a specific organization should provide financial and other resources for developing and implementing self-career programmes for its employees, particularly programmes emphasizing personal growth. This is not an easy question to answer. At first glance, there are clearly reasons for companies to undertake such programmes.

They provide recognition of the frequently temporary nature of contemporary work settings while at the same time encouraging positive relationships between individuals and organizations over the long run. Both of these outcomes may serve the individual and the organization in good stead at once or at some time in the future. In addition, these programmes may serve to illuminate and develop skills in the participants not previously realized and thus eventually prove beneficial to the individual and the organization. Finally, such programmes help the organization in situations where downsizing may become inevitable. Clearly, preparing individuals to deal with the loss of employment before it happens is to be preferred over sudden notices of termination.

Still, some negative aspects also need to be recognized before a corporate decision is made to undertake a personal growth programme encouraging self-career management. One obvious problem is the cost involved. The cost may be considerable, depending on the number of individuals involved and the type of programmes chosen. Second, there is the continuing reality that all the benefits the programmes may provide to employees may never be of value to the organization that pays for them (and, indeed, may turn out to be of value to competitors).

Third, it needs to be realized right from the beginning that such programmes are not for everyone. They should not be oversold as "the answer" to the problems of the new world of work. Rather, companies need to keep in mind that other programmes will be necessary regardless of what they decide about self-career management programmes. To be blunt, self-career management is not and cannot be appropriate for those who have neither the personality nor the technical skills, educational levels, or likelihood of developing the skills to the degree needed to make the approach fruitful. For these individuals, other alternatives will be necessary.

Assuming these pros and cons have been considered and the company decides to proceed with such programmes, how might they do so? One possible procedure is to make self-career management programmes a voluntary aspect of the HRM process. Such an approach would increase the probability of successful outcomes by making it likely that the individuals participating in the programmes possess the skills, abilities, interests, or personality that would enable them to benefit from the programmes.

In addition, once the decision to proceed is made, HRM can increase the effectiveness of self-career management programmes by generating and making available as much information as possible about the nature of potential and actual career possibilities in a particular job market for those participating in the programmes. Self career management programmes are much concerned with personal growth but are not aimed at personal growth alone. They also have career and work-oriented goals.

The more work opportunities available that the participant knows about and the more the participant has the time, knowledge, and personal characteristics to carry out a job or career search, the more self-management career programmes will be useful. A further advantage of providing job knowledge to those undergoing self-career management is that doing so will help identify those for whom such programmes might not be useful, that is, those who will not have job opportunities for the skills they have or are likely to develop. For this latter group, other types of programmes will be necessary, perhaps programmes of the type we now turn to.

Labour Pool Associations

HRM also needs to begin to develop mechanisms that are appropriate in assisting the adaptation of current and potential employees for whom the concept of self-career management is inapplicable. Among these are the unskilled and semiskilled, immigrant workers, single parents whose job freedom is limited, and people with little growth potential. Two factors concerning these individuals are crucial. First, there are great numbers of such employees and they may, in fact, be increasing relative to the population at large. Second, despite their numbers, economically they are falling farther and farther behind people with higher skill levels, as evidenced by the findings of an increasing disparity in income between those at the higher and lower levels of our population.

Yet despite their numbers and this disparity, it is fair to say that little attention has been paid to how the new world of work can meet the needs of these people. For these individuals, basic educational training may have been insufficient, job training opportunities may not be available, and financial resources to keep up skill development may not be there. Also, the habit and encouragement of self-reliance in the occupational sphere may be more foreign to these individuals than those who are higher on the occupational hierarchy.

Rather, these individuals may have, perhaps, more of a tendency to rely on traditional employment relationships and organizational reward systems as sources of meeting self enhancement and self-protection needs. Because the characteristics of the emerging world of work makes this pattern increasingly unlikely, it is even more important to pay attention to helping these groups adapt to the new and different setting.

A new type of organization be developed with the aid of HR professionals in response to these considerations. Let's call them labor pool associations. Such associations can be conceived of as organizations based on cooperative relations among different companies (and perhaps government agencies) that focus on maximizing the human resources available to all of them. As cooperatively managed HR personnel from different organizations, labor pool associations would have several objectives. First, they would keep a continuing registry of individuals and their skills, thus ensuring a labor supply as needed by member organizations, large or small.

Second, they would serve as training-retraining-counseling centers for occupational entry and upgrading as desired and available. Third, and perhaps most uniquely, they would serve as "permanent employers" who, besides supplying and making available job and training opportunities, would also provide such "security type" benefits as health insurance and pension plans. These benefits would be paid into accounts maintained for each individual by the organizations. They would thus replace the security systems traditionally used by organizations, which are increasingly difficult to maintain in this era of downsizing and rapid corporate change.

One step toward this type of organization is the Talent Alliance (TA), an association of hotels that has been operating since spring 1997. One is to keep individuals employed in hotels and settings where they are most needed when they are needed. It is therefore an employee allocation system (or labour pool association) of the type we envision here. A second objective is to increase employee marketability; this is done in a number of ways, including through career growth counselors, training and retraining programmes for employees, and strategic planning seminars for corporate management aimed at adapting HR practices to the new world of work.

The TA is, therefore, a step toward the type of organization suggest here because it has some of the aspects recommend. However, it lacks at this time a focus on the necessity of meeting the needs underlying self-protective motivation, that is, the desire for the security of health and welfare benefits and pensions. A second possible limitation is that it is designed for the occupational spectrum of relatively big organizations employing large numbers of individuals, a considerable percentage of whom may be at a high technical level.

Such organizations are, of course, crucial as major employers and these occupational groups are of legitimate concern. However, believe that labour pool associations need also be concerned with those individuals who, though working for small, sometimes marginal organizations, nevertheless have traditionally looked to organizations as the mechanisms through which they will meet their needs for both enhancement and protection.

One further note

Labour pool associations may be of value to those for whom self-career management programmes are appropriate as well as for those for whom it is not. This is because systems need to be developed to bring individuals and organizations at all levels together for their mutual benefit in this emerging world of short-range assignments as well as long-range jobs and rapidly changing skill and competency demands. Labor pool associations, as we have envisioned them, would satisfy this need.

In sum, we need organizations like the TA and others like it, such as Job Link in Louisville, Kentucky, to meet self-enhancement needs but also to meet the need for self-protection. (Job Link is a one-step career center established by the nonprofit Louisville Private Industry Council in 1989. It is basically a referral and counseling center that makes training available as a final resort.) We need organizations such as the TA and Job Link because the two major motivations in work settings—self-enhancement and self-protection—increasingly may not be met by individual companies. For some organizations, self-career management will be an appropriate alternative mechanism.

However, for others, cooperative efforts like labor pool associations will be needed to help them find qualified workers and to help workers find jobs that meet both self-enhancing and self-protective needs. Key here is the need for cooperative activity among different organizations, including accepting the principle of having these associations serving as an "employer" designed to meet self-protective concerns. This is perhaps a somewhat different perspective from that we are used to, but it is an idea that reflects the new world of work and the needs it has generated.

Nonorganizationally Linked Incentive Systems

Financial incentive systems for performance have long been one of the staples of HRM and there is little reason to think they would or should lose their relevance in the new world of work. On the contrary, they may become even more relevant as other types of incentives—those that assume organizational links and commitment, such as promotion and transfer opportunities—will become less relevant to those who see their future as falling into the self-career management pattern or who are attaining employment through "labour pool associations."

Purely financial incentives, on the other hand, are not limited to any specific type of setting. Bonuses tied to individual or unit performance are innately transferable (or fungible) and do not have to be linked to any particular organization. That is, the value of financial incentives as mechanisms to self-enhancement are not limited to any particular context and will usually hold their meaning regardless of where they are offered. Financial incentives will, then, retain significance in the new world of work and may become even more significant as the ties of organizational loyalty become less common and less relevant. First, direct monetary income in this changing world of fewer commitments will gain increased significance.

Second, incentive programmes that enable individuals to meet their needs for self-protection will have increased value. Such needs might be met by developing and applying incentive payments directly into health, welfare, and pension programmes even though the employees involved may be temporary workers who frequently change employers. Consistent with the logic underlying the labor pool associations described earlier, HR professionals might well consider developing financial incentive programmes using individual "benefit" accounts into which employers (and employees) would contribute based on employment, no matter how temporary or varying that employment might be.

These would be financial incentives for performance designed to satisfy self-protection needs by paying into health, welfare, and pension accounts maintained by the labor pool association. In addition to being of value to the individuals involved, such contributions are likely to increase commitment and loyalty to an organization's needs. (One might note that the type of account we are referring to here is somewhat analogous to Social Security accounts. However, there are two major differences. First, these accounts are linked to individual work patterns and individual work behaviour in a more immediate manner. Second, these plans focus on health and welfare benefits as much as if not more than pay and pension concerns.)

Insider-Outsider Training Programmes

Training programmes designed to integrate individuals of diverse backgrounds and views into cohesive work teams are not new. They have been a standard part of HRM programmes in recent years as cultural and ethnic diversity has become a major challenge for organizations. Some of these training programmes have proved fruitful and some have not.

However, the challenge to HRM here is somewhat different in that the programmes we refer to have generally made one major assumption that we cannot make in the new context: that the individuals and groups in these programmes, diverse though they may be, all wish to maximize the effectiveness of the same organization, that is, the organization to which they are all committed by reason of employment.

In the new world of work, group members may include permanent employees committed to the same organization and work unit as well as temporarily assigned employees who rotate from assignment to assignment within the same organization and are sent to different units with not always consistent goals.

Even more difficult, however, will be dealing with people who are individual contractors or temporary workers who go to different organizations once a specific job is finished. It is not just that there will be changing memberships and changing interaction patterns in these organizational settings. Rather, there are and will also be individuals working together who have different, perhaps even conflicting loyalties. How does one get these groups to work together for some super ordinate goal when some are truly insiders and some outsiders?

It is not clear how one proceeds here. Appeals to super ordinate goals may not be appropriate over the long run (although they may be for the short run). In addition, the need for emotional cohesion may not be great because the groups may not be conceived of as even quasi-permanent. It is also uncertain which type of development programme might be most appropriate and which type of incentive programme might be best. One possibility may be the extensive use of financial incentives to integrate such groups into a common effort because financial benefits are not tied to any particular organization or setting. These incentives may be performance based, perhaps even providing stock options keyed to the length, level, and quality of performance in a particular setting.

We really do not have any answers to these questions at this time, but the potential for conflict between insider-outsider groups within organizations is great, as is the potential for conflict among those with different perspectives who also need to work together, such as suppliers and vendors. Hence, it is in the development of appropriate training and performance incentive programmes to meet this need that HRM may make another significant contribution in the new world of work. A work setting is beginning to emerge that is radically different from the one that has traditionally provided the context for HRM policies and practices. In this world downsizing is a tool of managerial decision making, work-family conflict is a fact of life for millions and, increasingly, contingent workers, part-time workers, and outsourcing are used. It is a work setting where opportunities to meet self-enhancement and growth needs exist for some individuals but not for all, and where opportunities for self-protection such as job and benefit security are increasingly difficult to come by.

These changes have made it necessary for HRM as a profession to reevaluate its traditional practices and begin to develop and implement programmes that meet these needs for self-enhancement and self-protection in the new work setting.

This chapter offered illustrations of such programmes, including effective self-career management programmes based on personal growth principles; labor pool associations for those for whom self-career management is inappropriate; performance incentive programmes not based on organizational commitment, including financial rewards of both direct income and health, welfare, and pension benefits; and insider outsider training programmes.

Underlying these recommendations is my view that HRM professionals, regardless of specific training, need to take an active role in meeting the demands of the new world of work.

Key to this process is recognizing that the opportunities for meeting and satisfying the primary motivational patterns of self-enhancement and self-protection are no longer what they used to be, whatever level of the occupational spectrum we are focusing on.

For the benefit of both organizations and individuals, developing new mechanisms for responding to these changes is a major challenge facing HRM today.

Chapter 5

HR Professionals in Managing Performance of Hotel

Most Fortune 1000 employees have been affected by the widespread proliferation of work teams. This holds true also for the millions of employees and managers who work outside the Fortune 1000. Recent evidence about the growth in work teams reinforces the notion that they have become a way of life in many organizations. For example, Osterman (1994) found that over 50 percent of the seven hundred firms he studied were using teams and that over 40 percent had more than half of their employees working in teams. As the use of teams continues to grow, human resource (HR) professionals need more knowledge about teams in general and, more specifically, information about the HR practices that enhance team performance. Human resources play a critical role in developing and implementing organizational strategies and structures. Successful HR professionals will be those who can align their organizational HR practices with the unique demands of team-based organizational structures.

First, we provide HR professionals with a brief history of the use of teams in the United States, reviewing definitions and types of teams, evidence regarding the impact of teams, and the factors that led to their proliferation. Second, we aim to provide the HR professional with tools to increase the effectiveness of teams, discussing the key assumptions underlying supportive conditions for teams. Third, we review modifications in HR practices that are necessary to implement teams effectively. Finally, we discuss potential challenges that HR practitioners may face in implementing teams in multinational organizations; looking to the future, we present guidelines for meeting these challenges. We conclude with some predictions about the use of teams that will likely develop as our team-based organizations continue to evolve.

What Teams Are, How Teams Contribute, and When to Use Them

In general, a work team can be defined as a group of individuals working interdependently to solve problems or accomplish tasks. However, a single definition is not sufficient to capture the key differences that exist between the various types of teams being used in organizations. A number of key differences between these types of teams will determine the efficacy of HR practices designed to enhance their effectiveness. For example, compensation structures are normally altered for self-managing work teams to include team-based rewards to encourage cooperation between members and motivate them to reach team goals. Because self-managing members are working on permanent teams, the effort and expense involved in changing compensation structures is often justified. However, in more temporary teams, such as cross-functional or problem solving teams, other types of HR policy changes (for example, altering an evaluation system to include team behaviors) may be more appropriate to encourage positive behaviours.

Our point here is not to review all of the appropriate HR policies for each type of team but rather to acknowledge that our use of the term work team includes several different types of teams.

Contrary to popular belief, teams are not a new phenomenon. The origins of teams can be traced to the Tavistock studies of post–World War II and the Swedish socio technical movement generally associated with the Volvo Corporation. The first work teams in the United States were found in the Procter & Gamble Company in the early 1960s, the Topeka work system at a General Foods pet food plant in the late 1960s, and the Rushton Quality of Work Project in Pennsylvania in the mid–1970s. Given that teams were identified as a mechanism for improving employee performance as early as the 1960s, why has it taken over thirty years to implement work teams on a large scale in the United States?

We attribute the recent rise in the interest in and use of teams over the last ten years to three factors: a higher concern for the social component of work; the globalization of the U.S. economy and resulting downsizing; and the early adoption of work teams by highly visible hotels. Although many believe that organizations have adopted work teams to improve employee morale or productivity, the forces behind their adoption have been much larger in scale and much more connected to global patterns of international business. Organizations have adopted work teams because many had no choice. Dramatically reduced numbers of managers could not keep up with employee activities on a day-today basis.

Furthermore, the increased use of teams can be attributed, in part, to evidence of their success. Work teams have been associated with higher levels of productivity. It should be noted, however, that most of these studies have been conducted with self-managing work teams that have considerable control over their own structure and process. For traditional work teams, much of the evidence of impact has been collected on a case-by-case basis. Wellins, Byham, and Dixon (1994), for example, chronicle the pervasive positive impact teams have had in twenty companies. These companies claim that implementing teams resulted in improvements in bottom-line indicators such as cost savings, quality and service improvement, speed, absenteeism, and turnover.

This is not to say that teams are a panacea. Several studies on the impact of teams have failed to find effects for performance on more quantitative measures, such as productivity; others report only modest findings for productivity. Smaller effect sizes for productivity may be the result of using work teams in contexts where they are not appropriate. Clearly, work teams are not ideal for every task (even if you have a hammer, not every problem is a nail). Work teams are more effective under the right circumstances and situations.

For example, work teams are most effective when there is high task interdependence or a high degree of coordination and collaboration required between team members to accomplish tasks. Thus, a group of insurance sales agents who are geographically dispersed and have little interaction with one another to carry out their tasks would most likely be an inappropriate context in which to implement teams. The agents would probably see such an effort as an empty, poorly developed strategy designed to capitalize on a management fad.

Work teams are also more appropriate when the tasks that their members carry out are complex and well designed. If a group's work is routine and unchallenging, of dubious importance, and wholly preprogrammemed with no opportunity for feedback, teams will probably not make much difference in productivity. As Johns (1996) has stated, "Taking a bunch of olive stuffers on a food processing assembly line, putting them in distinctive jumpsuits, calling them the Olive Squad, and telling them to self-manage will be unlikely to yield dividends in terms of effort expended or brainpower employed". Work teams, especially those that increase autonomy and responsibility, are most effective when members are given complex tasks that capitalize on their diverse knowledge and skills. Thus, teams should view their tasks as significant, the tasks should require the use of a variety of skills, and members should, where possible, assemble an entire product or deliver a complete service.

The effectiveness of work teams also depends on whether an organization has high integration needs as a result of operating in a complex environment. Complex environments usually force organizations to serve a wide variety of customers, deal with rapidly changing technology, and satisfy large numbers of different stakeholders. IBM, for example, faces a much more complex environment than McDonald's (compare the rate of change in PCs with that of Big Macs over the last fifteen years). Organizations must simultaneously deal with all of these issues—in other words, differentiate into smaller, more responsive units—and then integrate these widely dispersed efforts and units back into one cohesive organization. Teams will be most effective when a team structure is the best solution to obtaining the integration required to accomplish goals in a complex organizational environment. Without effective integration, the benefits attributed to work teams (increased productivity, higher quality, better job satisfaction) will not be realized.

Thus, companies implementing teams from a "bandwagon" perspective will not realize the benefits to be had from an appropriate fit between teams and context. In fact, many organizations are currently struggling with team effectiveness. We argue that this is the result, in part, of traditional assumptions about work that still prevail. In order to implement teams effectively, assumptions must change. We next discuss these adaptations.

The Need to Adapt Our Assumptions

We discuss the assumptions that shaped the decisions made by HR professionals in traditional hierarchical organizations in three areas: motivation; structure of work; and accountability. Traditional assumptions must be adapted in order to support effective implementation of teams.

Motivation

The first set of assumptions that must be examined pertain to motivation. National culture helps determine what motivates people. For example, some cultures can be classified as individualistic, where people tend to value their own self-interest and welfare over the interests of groups or societies; other cultures are known as collectivistic, where people tend to value the welfare of groups more than their own.

Individualists are motivated by the opportunity to gain personal recognition. They resist working in teams more than people from collectivistic cultures. Such resistance lowers team effectiveness on outcomes such as productivity, job satisfaction, cooperativeness, and organizational commitment. It takes time and experience for people to adjust their notions of fairness and equity to include collective accountability. Taking a longer-term focus and understanding the eventual payoffs for early investments in team-based systems is essential for harnessing the motivational power of teams.

In understanding motivational assumptions, it is also important to consider expectations. Research attests to the importance of collective expectations in determining our level of motivation and subsequently our performance. When we believe we can accomplish objectives as a team, we are motivated to stick with our work tasks and prevail. But sometimes these high expectations get out of hand, to the point that teams hold unrealistic expectations. Cohesive teams often fall prey to this phenomenon, which is referred to as groupthink. Coinciding with extremely high expectations, teams suffering from groupthink also hold illusions of invulnerability.

They ignore important external information sources that might help them adjust their performance to fit the needs of customers better. Teams in individualistic cultures appear to be particularly susceptible to overconfidence. This may be because individualists view their team as an entity in and of itself rather than one that is connected to the external context and are therefore even less apt to use external sources of information to make corrections in their behaviour and improve their performance. Particularly in individualistic cultures, team-based organizations need to have systems that help teams set realistic expectations. This allows them to stay motivated while at the same time remaining open to learning from feedback and mistakes.

Work Structure

A second domain of assumptions concerns the structure of work. Traditional work groups were generally formed around common technical or functional skills and areas of expertise (for example, accounting, finance, or production). In recent years, it has become apparent that organizing work around a process (for example, new product development) rather than around a specific task or function is more effective. Doing so often requires extending team members' task skills. Multi skilled teamwork involves teams made up of individuals with multiple and overlapping skills that are deployed around the performance of a whole task, which represents a significant part of a larger work flow. Members are multi skilled so that work can be flexibly allocated among them.

In organizing work around processes, organizational boundaries must often be renegotiated. Increasingly, work teams include external customers and suppliers. For example, General Electric Medical Systems invites representatives from leading health maintenance organizations (HMOs) to serve on its sales and service teams. The American Red Cross has members of communities serving on key committees that set organizational objectives. Eastman Kodak allies itself with key competitors to form market segment task forces. These types of work structures require a whole new notion of collaboration—collaboration with external constituencies. Those who were previously viewed as "them" are now viewed as "us."

The reorganization of work around processes and across boundaries has numerous benefits. For example, multi skilling (the learning of new skills in addition to functional expertise) can result in reduced staffing as fewer workers can perform the same range of tasks. It can create efficiencies through more flexible task assignment. Multi skilling also often leads to lower inventories because there is more effective work flow coordination. It also makes the team more flexible in meeting fluctuating market demand through operational flexibility.

Finally, it can lead to a more differentiated response to the needs of particular customer segments and so contribute to strategic flexibility. Multi skilling leads to greater awareness of the whole task and enables the team member to take part in problem solving, innovation, and strategic thinking. These same benefits do not accrue when tasks and organizations are structured under traditional assumptions of static, independent jobs.

Accountability

A third domain of assumptions that shape team effectiveness pertain to accountability. The focus of most HR departments has been on the individual. Individual accountability and responsibility have been the foundation on which all of the business practices in the United States have been built. Furthermore, accountability in traditional work organizations was vested in those with formal positions—the managers and supervisors. Individual employees showed deference to people in these positions, Reporting structures were vertical and a command-and-control philosophy reigned. Skills such as planning, coordination, personnel functions, quality management, health and safety, and boundary management were the domain of managers. But increasingly, these duties are becoming the domain of teams.

Managerial responsibility is shifting from individual accountability to collective, mutual accountability. As this has occurred, the notion of self-management has gained acceptance. Self-management grows as the team's operational tasks are delegated to the team itself. Many different terms have evolved to describe and distinguish varying degrees of autonomy, including self-directed work teams, empowered teams, and superior work teams. The common distinguishing characteristic of such teams is that they operate with some degree of autonomy.

As nonmanagers become collectively responsible for managerial duties, basic assumptions about the legitimacy of authority are challenged. Team members may begin to question what gives peers the right to set rules for others. They may have difficulty dealing with authority that does not stem from position. Rather than depending on a job description and direction from the manager, people work jointly with coworkers to determine what they do. Because personal success depends on collective success, an individual's fate is tied to coworkers. Feelings of mutual trust and partnership must develop. The organization must help people learn to deal with greater ambiguity, uncertainty, continual change, and collaborative relationships. Both managers and employees in the team-based organization need to adjust to this shift in accountability and responsibility. We discuss the HR systems that increase team effectiveness in the next section.

The Need to Modify HR Practices to Support Teams

In addition to recognizing and adapting the assumptions on which they base their practices, HR professionals must also modify those practices to support teams. The practices to be modified cluster in five areas: recruitment and selection; task design; training; evaluation; and compensation. In the following sections, we summarize the modifications and provide references for practitioners interested in exploring them in greater depth.

Recruitment and Selection

Working effectively in a team requires a particular set of knowledge, skills, and abilities (KSAs) that were not as critical in traditional organizations. Proficiency is needed in at least five areas: conflict resolution, collaborative problem solving, communication, goal setting and performance management, and planning and task coordination. During recruitment, organizations aspiring to create a workforce of effective team members should clearly communicate the importance of these proficiencies. Doing so provides a realistic job preview and can therefore help to reduce turnover. Recruiting individuals who prefer these activities also makes sense because team members' preferences for teamwork are related to team effectiveness.

It is also important to consider teamwork KSAs in the selection process. It might seem easy to include measures of KSAs in most selection systems, but most selection instruments focus on basic learning abilities (for example, math, language, perceptual skills) or specific technical abilities (for example, mechanical, electrical, and so on). In the last few years, employment tests designed to measure teamwork KSAs have been under development.

Early results suggest that the tests can predict subsequent performance beyond the level of prediction from a large battery of traditional employment aptitude tests. These initial findings offer encouraging support for such instruments. Interviews might also be a viable method of assessing social and interpersonal attributes that contribute to teamwork. There is evidence that a structured interview designed to measure social KSAs can predict future team effectiveness. Finally, selection techniques that involve collecting biographical information may be another way to assess teamwork KSAs.

Task Design

The second set of practices that must be modified relate to task design. Effective teams are designed around the tasks they perform. Two key considerations are that teams should be relatively self contained and handle many aspects of their own functioning. First, teams should be collectively responsible for an identifiable and substantial part of the work of the organization. To the extent possible, support services should be included in the team so that it has the resources necessary to accomplish its goals. Members should be multi skilled and dedicated to the team so that they do not have to split priorities. Finally, the team should report as a unit so that members do not have conflicting directions from different managers.

Second, the team should be responsible for many aspects of its own functioning. For example, it should be able to determine how to apply the team's resources, strategies for completion of work, and quality monitoring. It should also be responsible for working with internal and external customers. Finally, part of the team's task should be performance evaluation. Whenever appropriate skill levels and task conditions exist, team members should be involved in reviewing their own performance and determining their own rewards.

Beyond these two fundamental design principles, a third issue is whether teams should be functional or cross-functional. Functional organizations group people by common specialties and break work down into functional packets that translate into individual assignment. Project organizations combine different specialties required to perform the entire project but then break the work down for members of functional groups within the project. Team-based organizations require a shift away from a hierarchical breakdown to focus instead on the lateral distribution and integration of work.

Whether teams should be functional or cross-functional is a choice to be based on an analysis of the work to be accomplished. Process analysis can be used to determine the sets of activities that have to be carried out and integrated to deliver value to customers. If within an identifiable set of activities coordination must occur across different functional areas, then teams should be cross-functional. In the cross-functional teams members can integrate work across disciplines and make trade-offs that require a multidisciplinary perspective. But if the process analysis indicates that an identifiable set of activities occurs within a functional area, then teams should be functional.

Training

Training constitutes a third set of practice modifications for effective team implementation. There is often a mistaken belief that people who are highly educated have the basic skills to work effectively in team settings. In fact, highly specialized individuals are often used to working alone and may lack some of the basic interpersonal skills necessary for collaboration. Training programmes designed for interpersonal skills in teams take one of two approaches: traditional classroom instruction in which a lecturer delivers material about techniques or strategies for working in teams and creative off-site team-building sessions in which teams participate in athletic, artistic, or competitive activities unrelated to their actual day-to-day responsibilities. What is generally missing is the development of hands-on team capabilities, which is best accomplished by treating the team as a whole and applying the training as the team performs its actual tasks. In this way, the value of the training is established in the context of the work that the team does.

In addition to teaching interpersonal skills, training must focus on establishing the skills necessary for self-management. First, considerable attention must be given to determining an optimal degree of autonomy. Self-managing teams are an appropriate response to situations where performance can be enhanced by taking decisions closer to the organization's environment. In contrast, self-management is not appropriate when the team is particularly large, when there is a high degree of functional diversity, or when the team is newly formed.

In these situations, the team is faced with a high level of complexity, information-processing requirements are extensive, and managerial tasks are particularly challenging. Having an external leader provide direction in these instances can improve team effectiveness. Perhaps the most substantial costs associated with increasing self-direction in teams are associated with the level of training and development needed to ensure that all or most of the members have the KSAs required to perform what were previously managerial responsibilities. In addition, on some teams employees are asked actually to carry out the training and development of their fellow members.

Another training focus pertains to learning. In a team-based system, multidirectional learning is required across functions, levels, and organizations. This requires norms that are far different from those that prevailed in the traditional organization. For example, learning requires the willingness to surface bad news and act on it. But that will not happen unless the traditional reaction— negatively evaluating the messengers of bad news—changes. Organizations that encourage experimentation and innovation and set up mechanisms for shared reflection can capitalize on this learning potential. Lateral learning must occur through dialogue and collaboration, and vertical learning must occur between teams at different levels in the organization. Local learning and innovation occurs through trial and error, but broader learning depends on whether organizations establish mechanisms for reflecting on and capturing learning from a variety of experiences.

Evaluation

A fourth set of practices that must be modified involves evaluation. If organizations wish to motivate teamwork, they must incorporate teamwork KSAs into their appraisal systems. It is important that the appraisal system not only reward good team players but also discourage behaviors that are not conducive to team effectiveness. An organization-specific job analysis should be conducted to determine the precise nature of the behavioral and performance measures to be included in the appraisal form for each individual team member. Categories of teamwork KSAs such as conflict resolution, collaborative problem solving, communication, goal setting, performance management, planning, and task coordination could be translated into critical work behaviors or performance dimensions and incorporated into such an appraisal form.

Equally important, however, is that team behaviors then be assessed. Imagine four teams, each performing the same task. In the first team, each team member is given an individual goal. In the second, a goal is set for the team as a whole only. The third team is given both individual and team goals. The fourth is given no specific goal at all. Which team will do the poorest work? In an experiment that replicated this situation, the team with individual goals only was the poorest performer among all four teams. The team with both individual and team goals performed the best. Most organizations might claim they have both individual and team goals if they have profit sharing or gain sharing. However, psychologically, these types of "team goals" are often overshadowed by individual goals, because the personal sense of control over performance lessens as one focuses on larger and larger groups, such as the entire organization.

Each team should identify a set of critical measures representing a combination of results and process-oriented outcomes. Focusing only on results (for example, return on sales, revenue growth, and so on) does not help inform the team about which behaviors should be adjusted. Process measures (time spent per call, days before call returned, and so on) identify key behaviors that the team can change in order to improve results. Teams should avoid developing too many measures. If a measure is not critical in guiding the team's behaviour, then discard it.

Most experts recommend that teams track six to ten performance areas. Finally, in team-based organizations, people are responsible for collective performance at multiple levels. Individual, team, and business unit performance must be evaluated. Optimizing performance at any one level may hurt performance at other levels. The link between behaviour at one level and performance at another may be uncertain. People are often concerned that they will not get adequate feedback on how they are performing when the focus is on collective performance. Therefore, appraisal systems should assess behaviors that contribute to performance of other units or other levels within the organization.

Team members should receive feedback from multiple sources, not just a manager. In small teams, each person can receive peer feedback, that is, feedback from all other team members and, where appropriate, feedback from customers.

Customers may be external to the organization (for example, a person who purchases a product or service) or internal (a person downstream in the process who receives the work of the team). It is also critical that feedback be given on multiple levels. It should be provided on individual performance, individual contributions to the team, team performance, and the team's contribution to the organization as a whole. Especially for the latter, feedback from customers and about competitors is critical. Whenever possible, it is best for teams themselves to document their own performance. This documentation should be developed and then discussed regularly at team meetings.

Compensation

A final set of HR practices that should be examined when implementing teams pertains to compensation. Good practices for rewarding team performance require good processes for defining what the performance should be and for measuring and evaluating the performance. Some researchers have advocated that rewards should be the last component put in place in the transition to teams. This argument is made because team rewards are difficult to develop and have to be tailored to the organization.

We recommend that organizations begin by introducing teamwork as a central objective in each individual's performance evaluation. Individual compensation should then be based on the accomplishment of these objectives. This is an intermediary step on the path toward team-based rewards; it allows recognition for teamwork and allows time for the organization to adjust other systems. Next, HR professionals can work to change the organizational compensation and reward practices. For example, team awards and team bonuses help team members focus on the performance of their own team. Profit sharing and gain sharing help team members focus on unit wide performance and orient employees to the larger performing unit by making it in everyone's interest to improve the performance of the enterprise as a whole.

We argue that the most effective compensation systems incorporate an element of all three of these approaches (individual rewards, team rewards, and unit rewards). This combination ensures that performance at each level is recognized and encouraged, in turn ensuring that individual behaviour is in the best interest of the team and that team behaviour is in the best interest of the organization.

Impediments, Facilitators, and Challenges for the Future of Work Teams

HR professionals may face several additional impediments. We see four challenges in particular: the inability of work teams to make a dramatic improvement in organizational performance quickly; the inevitable inter team conflict inherent in team-based organizations; resistance to work teams in foreign affiliates; and North American cultural barriers to working in teams.

Time Lag

The first stumbling block to the further proliferation of work teams in organizations is the time lag between their implementation and positive results on productivity and employee morale. As with most large-scale organizational changes, team implementation may make things worse initially. Employee productivity and morale may drop and absenteeism and turnover may increase. This time lag is problematic for two reasons. First, many managers focus heavily on quarterly results.

Such a focus may cause extreme disappointment in top managers looking to maximize short-term profitability. Second, because the popular press contains so many positive stories about teams, many top managers are likely to be shocked by the initial drop in organizational performance. After reading The Greatest Team Success Stories (a fictional title but probably not far off from the real thing!), patience is likely to wear thin by the time improvements in productivity or morale are actually realized. HR professionals need to arm themselves with concrete evidence about what really happens when work teams get implemented. They must inform top managers that work teams will not be an overnight success. In fact, many leading researchers have suggested that three to five years is not an unreasonable time frame for work teams to be fully and successfully implemented.

Inward Focus

The second likely impediment to successful work teams is a common phenomenon in sports. When individuals are divided up, given team names, granted a set of distinct responsibilities, and told to perform well as a team, they naturally tend to become more inwardly focused and concerned about their own team than about others. Football players shout insults, hockey players brawl, and work teams occasionally place their own interests above that of other teams and the organization as a whole. Such inter team conflict can result in lack of cooperation, refusal to assist other teams in need, or worse, outright sabotage of other teams' efforts. In other words, too much team commitment can be detrimental. An unwillingness to communicate between teams destroys one of the reasons that organizations implement teams in the first place: to create a higher level of integration in a complex organizational environment. Inwardly focused teams that fail to collaborate with others or communicate with external customers perform more poorly than externally focused teams.

Several strategies are available to the HR professional for overcoming problematic inwardly focused teams. First, managers should keep teams focused on a higher level, or super ordinate, goal. Such a goal can be organization-, plant-, or unitwide. A super ordinate goal keeps teams focused on the big picture, lowers competition between teams, and ties everything that all do more closely to overall organizational success. A second strategy is to implement rewards (possibly based on goals) that are tied to the success of a set of teams as whole (a work unit, for example).

Unit-level rewards are tricky in that all team members have to know how their contribution affects their rewards (also known as line of sight). A final strategy is to create linking or integrating teams composed of members from each of the competitive teams. Integrating teams tend to dilute original team member loyalties and ensure that each team's concerns are heard. Regardless of the strategy chosen, ignoring the problem of combative teams will inevitably erode any potential gains to be realized from the implementation of work teams. HR professionals should take a proactive stand by designing strategies to reduce competition before the teams are allowed to become inwardly focused.

Resistance

A third impediment may arise when multinational organizations use work teams in their foreign affiliates. Organizations often wish to "export" their management practices because having similar HR practices in each country streamlines operations and reduces costs. For example, the Goodyear Tire and Rubber Company has begun using work teams in Europe, Latin America, and Asia; Sara Lee Corporation currently uses teams in Puerto Rico and Mexico; and Texas Instruments Malaysia has organized its entire workforce into teams.

Organizational scholars have pointed to national culture as a determinant of the success or failure of management initiatives that are developed in one culture and implemented in another. Some employees may resist management initiatives or react angrily when those initiatives clash with their deeply held cultural values.

HR professionals should learn about the cultures in which the company's work teams will operate. Through better understanding of cultural differences comes the knowledge of potential stumbling blocks to successful implementation before attempts are made to export work teams. Success stories about work teams in foreign affiliates exist, but that success depends on an understanding of the cultural forces that shape employee reaction to teams.

Values

A final potential impediment to the success of work teams comes from differences in employee preferences and values within the United States. Just as some cultures are more individualistic or more collectivistic than others, individuals within cultures also vary on this dimension—even though there is, on average, more variation across cultures than within cultures. For example, when faced with the prospect of moving to a team-based work environment, some employees in a study conducted in the United States expressed concerns that reflected their individualistic values. Their comments included these: "Why should someone else's performance affect my pay?" "Will the team get credit for what I do?" "Individual achievement won't count anymore." "My achievement will be diluted by overall team success."

These comments suggest that some employees may resist work teams because they are not compatible with their own work-related values. Tests exist for measuring individualistic and collectivistic values at the individual level. Other measures such as preference for teams could be used as selection tools to evaluate prospective team members before they are placed on a team. If the teams are self-managing or autonomous, measures such as need for growth or need for achievement could be used to assess prospective member preferences for increased autonomy and responsibility. Whatever the measures used, HR professionals need to be aware of the role of individual differences in a team's success or failure in order to select more carefully individuals who are suited to working in a team. Barring the availability of such individuals, training must attempt to enhance employee receptivity to work teams.

Facilitators

We see three forces that will continue to enhance the use of teams: the sharing of business practices across organizational units and across different organizations, organizational environment trends, and cultural change.

First, in the years during which Total Quality Management enjoyed its heyday (the 1980s), many companies began a practice that had previously seemed contradictory to maintaining competitive advantage: benchmarking HR practices in other organizations. In years past companies viewed their internal operations as sources of extreme value. But with the growth in international competition—especially in automobiles, electronics, and textiles—some businesses in the United States have realized the benefits of sharing information more openly to increase the global competitiveness of entire industries.

This realization coupled with the work team success stories in the popular press have fueled an unprecedented exchange of both ideas and visits between companies and even competitors interested in adopting or improving work teams. For example, companies such as General Electric have looked to other seemingly unrelated businesses, such as Southwest Airlines, in order to adapt team-based practices. The benchmarking of HR practices also occurs within industries. Several major semiconductor manufacturers (for example, Intel, DEC, Texas Instruments) have benchmarking agreements that allow for information exchange around HR best practices.

Second, in many industries, organizational environments are becoming exceedingly dynamic and complex. Scholars and practitioners alike have long realized the importance of aligning organizational structures with environmental characteristics. For example, the rapid changes witnessed in the computer industry forced companies such as IBM to restructure to achieve a better organizational structure-environment fit. There is general consensus that increasing environmental complexity will continue for the foreseeable future for organizations in many industries. As these changes continue, the use of work teams will continue to serve as an integrated and flexible means of responding to organizational environments.

Finally, regarding cultural change, researchers have suggested that there may be a substantial amount of cross-national convergence of management practices, values, and beliefs as a result of the interactions between organizations across cultures. As cultural convergence continues, a common set of values and assumptions may develop across national boundaries. This implies that eventually it may be possible to develop a universal set of best practices that will be appropriate no matter the cultural setting. In other words, less cultural adaptation may be necessary.

Thus, HR practitioners in multinational corporations may gradually have an easier time dealing with cultural impediments. We caution, however, that although some convergence is likely to take place, there are fundamental cultural values within nations that will remain stable. Researchers have referred to this phenomenon as the distinction between peripheral and core values. Therefore, it will always be necessary to adapt HR practices to some degree to fit the cultural context if the effectiveness of those practices across national boundaries is to be enhanced.

The Future of Work Teams

We expect the work teams of the twenty-first century to take on new characteristics that are not currently in common practice but exist in the early adoption phase in the Fortune 1000. First, as the environment grows increasingly complex, temporary team structures will supplant more permanent work teams. As the forces outside organizations continue to change, the structures inside organizations will become more fluid. Rather than permanently assigning people to work teams, team composition will shift as projects, problems, or customers demand. Ad hoc teams or project teams will be more prevalent, placing extraordinary demands on employees to be flexible and demonstrate their value to organizations consistently through their team efforts. The challenge for HR managers will certainly involve compensation and evaluation for employees who may be constantly moving from one project team to another without a regular supervisor or team members with whom they have any long-term contact.

Second, the use of multicultural teams (composed of members from different cultures) and globalized teams (composed of same culture members in a variety of countries) is likely to rise as trade barriers continue to fall (as, for example, with NAFTA and the European Union). National culture plays a strong role in determining employee attitudes and behaviour. If a significant rise in these more culturally diverse teams occurs—and we feel strongly that it will—then HR managers must familiarize themselves with the cultures in which their organization operates. For example, if peer evaluations are part of the performance appraisal process on a multicultural team, HR managers must identify the key cultural characteristics that may serve as stumbling blocks to these evaluations. If globalized teams are used, it is likely that entirely different compensation systems will be needed depending on the dominant cultural values of the areas in which an organization has business.

Finally, with more telecommuting and flextime there will be less face-to-face time in work teams. We predict that traditional work teams will be replaced by virtual teams, whose members may seldom or never meet in person. Also referred to as "mobile, " these teams have no geographic center. The members work out of their homes, automobiles, and clients' facilities and communicate via e-mail, fax, telephone, and videoconference. Team meetings may take place only once each quarter. The challenge for HR professionals is to assist managers in integrating team members, building cohesive teams, and facilitating communication and information exchange without having team members together in one place.

Teams are a powerful design option for organizations that hope to meet the challenges of increased global competition, improve output quality, and address the social needs of the ever-changing global workforce. However, the success or failure of work teams in multinational organizations will depend largely on the HR professional. Effective implementation of teams requires that HR practitioners adapt key assumptions about motivation, structure, and accountability. Adapted assumptions must support lateral thinking, collaboration, interdependence, a focus on process, permeable boundaries, and mutual responsibility.

At the same time, HR practices must evolve to support teambased systems. Modifications in recruitment and selection, task design, training, evaluation, and compensation are all key to the effective use of teams in multinational organizations. Key to effective selection and recruitment for teams is the identification of teamwork KSAs. Critical for task design is the development of teams around task processes and the integration of functional areas. Developing interpersonal, managerial, and learning skills are important training needs in team-based organizations. Finally, effective evaluation and compensation for teams requires a multilevel perspective and a balance between individual and team-based systems.

Numerous impediments will challenge the effective implementation of teams across national contexts, including the inherent time lag between implementation and results, the often tenuous relationships between teams, cultural differences that require adaptations in practices to fit the context, and increasing domestic demographic diversity within nations. To address these potential impediments, HR practitioners can encourage sharing practices within and between organizations, observe and adapt to organizational environmental trends, and maintain awareness of cultural convergence.

HR professionals who can change their assumptions and are adept at modifying basic HR practices will be better poised to face future trends in the use of teams that are just on the horizon. As temporary team structures, multicultural teams, and virtual teams proliferate, these team-savvy practitioners will be able to lead their organizations through successful implementation and use of teams in multinational contexts.

LESSONS FROM GLOBAL HUMAN RESOURCE PRACTICES IN HOTELS

Given the substantial issues of diversity that all organizations are confronting today, the successful human resource (HR) practitioner needs a conceptual framework to deal with them in both global and single-country business environments. Diversity should be viewed not as a confounding factor but rather as a source of energy that drives change and growth. Rhinesmith (1993) points out that globalization has arrived and that "diversity—both domestic and international—will be the engine that drives the creative energy of the corporation of the twenty-first century. Successful HR managers will be those who are able to manage this diversity for the innovative and competitive edge of their corporation."

We believe that diversity can no longer be discussed only from a single-country perspective. Workforces in all countries are be- coming more diverse, not just in gender, age, and race but also in culture. The workforce of any industrialized or developing nation will increasingly be a mix of domestic and international ethnicities. To deal with this challenge, the HR practitioner of tomorrow will have to understand the impact of cultural or global diversity, as well as of country-specific diversity, on the effectiveness of the organization and the workforce.

HOSPITALITY AND LOADGING

Organizing, the process of structuring human and physical resources in order to accomplish organizational objectives, involves dividing tasks into jobs, specifying the appropriate department for each job, determining the optimum number of jobs in each department, and delegating authority within and among departments. One of the most critical challenges facing lodging managers today is the development of a responsive organizational structure that is committed to quality.

The framework of jobs and departments that make up any organization must be directed toward achieving the organization's objectives. In other words, the structure of a lodging business must be consistent with its strategy. Managers give structure to a hotel and lodging through job specialization, organization, and establishment of patterns of authority and span of control.

Job Specialization

There are as many degrees of job specialization within the lodging industry as there are types of organizations—and there are many types of organizations. One extreme is the case of a hotel where the owner/operator is responsible for checking in the guests, servicing their needs, taking care of the housekeeping for the guest rooms, maintaining the building and grounds, and checking out the guests. There is, to be sure, much to recommend this method of work. It is rewarding to have total control over a project from beginning to end, and many people find it motivating to see the results of their efforts.

However, as the demand for additional products or services increases (i.e., if additional rooms are added or another hotel is purchased), it becomes more and more difficult for an individual to do his or her job well. One benefit of the increased workload is increased revenue, which would enable the individual hotel operator to add housekeeping staff, one or more front desk agents to check in and check out the additional guests, and engineering and maintenance personnel to care for the building and grounds.

As a general rule, specialization increases worker productivity and efficiency. On the other hand, delegating jobs increases the need for managerial control and coordination. Someone has to make sure that housekeeping staff come in after the painters have repainted a room (and that the paint is dry), not before! A crucial element of hotel and lodging management is coordinating the many specialized functions within hotels so that the organization runs smoothly.

Specialization has its own set of problems; it can result in workers performing the same tasks over and over again. A point can be reached where the degree of specialization so narrows a job's scope that the worker finds little joy or satisfaction in it. Signs of overspecialization include workers' loss of interest, lowered morale, increasing error rate, and reduction in service and product quality.

One solution to this problem is to modify jobs so that teams can perform them. Instead of a single guest room attendant being assigned to a group of rooms, a work team in a hotel housekeeping department might clean all of the rooms on a particular floor. Some establishments use teams regularly throughout the organization; others use teams more selectively. Teams can be directed by a manager or can be self managed. The idea behind self-managed work teams is for workers to become their own managers, which increases their self-reliance as well as develops a talent pool.

A concept called the quality circle is based on the belief that the people who actually do the work, rather than their managers, are the ones who are best able to identify, analyze, and correct problems they encounter. The idea originated in Japan in 1962. The quality circle is a group of employees, usually fewer than ten, who perform similar jobs and meet once per week to discuss their work, identify problems, and present possible solutions to those problems. For example, a quality circle might be formed among front desk agents. The group forwards its findings and proposals to management for evaluation and action. Quality circles are most successful when they are part of an organization- wide improvement effort. American business picked up on the quality circle concept in the mid-1970s.

THE ORGANIZATION OF A LODGING ESTABLISHMENT

As their facilities grow in size, lodging managers are faced with the need to group certain jobs in order to ensure efficient coordination and control of activities. These job groupings are usually called departments. In general, departments might be grouped as front of the house (those departments in which employees have guest contact, such as front desk), and back of the house (where employees have little guest contact, such as accounting). However, separating departments by function is the most common method of organizing a hotel or a lodging business.

The limited-service hotel, a full-service hotel with under 500 rooms, and a full-service hotel with over 500 rooms. There may be as few as 2 or as many as 50 employees in a particular department. In a very small lodging business, such as a bed-and-breakfast, the owner can supervise each department. However, as the lodging business increases in size (i.e., above 20 rooms), it is most effective to create managerial positions within departments.

Typically, the rooms department (called the front desk department in a limited-service facility) includes reservations, the front office, housekeeping, and telephone or PBX. In smaller full-service hotels, security and engineering might also be included in the rooms department. Responsibilities of the rooms department include reservations, guest reception, room assignment, tracking the status of rooms (available or occupied), prompt forwarding of mail and phone messages, security, housekeeping of guest rooms and public spaces such as lobbies, and answering guests' questions. To perform these many duties effectively, the rooms department may be divided into a number of specialized subunits. To complicate matters, in many instances these subunits are also referred to as departments. For example, the laundry department

The front office is one of the most important departments in a hotel, as it often offers the only contact between guests and staff. A hotel's front office is where guests are greeted when they arrive, where they are registered and assigned to a room, and where they check out. Usually, the telephone operator, other guest communications functions, and the bell staff or those employees responsible for delivering luggage and messages and attending to special guest requests also fall under the front office umbrella. The reservations department takes and tracks the hotel's future bookings. The housekeeping department is responsible for cleaning guest rooms and public spaces. Because of their specialized nature, the security and engineering departments are discussed in separate sections.

A great deal of interdependence exists among the subunits of the rooms department. For example, reservations must inform the front office of the number of presold rooms each day to ensure that a current inventory of salable rooms is always available. On the other hand, the front office must let reservations know whenever walk-in guests (those who do not have reservations) register. A similar level of cooperation is required between the front office and housekeeping. When a guest checks out, the front office must inform housekeeping so that the room may be cleaned.

Once a room is cleaned, housekeeping must inform the front office so that the room may be sold. Certain tasks within the rooms department must occur in a specific order. For example, housekeeping cannot properly provision a guest room if the laundry does not supply enough clean towels or bed sheets. Engineering cannot replace a defective light switch in a guest room if housekeeping does not report the problem. Effective management of this busy department calls for standardized plans, procedures, schedules, and deadlines, as well as frequent direct communication between the executives who manage the key operating units of the rooms department.

Security

The hotel and lodging business is vulnerable to security and safety problems. Problems can be created by guests, employees, or intruders. Security breaches can result in embezzlement, theft, arson, robbery, and even terrorism. Depending on the size of a hotel or a lodging establishment, the security function may be handled by a fully staffed department on site, contracted to an outside security company, or assigned to designated staff members or on-premises supervisory personnel in the rooms department. In a larger, full-service hotel, the director of security may report directly to the general manager. In smaller hotels, the security function might become a task of the rooms department.

Engineering.

Typically, the engineering department's responsibilities include preventive maintenance; repair; replacement; improvement and modification to furniture, fixtures, and equipment (FFE); and ensuring uninterrupted provision of utilities (gas, electricity, water). Preventive maintenance involves routine checks and inspection of the key components of all equipment. Maintenance of recreational facilities may be part of the engineering department's responsibilities. In particular, swimming pools require extensive maintenance to ensure proper filtration and to prevent the accumulation of algae and other conditions unsuitable for swimming.

Prompt repair minimizes loss of productivity in other hotel operating departments and inconvenience to hotel guests. When a particular FFE has reached the end of its useful life and repair is no longer cost-effective, replacement is indicated. Improvement projects enhance the existing operation or reduce operating costs of the facility. Modification projects alter the existing operation to accommodate one or more new functions.

One hotel might have a large engineering staff that includes plumbers, carpenters, painters, electricians, and other technicians. Another might have maintenance personnel who have general knowledge and understanding of the hotel's operations but rely on outside contractors for specialized jobs. In larger, full-service hotels, engineering may be a separate department, with a director who reports directly to the resident manager.

The primary function of the food and beverage department is to provide food and drink to a hotel's guests. In earlier times, when an inn had a single dining room that could hold a limited number of guests, this was a fairly simple task. Today, however, providing food and drink is much more complicated.

A large hotel might well have a coffee shop, a gourmet restaurant, a poolside snack bar, room service, two banquet halls, and ten function rooms where food and beverages are served. It might also have a lounge, a nightclub, and a lobby bar. On a busy day (or night), it's quite likely that functions will be booked in many outlets at the same time. In addition, some outlets may have multiple events scheduled for a single day. As you can see, there is great diversity in the types of activities performed by a food and beverage department, requiring a significant variety of skills on the part of its workers.

FOOD AND BEVERAGE DEPARTMENT

Because of the diversity of services provided, the food and beverage department is typically split into subunits. The executive chef, a person of considerable importance and authority in any full-service hotel, runs the food production, or kitchen, department. A variety of culinary specialists who are responsible for different aspects of food preparation report to the executive chef.

The actual serving of food in a large hotel's restaurants is usually the responsibility of a separate department, headed by the assistant food and beverage director. The food service department is composed of the individual restaurant and outlet managers, maitre d's, waiters, waitresses, and bus help.

Because of their special duties and concerns, many large hotels have a separate subunit that is responsible only for room service. Because of the high value and profit margins associated with the sale of alcoholic beverages, some hotels have a separate department that assumes responsibility for all outlets where alcoholic beverages are sold. The person responsible for this department is the beverage manager. Most full-service hotels also do a considerable convention and catering business. The typical convention uses small function rooms for meetings and larger rooms for general sessions, trade shows, exhibits, and banquets. As a hotel or lodging business increases the use of its facilities for conventions and meetings, it may form a separate convention services department.

The convention services department and its personnel are introduced to the client, a meeting planner, or an association executive by the marketing and sales department. The convention services department then handles all of the client's meeting and catering requirements. Individually catered events include parties, wedding receptions, business meetings, and other functions held by groups. To provide for the unique needs of these types of customers, hotels often organize separate catering and convention departments. Depending on the size of the hotel, the job of cleaning the food and beverage outlets themselves as well as of washing pots and pans, dishes, glasses, and utensils is often delegated to a subunit known as the stewarding department.

It is only through continuous cooperation and coordination that a hotel's food service function can be carried out effectively. A guest who is dining in a hotel restaurant requires the joint efforts of the kitchen, food service, beverage, and stewarding departments. A convention banquet cannot be held without the efforts of the convention and catering department along with the food production, beverage, and stewarding departments. The sequence of events and cooperation required among the food and beverage staff is even more important than in the rooms department, thus increasing the importance of communication between managers and employees alike.

Another challenge faced by management is the diversity of the employees in the food and beverage department; the dishwasher in the stewarding department is at a dramatically different level than the sous chef in the kitchen. Coordination is not as important an issue in the marketing and sales department, which is generally much smaller than the food and beverage department. The primary responsibility of the sales managers who make up the marketing and sales department is sales, or the selling of the hotel facilities and services to individuals and groups. Sales managers sell rooms, food, and beverages to potential clients through advertising, attendance at association and conference meetings, and direct contacts.

The marketing and sales department is also removed from most of the day-to-day operational problems faced by other departments. The division of work among the sales managers is based on the type of customers a hotel is attempting to attract. Individual sales managers often specialize in corporate accounts, conventions, or tour and travel markets. Sales managers' accounts are sometimes subdivided along geographical lines into regional or national accounts. The sales staff of the largest full-service hotels usually does not exceed a dozen or so. These sales managers work more or less independently in their particular market segments.

The human resources department serves no customers, books no business, and prepares no meals, yet it plays a vital role in a hotel's efficient operation. The three functions of the human resources department are employee recruitment, benefits administration, and training. The director of human resources is also expected to be an expert on federal and state labor laws and to advise managers in other departments on these topics. The human resources department's major challenge is in its interactions with other hotel departments. Although the human resources department recruits, interviews, and screens prospective employees, the final hiring decision rests within the department in which the potential employee will be working. The same is true of promotion and disciplinary decisions; the human resources department's input is, in most cases, limited to advice and interpretation of legal questions.

The human resources department's effectiveness depends on its manager's ability to form effective working relationships with managers of other departments. In many hotels, the accounting department combines staff functions and line functions, or those functions directly responsible for servicing guests. The accounting department's traditional role is recording financial transactions, preparing and interpreting financial statements, and providing the managers of other departments with timely reports of operating results (line functions). Other responsibilities, carried out by the assistant controller for finance, include payroll preparation, accounts receivable, and accounts payable (staff functions). Another dimension of the accounting department's responsibilities deals with various aspects of hotel operations, cost accounting, and cost control throughout the hotel.

The two areas of central concern to the accounting department are rooms and food and beverage. The accounting department's front office cashier is responsible for tracking all charges to guest accounts. At the close of each business day, which varies by hotel but typically occurs at midnight or after the bulk of guests' transactions have been completed (i.e., check-in, restaurant charges, retail charges, etc.), the night auditor is responsible for reconciling all guest bills with the charges from the various hotel departments.

Although the front office cashier and the night auditor physically work at the front desk and, in the case of the cashier, have direct contact with guests, they are members of the accounting department and report to the assistant controller of operations.

The food and beverage department may be responsible for food preparation and service, but the accounting department is responsible for collecting revenues. The food and beverage controller and the food and beverage cashiers keep track of both the revenues and expenses of the food and beverage department. The food and beverage controller's job is to verify the accuracy and reasonableness of all food and beverage revenues. In addition to tracking and preparing daily reports on the costs of the food and beverages used in the hotel, in many cases the accounting department is also responsible for purchasing and storeroom operations.

Finally, the director of systems is responsible for designing the accounting and control systems used throughout the hotel. As you can see, the accounting department is anything but a passive staff unit contending with routine recordkeeping. The accounting department is also responsible for collecting and reporting most of a hotel's operational and financial statistics, which provide important data for decision making and budget preparation purposes.

The head of the accounting department may report not only to the hotel's general manager but also to the hotel chain's financial vice president or to the hotel's owner. The reason for this dual responsibility and reporting relationship is to afford the hotel corporation an independent verification of the financial and operating results of the hotel. In addition to being in charge of overseeing all of the departments that we have discussed, the hotel's general manager (GM) is responsible for defining and interpreting the policies established by top management.

The general manager serves as a liaison to the hotel's owner or corporate parent, sets (or communicates) the overall strategic course of the hotel, sets hotel-wide goals, coordinates activities between departments, and arbitrates interdepartmental disputes. It is common practice in a large, full-service hotel for a director of public relations to report directly to the GM. The GM also has corporate-level responsibilities, participates on civic boards and committees, and engages in industry-related activities such as serving on the local tourism commission or hotel-motel association.

In addition to possessing a high level of technical skill (i.e., a thorough understanding of each operating department in the hotel), the general manager must also be decisive, analytical, and skilled with both computers and people. He or she must be able to see the big picture and how all of the parts of the hotel fit into the overall organization. An executive may be promoted to relieve the general manager of some operational duties. This is often accomplished by elevating the duties and responsibilities of one particular department head without relieving that person of regular departmental duties. The title of this position is usually resident manager. It is quite common (and logical) for the general manager to select the manager of the rooms department to be resident manager. Responsibilities of the resident manager include serving as acting GM in the GM's absence, representing the GM on interdepartmental hotel committees, and taking responsibility for important special projects such as major hotel renovations, VIP guests, and operating reports that require in-depth analysis for the regional or corporate offices.

PATTERNS OF AUTHORITY

The delegation of authority creates a chain of command, the formal channel that defines the lines of authority from the top to the bottom of an organization. The chain of command consists of a series of relationships from the highest position in the organization to the lowest. The chain of command specifies a clear reporting relationship for each person in the organization and should be followed in both downward and upward communication. Following the chain of command enables each new employee, no matter what his or her position, to know exactly for whom and to whom he or she is responsible.

When designing an organizational structure, managers must consider the distribution of authority. Defined simply, authority is the organizationally sanctioned right to make a decision. Authority can be distributed throughout an organization or held in the hands of a few select employees. Decentralization is the process of distributing authority throughout an organization. In a decentralized organization, an organization member has the right to make a decision without obtaining approval from a higher-level manager. Centralization is the retention of decision-making authority by a high-level manager. Traditionally, hotel and lodging management has been very centralized, probably due to its roots in small, owner-operated lodging. In recent years, as the hotel and lodging industry has expanded, decentralization has become a more frequent style of operation.

Decentralization has several advantages. Managers are encouraged to develop decision-making skills, which help them advance in their careers. The autonomy afforded by this style of operation also increases job satisfaction and motivation. When employees are encouraged to perform well, the profitability of the organization increases. Many hotel and lodging organizations have begun to empower employees and supervisors to make decisions that typically have been made by managers. One example that we have already discussed is the use of the quality circle. For example, if a front desk agent determines that a guest's bill is incorrect, in a decentralized organization the agent has the power to make the correction immediately. If that same front desk agent determines that a guest's stay has been unsatisfactory, he or she has the power to reduce the guest's bill by an amount previously specified by management.

Additional challenges, control of the process, and quality assessment become part of everyone's job, and each employee is given the authority to take positive actions that will lead to high quality and improved performance.

Span of Control

Span of control refers to the number of people who report to one manager or supervisor. A wide span of control results in a flat organization— that is, a large number of employees reporting to one supervisor. A narrow span of control results in a tall organization, in which a small number of employees report to a supervisor, necessitating a larger number of supervisors. No formula exists for determining the ideal span of control. The following factors determine the most appropriate span of control: task similarity, training and professionalism, task certainty, frequency of interaction, task integration, and physical dispersion.

When a large number of employees perform similar tasks, the span of control can be increased. When the employees perform very different tasks, the supervisor must give each subordinate more individual attention in order to keep in touch with the different types of tasks; this requires a narrower span of control.

For example, the rooms department manager might easily manage the front desk agents and housekeepers until the brand standards for check-in or checkout of a guest increase in complexity and the standards for the various types of rooms and their cleaning procedure increase in detail. At this time, the rooms department manager's span of control must be narrowed. The better trained and more skilled a subordinate is, the less supervision is required. For example, a front desk agent might require a higher level of training and skill than a room service waiter. Thus, a front desk supervisor can supervise more employees (wider span of control) than the room service supervisor (narrower span of control).

Task certainty refers to the predictability of a task. Routine tasks allow management to devise standard procedures for subordinates to follow, minimizing questions about the job and widening the span of control. On the other hand, close supervision is called for when tasks are ambiguous and uncertainty is great. For example, the task of checking a guest in or out of the hotel can be documented and standard procedures can be created, so the front desk manager can have a relatively wide span of control over the front desk agents.

However, because of the diversity of customers the sales manager encounters, the tasks of a hotel sales manager are less certain. The director of sales is responsible for coaching the sales managers, observing sales calls, and ensuring deal closings; these tasks require a hands-on approach that limits the number of employees the director of sales can handle, narrowing the span of control.

If the supervisor-subordinate relationship requires frequent interaction, the span of control must be narrow. If interaction is infrequent, the span of control can be wide. For example, the hotel controller must review regularly the status of collections and payments with staff.

In contrast, the frequency of interaction between the chief engineer and his or her subordinates is directed by written work orders in most circumstances and thus requires less direct communication, enabling a wider span of control.

If the supervisor must integrate and coordinate the tasks of subordinates, the span of control narrows. For example, in the production of a meal for one table of four guests with different appetizers, salads, and entrées, the chef must have a narrow span of control to ensure that each component of the meal is assembled correctly and delivered to service personnel on a timely basis. The span of control of the executive housekeeper can be much wider because the procedure for cleaning and preparing each guest room is similar, if not exactly the same, for every room.

Physical dispersion refers to the distribution of employees within the lodging establishment. For example, if the executive housekeeper has guest room attendants on 20 floors in two buildings and the front desk manager has all front desk agents located in one place, the span of control would narrow for the executive housekeeper and widen for the front desk manager.

The ideal number of people that one person can supervise depends on a variety of factors. Consistent with trends in organizational structure such as teams, quality circles, and employee empowerment, many hotel and lodging organizations are widening their span of control. The objective behind these trends is to develop a flatter, more responsive organizational structure in which employees can make decisions without going through several levels of management.

Functional Organization Design

The most important strength of a functional organizational design is efficiency. The performance of common tasks allows for work specialization, which increases overall productivity. Workers develop specialized skills and knowledge more rapidly. Training is easier because of the similarity of tasks and the resulting opportunities for inexperienced workers to learn from experienced workers. This helps new employees quickly learn the kinds of behaviour that lead to success and promotion. Coordination of activities within functional departments is easier than in more broadly based organizations.

A functional organization fosters efficiency, teamwork, and coordination of activities within individual units. However, the functional organization's most important strength is also the source of its greatest shortcoming. The success of a hotel as a business is measured by its overall performance and not by the performance of any one department. A hotel with spotless guest rooms will not be successful if guests' front desk experiences are not up to par. Even if guests' dining experiences are superb, the hotel will fall flat on its face if its rooms are dismal. It is sometimes difficult for each department to fully appreciate its role in the overall success of the organization. It is vital that each department keep in mind the hotel-wide goals of customer service and profitability rather than focus narrowly on its own concerns. Some means must be found to coordinate the activities of functional departments and to set hotel-wide strategies and goals. A hotel's functional organization demands strong leadership.

New initiatives in hotels often require cooperation and coordination between functional departments. New ideas tend to be stillborn if department heads lack a hotel-wide perspective or have difficulty coordinating their activities. The tendency to concentrate on doing things right often overshadows the organization's ability to do the right thing.

The GM, as the chief executive of the hotel, emerges as the single person capable of providing the overall organizational direction, decision making, coordination, and arbitration needed to make a hotel's functional departments work together effectively. A hotel simply cannot run itself from the departmental level. Thus, the GM must be a strong leader to be effective.

Meetings and Commitees

An organizational chart is useful in identifying the formal reporting and authority relationships of a hotel or a lodging enterprise. However, it is not of much help in coordinating administrative units at the department and subdepartment level.

Consider this scenario. If the director of sales increases group bookings without consulting other hotel departments, a disaster is in the making. If the reservations department is not consulted, the sales department might guarantee more rooms to a group than are actually available at a price lower than the reservations department's quarterly goal. If the convention services manager is not consulted, necessary meeting rooms might not be available. If the food and beverage department is not consulted, the group might be sold a banquet that exceeds the hotel's capabilities. If the accounting department is not consulted, credit terms might be extended that violate the credit manager's policies. If the front office is not consulted, the group might experience lengthy delays at check-in (groups are usually preassigned rooms and keys).

The executive operating committee (EOC) of a hotel, made up of the general manager and senior executives from each department, is designed to increase the level of coordination between departments. There is no standard membership for this committee, but it usually comprises those executives who report directly to the general manager. The EOC is also responsible for a hotel's major budgetary units, such as the food and beverage and housekeeping units. EOC functions depend on how the hotel GM chooses to use the group, the GM's style, and the structure of other management meetings in the hotel.

Typically, the EOC meets weekly, focusing on matters ranging from day-today operational issues (daily function schedules and labor and food cost control) to comparing budgets with actual operating results. Many hotels increase communications through an elaborate structure of additional committees and meetings, including some or all of the following: operations, staff, sales forecast and marketing, departmental, sub departmental, credit, safety, energy conservation, and employee meetings.

The operations committee comprises the general manager, department heads, front office manager, manager on duty, and representatives from housekeeping, security, engineering, and food and beverage. This committee might meet four or five times per week for 15 to 20 minutes to review upcoming activities and assess the results of previous activities.

The staff committee might include the GM, department heads, and all sub department heads who report to the department heads. This committee, which might meet weekly for one or two hours, reviews the prior week's performance, the current week's activities, the next week's plans, and special projects. The staff committee also presents performance awards to employees.

The sales forecast and marketing committee might meet one to four times per month for several hours so the GM and department heads can review room demand for the coming 90 days and devise strategies to increase room nights (and thus bring in more revenue) and to increase average daily rates by up-selling potential guests to higher-rated rooms with perhaps more amenities or services.

The departmental committee consists of the department head and his or her sub department heads, managers, and supervisors. Meeting once or twice per month for an hour or so, the group reviews departmental issues. Similarly, sub department committees meet monthly for about an hour so the sub department head, managers, and supervisors can address issues unique to their sub department, such as the selection of a new type of floor cleaner by the housekeeping department or a more energy-efficient light bulb by the engineering department.

The credit committee includes the general manager, the controller, sales, the front office, reservations, catering, and the credit manager. Meeting monthly for an hour, the committee reviews those guests and clients of the hotel who were granted credit but have not settled their account. The safety committee typically comprises representatives from human resources, food and beverage, housekeeping, and engineering. Meeting monthly for an hour or so, the committee reviews safety programmes and safety records, addresses problems, and discusses the implementation of new safety regulations.

In some full-service hotels, an energy conservation committee includes the chief engineer, resident manager, food and beverage staff, human resource representatives, rooms staff, and housekeeping representatives. The committee typically meets monthly for an hour to discuss strategies and programmes for controlling energy costs. Most full-service hotels convene a monthly meeting or at least an annual meeting of all hotel management and employees to review performance and to distribute awards. This event ranges from an hour long meeting to a company-wide celebration lasting several hours.

THE FUTURE ORGANIZATION OF HOTELS

As new business practices are evolving as fast as our technologies, resistance to change has become a primary cause of business failure. The future success of a hotel will be driven in large part by the ability to foresee and capitalize on change. As we go through global transitions, the successful hotel will examine the key factors that will not only define success but also the ability to survive in coming years. These key organizational trends must be acknowledged by the successful hotel organization: visionary leadership, globalization, diversity, flexibility, flat structure, customer focus, zero defects, network orientation, and being in the information fast lane.

The organization must be able to respond to increasingly globalized sales, the movement to maintaining sales offices in many countries and hotel properties across the globe, and an increasingly globalized labor market. Intercontinental Hotels Group recently introduced a new organization structure to more efficiently use regional and global resources to drive higher levels of innovation, customer focus, and revenues.

Diversity means the organization must respond to a workforce that is heterogeneous sexually, racially, and chronologically; innovation and conflict/communication issues; and different styles of interaction, dress, presentation, and physical appearance. Flexibility in the modern hotel organization means assuring that systems, processes, and people can respond differently to different situations; fewer detailed rules and procedures; greater autonomy and encouragement of initiative; customizing employment relationships to include telecommuting and job-sharing; and lifetime employability rather than lifetime employment.

The trend toward flatness in hotel organizations means fewer levels of management, workers empowered to make decisions, and fewer differences in responsibility. The organization's employees need to believe in a sense of entrepreneurship that reacts proactively to market diversity. Traditional organizations that follow well-documented rules must give way to leaders who can balance a sense of discipline with one of flexibility.

If the customer is king or queen in the 21st century, hotel organizaions will be best served by focusing less on their hotel assets as measures of success and more on their customers. This involves a fundamental shift from viewing the real estate asset as the wealth creator to seeing the customer as the key to building shareholder wealth. A customer focus must reflect business decisions at all levels of developing and operating a hotel organization. Pursuing such a course will inevitably impact shareholder wealth.

The Japanese concept of zero defects in products and services can yield tremendous benefits for a hotel business organization. In practical terms, the hotel industry finds it extremely difficult to meet the standard of zero defects in service. Hotel services are based primarily on people, not on computers or other equipment. Twenty years ago, a business executive did not expect a consistent and predictable level of service wherever he or she traveled. Today that is the standard, not the exception, as is the expectation of sophisticated technology in hotel rooms to support business needs. With customer discrimination so acute, it is not surprising that brand loyalty is a diminishing commodity in the hotel industry.

Today's hotel organization must recognize the need for visionary leadership. The old command-and-control model of leadership is giving way to a focus on leadership in ideas, information, inspiration, vision, and teamwork. A failing hotel organization is overmanaged and underled. The networked hotel organization can facilitate direct communication across unit and property boundaries, ignoring the chain of command; cross-unit team structures; outsourcing and downsizing; strategic alliances with competitors and others; customization; and decentralization. Being in the information fast lane is critical. The traditional role of information technology as a back office support for accounting and bookkeeping has clearly moved to front and center stage. Information technology today influences all aspects of business from corporate strategies to organizational structure.

Technology was once viewed as a way to reduce costs by replacing people. That attitude has been firmly supplanted by the idea of seeking information technology support for the creative work all organizations must pursue. Information technology must enable organizations to react more speedily to market needs and, of course, produce the fulfillment of customer demands both quickly and accurately. To do this it must operate on a decentralized basis. Information technology delivers, but it has to deliver the right information to the right people at the right time.

The Hotel Staffing System

Staffing, which is one of a hotel's most important management functions, is an ongoing challenge because of the high rate of employee and manager turnover. Full-service hotels can experience annual turnover rates in excess of 100 percent in certain employee classifications. Some managers consider an annual employee turnover rate of 33 percent low. (In other words, in a single year, one-third of a hotel's employees must be replaced.) At this rate, the entire hotel must be completely restaffed every three years. The higher the turnover rate, the larger the number of employees who must be replaced. For example, if a hotel with 450 employees has a 75 percent annual turnover rate, it will be completely restaffed every 16 months.

In an attempt to reduce employee turnover, hotel and lodging businesses are giving increasing attention to job design, seeking to enhance those job characteristics that give the employee the greatest satisfaction and motivation. Good job design must take into account the needs of employees as well as the demands of the job. Well-thought-out job design begins when management conducts a job analysis—that is, a thorough evaluation of the specific tasks performed for a particular job and the time required to perform them. Job analysis is an ongoing process, as many jobs change with improvements in technology and pressure to improve product quality.

The job analysis is the basis for the job description and job specification. A job description includes the job title, pay, a brief statement of duties and procedures, working conditions, and hours. The job specification is an outline of the qualifications necessary for a particular job. In response to the limits of specialization, organizations can redesign jobs to improve coordination, productivity, and product quality while responding to an employee's needs for learning, challenge, variety, increased responsibility, and achievement. Such job redesign often involves job rotation, the systematic movement of employees from one job to another; job enlargement, an increase in the number of tasks an employee will do in the job; job enrichment, the attempt to give the employee more control over job-related activities; and flextime, a flexible work schedule that permits employee input in establishing work schedules. In team-driven job redesign, a concept similar to job rotation, employees can transfer back and forth among teams that provide different services or products.

Hotels recruit employees from a variety of sources. Newspapers and employee referrals are used to recruit nonskilled hourly employees. Supervisory and management employees generally are recruited through colleges and universities, promotions from within, professional associations, and management recruiters. Hotels that take more time in making their selections are more successful in retaining employees. Discussions of employee training and development often concentrate on training techniques without giving a full explanation of what a hotel is trying to accomplish. As training and development impart job skills and educate employees, supervisors, and managers, they also improve current and future employee performance, which affects the bottom line. Effective training includes problem solving, problem analysis, quality measurement and feedback, and team building.

Performance evaluation, also called performance appraisal, is the systematic review of the strengths and weaknesses of an employee's performance. The major difficulty in a performance appraisal is quantifying those strengths and weaknesses. The performance of some jobs is easy to quantify, while for others it is more difficult. An important part of the appraisal process is a well-established job description, so that the employee and the supervisor have similar expectations. Compensation includes the monetary and nonmonetary rewards that managers, supervisors, and employees receive for performing their jobs. In order to set compensation levels, the human resources department must periodically conduct job evaluations, which determine the value of the job to the hotel. Knowledge of the value of the job to the organization and of wage rates for each job classification allows the hotel to establish a fair compensation policy.

Career Paths And Opportunities

If you complete your course of study and graduate with a bachelor of science degree in hotel management, most likely you will enter the business at the managerial level. Along the way you will have learned that a successful manager provides clear direction, encourages open communication, coaches and supports people, provides objective recognition, establishes ongoing controls, follows up and gives subordinates feedback, selects the right people to staff the organization, understands the financial implications of decisions, encourages innovation and new ideas, gives subordinates clear-cut decisions when needed, and consistently demonstrates a high level of integrity.

There are three levels of management careers in the hotel or lodging business: first-line, middle, and top. First-line refers to those who have day-to-day contact with the guests and clients of a lodging business.

The first-line manager oversees the work of the supervisors and line employees. In a hotel or lodging business, first-line positions may include assistant manager of housekeeping, assistant front office manager, and assistant restaurant manager. First-line managers are responsible for a hotel's basic work, such as checking guests in and out, making up the guests' rooms, and preparing and serving the meals. First-line managers are in daily or near-daily contact with line employees. Middle management of most hotel or lodging businesses includes the department manager, general manager, and any position between those levels.

Depending on the size of the hotel, the regional manager (who supervises the general managers of the hotels in his or her region) can also fall into this category. Unlike first-line managers, those in middle management plan, organize, lead, and control other managers' activities and are responsible for the performance of their departments. Top management comprises a small group of managers such as the chief executive officer, president, or vice president. Top management is responsible for the performance of the entire hotel business as well as for supervision of the middle managers. The top manager is accountable to the owners of the financial resources used by the organization, such as the stockholders or executive board.

As you have already seen, there are numerous attractive careers in the hotel and lodging business.

The following is one of the many paths your career might follow:

1. Assistant manager of the reservations department
2. Reservations department manager
3. Rooms department manager
4. Resident manager

5. General manager
6. Regional manager

In a full-service hotel or lodging business, the movement from entry-level position to general manager might encompass 15 years. Career advancement in a limited-service hotel or lodging business can occur more rapidly. A career in a limited-service hotel or lodging establishment might commence at the assistant general manager level, with movement to general manager within three years and to district or regional manager within five to eight years. This accelerated pace is due in large part to the more restricted range of services the manager must master before advancing.

The four basic components of organizational structure include job specialization, departmentalization, patterns of authority, and span of control. Job specialization includes increased worker productivity and efficiency, but it increases the need for managerial control and coordination. Work teams can be used to alleviate the routine caused by job specialization. A similar concept, the quality circle, can also enhance employee productivity.

The departments of a full-service hotel and lodging establishment include rooms, food and beverage, marketing and sales, human resources, and accounting. These departments report directly to the general manager or to a resident manager who is responsible to the general manager. In smaller hotel or lodging businesses, the audit, front desk, housekeeping, maintenance, and sales departments all might report directly to the general manager.

While patterns of authority remain centralized in many hotel or lodging businesses, increasingly employees have become empowered to make decisions that typically have been made by managers. Decentralization is the distribution of authority throughout an organization. Centralization is the retention of decision-making authority by a high-level manager. Span of control refers to the number of people who report to one manager or supervisor. In a narrow span of control, fewer subordinates report to each supervisor, resulting in a tall organization. In a wide span of control, a larger number of subordinates report to each supervisor, resulting in a flat organization.

The level of coordination and communication between departments can be increased by the activities of committees. The executive operating committee includes the general manager and designated department heads. Other committees include operations, staff, sales forecasting and marketing, departmental, subdepartmental, credit, safety, and energy conservation. Larger organizations conduct an annual meeting for all employees of the organization, to discuss company performance and to distribute awards.

Staffing is an ongoing challenge in the hotel and lodging industry because of the high percentage of employee turnover. Successful staffing depends on providing adequate job descriptions, including job specifications, as well as realizing that job descriptions must be flexible. In some cases, it becomes necessary to redesign jobs; this can involve job rotation, job enlargement, job enrichment, and flextime. Employees must be properly trained; effective training includes problem solving, problem analysis, quality measurement, feedback, and team building. Successful managers enjoy certain common characteristics including providing clear direction, feedback, and recognition; encouraging open communication and innovation; and establishing ongoing controls. The management of a hotel or a lodging business falls into one of three categories: first-line, middle, or top.

Chapter 6

Human Resource Management in Tourism

Most of the tourism activity also involves economic costs, including the direct costs incurred by tourism businesses, government costs for infrastructure to better serve tourists, as well as congestion and related costs borne by individuals in the community. Community decisions over tourism often involve debates between industry proponents touting tourism's economic impacts (benefits) and detractors emphasizing tourism's costs.

Sound decisions rest on a balanced and objective assessment of both benefits and costs and an understanding of who benefits from tourism and who pays for it. Businesses and public organizations are increasingly interested in the economic impacts of tourism at national, state, and local levels. One regularly hears claims that tourism supports X jobs in an area or that a festival or special event generated Y million dollars in sales or income in a community. "Multiplier effects" are often cited to capture secondary effects of tourism spending and show the wide range of sectors in a community that may benefit from tourism. Tourism's economic benefits are touted by the industry for a variety of reasons. Claims of tourism's economic significance give the industry greater respect among the business community, public officials, and the public in general. This often translates into decisions or public policies that are favourable to tourism.

Community support is important for tourism, as it is an activity that affects the entire community. Tourism businesses depend extensively on each other as well as on other businesses, government and residents of the local community. Economic benefits and costs of tourism reach virtually everyone in the region in one way or another. Economic impact analyses provide tangible estimates of these economic interdependencies and a better understanding of the role and importance of tourism in a region's economy.

Tourism's economic impacts are therefore an important consideration in state, regional and community planning and economic development. Economic impacts are also important factors in marketing and management decisions. Communities therefore need to understand the relative importance of tourism to their region, including tourism's contribution to economic activity in the area.

A variety of methods, ranging from pure guesswork to complex mathematical models, are used to estimate tourism's economic impacts. Studies vary extensively in quality and accuracy, as well as which aspects of tourism are included. Technical reports often are filled with economic terms and methods that non-economists do not understand. On the other hand, media coverage of these studies tend to oversimplify and frequently misinterpret the results, leaving decision makers and the general public with a sometimes distorted and incomplete understanding of tourism's economic effects.

How can the average person understand these studies sufficiently to separate good studies from bad ones and make informed choices? The purpose of this bulletin is to present a systematic introduction to economic impact concepts and methods. The presentation is written for tourism industry analysts and public officials, who would like to better understand, evaluate, or possibly conduct an economic impact assessment. The bulletin is organized around ten basic questions that either are asked or should be asked about the economic impacts of tourism.

ECONOMIC IMPACT ANALYSIS

A variety of economic analyses are carried out to support tourism decisions. As these different kinds of economic analysis are frequently confused, let's begin by positioning economic impact studies within the broader set of economic problems and techniques relevant to tourism. These same techniques may be applied to any policy or action, but we will define them here in the context of tourism. Each type of analysis is identified by the basic question(s) it answers and the types of methods and models that are appropriate. Benefit cost analysis and economic impact analysis are frequently confused as both discuss economic "benefits".

There are two clear distinctions between the two techniques. B/C analysis addresses the benefits from economic efficiency while economic impact analysis focuses on the regional distribution of economic activity. The income received from tourism by a destination region is largely off-set by corresponding losses in the origin regions, yielding only modest contributions to net social welfare and efficiency. B/C analysis includes market and non-market values (consumer surplus), while economic impact analysis is restricted to actual flows of money from market transactions.

While each type of economic analysis is somewhat distinct, a given problem often calls for several different kinds of economic analysis. An economic impact study will frequently involve a demand analysis to project levels of tourism activity. In other cases demand is treated as exogenous and the analysis simply estimates impacts if a given number of visitors are attracted to the area. A comprehensive impact assessment will also examine fiscal impacts, as well as social and environmental impacts. Be aware that an economic impact analysis, by itself, provides a rather narrow and often one-sided perspective on the impacts of tourism.

Studies of the economic impacts of tourism tend to emphasize the positive benefits of tourism. On the other hand environmental, social, cultural and fiscal impact studies tend to focus more on negative impacts of tourism. This is in spite of the fact that there are negative economic impacts of tourism (e.g., seasonality and lower wage jobs) and in many cases positive environmental and social impacts (e.g., protection of natural & cultural resources in the area and education of both tourists and local residents). An economic impact assessment (EIA) traces changes in economic activity resulting from some action.

An EIA will identify which economic sectors benefit from tourism and estimate resulting changes in income and employment in the region. Economic impact assessment procedures do not assess economic efficiency and also do not generally produce estimates of the fiscal costs of an action. For many problems economic impact analysis will be part of a broader analysis. Environmental, social, and fiscal impacts are often equally important concerns in a balanced assessment of impacts.

An economic impact analysis will assess the contribution of tourism activity to a region's economy. The basic questions an economic impact study usually addresses are:

- How many jobs in the area does tourism support?
- How much tax revenue is generated from tourism?
- How much do tourists spend in the area?
- What portion of sales by local businesses is due to tourism?
- How much income does tourism generate for households and businesses in the area?

An economic impact analysis also reveals the interrelationships among economic sectors and provides estimates of the changes that take place in an economy due to some existing or proposed action. The most common applications of economic impact analysis to tourism are:

1. To evaluate the economic impacts of changes in the supply of recreation and tourism opportunities. Supply changes may involve a change in quantity,

such as the opening of new facilities, closing of existing ones, or expansions and contraction in capacity. Supply changes may also involve changes in quality, including changes in (a) the quality of the environment, (b) the local infrastructure and public services to support tourism, or (c) the nature of the tourism products and services that are provided in an area.

2. To evaluate the economic impacts of changes in tourism demand. Population changes, changes in the competitive position of the region, marketing activity or changing consumer tastes and preferences can alter levels of tourism activity, spending, and associated economic activity. An economic impact study can estimate the magnitude and nature of these impacts.
3. To evaluate the effects of policies and actions which affect tourism activity either directly or indirectly. Tourism depends on many factors at both origins and destinations that are frequently outside the direct control of the tourism industry itself. Economic impact studies provide information to help decision makers better understand the consequences of various actions on the tourism industry as well as on other sectors of the economy. For example, increased air pollution standards have been opposed in some regions due to the predicted economic consequences of the closing of plants that cannot meet the new standards. Tourism interests counter these arguments with estimates of the potential gains in income and jobs in tourism industries that depend on good air quality and visibility.
4. To understand the economic structure and interdependencies of different sectors of the economy. Economic studies help us better understand the size and structure of the tourism industry in a given region and its linkages to other sectors of the economy. Such understandings are helpful in

identifying potential partners for the tourism industry as well as in targeting industries as part of regional economic development strategies. Issues such as economic growth, stability, and seasonality may be addressed as part of these studies.

5. To argue for favourable treatment in allocation of resources or local tax, zoning or other policy decisions. By showing that tourism has significant economic impacts, tourism interests can often convince decision-makers to allocate more resources for tourism or to establish policies that encourage tourism. Tax abatements and other incentives frequently given to manufacturing firms have also been granted to hotels, marinas and other tourism businesses based on demonstrated economic impacts in the local area.
6. To compare the economic impacts of alternative resource allocation, policy, management or development proposals. Economic impact analyses are commonly used to assess the relative merits of distinct alternatives. The economic contribution of expanded tourism offerings may be compared for example with alternatives such as resource extraction activities (mining, timber harvesting) or manufacturing. Impacts of alternative tourism development proposals may also be evaluated, e.g., tourism strategies that emphasize outdoor recreation, camping development, a convention facility, or a factory outlet mall.

Tourism has a variety of economic impacts. Tourists contribute to sales, profits, jobs, tax revenues, and income in an area. The most direct effects occur within the primary tourism sectors —lodging, restaurants, transportation, amusements, and retail trade. Through secondary effects, tourism affects most sectors of the economy. An economic impact analysis of tourism activity normally focuses on changes in sales, income, and employment in a region resulting from tourism activity.

A simple tourism impact scenario illustrates. Let's say a region attracts an additional 100 tourists, each spending $100 per day. That's $10,000 in new spending per day in the area. If sustained over a 100 day season, the region would accumulate a million dollars in new sales. The million dollars in spending would be distributed to lodging, restaurant, amusement and retail trade sectors in proportion to how the visitor spends the $100. Perhaps 30% of the million dollars would leak out of the region immediately to cover the costs of goods purchased by tourists that are not made in the local area (only the retail margins for such items should normally be included as direct sales effects). The remaining $700,000 in direct sales might yield $350,000 in income within tourism industries and support 20 direct tourism jobs. Tourism industries are labor and income intensive, translating a high proportion of sales into income and corresponding jobs.

The tourism industry, in turn, buys goods and services from other businesses in the area, and pays out most of the $350,000 in income as wages and salaries to its employees. This creates secondary economic effects in the region. The study might use a sales multiplier of 2.0 to indicate that each dollar of direct sales generates another dollar in secondary sales in this region. Through multiplier effects, the $700,000 in direct sales produces $1.4 million in total sales. These secondary sales create additional income and employment, resulting in a total impact on the region of $1.4 million in sales, $650,000 in income and 35 jobs.

While hypothetical, the numbers used here are fairly typical of what one might find in a tourism economic impact study. A more complete study might identify which sectors receive the direct and secondary effects and possibly identify differences in spending and impacts of distinct subgroups of tourists (market segments). One can also estimate the tax effects of this spending by applying local tax rates to the appropriate changes in sales or income. Instead of focusing on visitor spending, one could also estimate impacts of construction or government activity associated with tourism.

There are several other categories of economic impacts that are not typically covered in economic impact assessments, at least not directly. For example:

Changes in prices — tourism can sometimes inflate the cost of housing and retail prices in the area, frequently on a seasonal basis.

Changes in the quality and quantity of goods and services — tourism may lead to a wider array of goods and services available in an area (of either higher or lower quality than without tourism).

Changes in property and other taxes — taxes to cover the cost of local services may be higher or lower in the presence of tourism activity. In some cases, taxes collected directly or indirectly from tourists may yield reduced local taxes for schools, roads, etc. In other cases, locals may be taxed more heavily to cover the added infrastructure and service costs. The impacts of tourism on local government costs and revenues are addressed more fully in a fiscal impact analysis.

Economic dimensions of "social" and "environmental" impacts — There are also economic consequences of most social and environmental impacts that are not usually addressed in an economic impact analysis. These can be positive or negative. For example, traffic congestion will increase costs of moving around for both households and businesses. Improved amenities that attract tourists may also encourage retirees or other kinds of businesses to locate in the area.

Induced Effects

A standard economic impact analysis traces flows of money from tourism spending, first to businesses and government agencies where tourists spend their money and then to:

Other businesses — supplying goods and services to tourist businesses,

Households — earning income by working in tourism or supporting industries, and

Government — through various taxes and charges on tourists, businesses and households

Formally, regional economists distinguish direct, indirect, and induced economic effects. Indirect and induced effects are sometimes collectively called secondary effects. The total economic impact of tourism is the sum of direct, indirect, and induced effects within a region. Any of these impacts may be measured as gross output or sales, income, employment, or value added. Direct effects are production changes associated with the immediate effects of changes in tourism expenditures.

For example, an increase in the number of tourists staying overnight in hotels would directly yield increased sales in the hotel sector. The additional hotel sales and associated changes in hotel payments for wages and salaries, taxes, and supplies and services are direct effects of the tourist spending.

Indirect effects are the production changes resulting from various rounds of re-spending of the hotel industry's receipts in other backward-linked industries (i.e., industries supplying products and services to hotels). Changes in sales, jobs, and income in the linen supply industry, for example, represent indirect effects of changes in hotel sales. Businesses supplying products and services to the linen supply industry represent another round of indirect effects, eventually linking hotels to varying degrees to many other economic sectors in the region. Induced effects are the changes in economic activity resulting from household spending of income earned directly or indirectly as a result of tourism spending. For example, hotel and linen supply employees supported directly or indirectly by tourism, spend their income in the local region for housing, food, transportation, and the usual array of household product and service needs. The sales, income, and jobs that result from household spending of added wage, salary, or proprietor's income are induced effects.

By means of indirect and induced effects, changes in tourist spending can impact virtually every sector of the economy in one way or another. The magnitude of secondary effects depends on the propensity of businesses and households in the region to purchase goods and services from local suppliers. Induced effects are particularly noticed when a large employer in a region closes a plant. Not only are supporting industries (indirect effects) hurt, but the entire local economy suffers due to the reduction in household income within the region. Retail stores close and leakages of money from the region increase as consumers go outside the region for more and more goods and services.

Similar effects in the opposite direction are observed when there is a significant increase in jobs and household income. Final demand is the term used by economists for sales to the final consumers of goods and services. In almost all cases, the final consumers of tourism goods and services are households. Government spending is also considered as final demand. The same methods for estimating impacts of visitor spending can be applied to estimate the economic impacts of government spending, for example, to operate and maintain a park or visitor center.

Regional Models

An input-output model (I-O model) is a mathematical model that describes the flows of money between sectors within a region's economy. Flows are predicted by knowing what each industry must buy from every other industry to produce a dollar's worth of output. Using each industry's production function, I-O models also determine the proportions of sales that go to wage and salary income, proprietor's income, and taxes. Multipliers can be estimated from input-output models based on the estimated re-circulation of spending within the region. Exports and imports are determined based upon estimates of the propensity of households and firms within the region to purchase goods and services from local sources (often called RPC's or regional purchase coefficients). The more a region is self-sufficient and purchases goods and services from within the region, the higher the multipliers for the region.

Input-output models make a number of assumptions. The basic ones are that:

- All firms in a given industry employ the same production technology (usually assumed to be the national average for that industry), and produce identical products.
- There are no economies or diseconomies of scale in production or factor substitution. I-O models are essentially linear — double the level of tourism activity/production and you double all of the inputs, the number of jobs, etc.
- The model doesn't explicitly keep track of time, but analysts generally report the impact estimates as if they represent activity within a single year.
- One must assume that the various model parameters are accurate and represent the current year.

I-O models are firmly grounded in the national system of accounts, which relies on a standard industrial classification system (SIC codes) and various federal government economic censuses, in which individual firms report sales, wage and salary payments and employment. I-O models will generally be at least a few years out-of-date, although this isn't usually a major problem unless the region's economy has changed significantly. An I-O model represents the region's economy at a particular point in time. Tourist spending estimates are generally price adjusted to the year of the model.

Multiplier computations for induced effects generally assume that jobs created by additional spending are new jobs, involving new households in the area. Induced effects are computed assuming linear changes in household spending with changes in income. Estimates of induced effects may be inflated due to the violation of these assumptions. Induced effects tend to account for the vast majority of the secondary effects of tourism, and therefore should be used with caution.

Multipliers Effects of Tourism

Multipliers capture the secondary economic effects (indirect and induced) of tourism activity. Multipliers have been frequently misused and misinterpreted in tourism studies (Archer 1984) and are a considerable source of confusion among non-economists. Multipliers represent the economic interdependencies between sectors within a particular region's economy. They vary considerably from region to region and sector to sector. There are many different kinds of multipliers reflecting which secondary effects are included and which measure of economic activity is used (sales, income, or employment).

For example,

- The Type I sales multiplier = direct sales + indirect sales direct sales.
- The Type II or III sales multiplier[1] = direct sales + indirect sales + induced sales direct sales.

Multiplying a Type I sales multiplier times the direct sales gives direct plus indirect sales. Multiplying a Type II or III sales multiplier times the direct sales gives total sales impacts including direct, indirect and induced effects. The multipliers defined above are called ratio type multipliers as they measure the ratio of a total impact measure to the corresponding direct impact. Comparable income and employment ratio type multipliers may be defined by replacing sales with measures of income or employment in the above equations. Ratio multipliers should be used with caution.

A common error is to multiply a sales multiplier times tourist spending to get total sales effects. This will generate an inflated estimate of tourism impacts. The problem is that tourism spending or sales is not exactly the same as the "direct effects", appearing in the multiplier formula. Tourist purchases of goods (vs. services) are the primary source of the problem. To properly apply tourist purchases of goods to an input-output model (or corresponding multipliers), various margins (retail, wholesale and transportation) must be deducted from the "purchaser price" of the good to separate out the "producer price".

In an I-O model, retail margins accrue to the retail trade sector, wholesale margins to wholesale trade, transportation margins to transportation sectors (trucking, rail, air etc.) and the producer prices of goods are assigned to the sector that produces the good. In most cases the factory that produces the good bought by a tourist lies outside of the local region, creating an immediate "leakage" in the first round of spending and therefore no local impact from production of the good. Before applying a multiplier to tourist spending, one must first deduct the producer prices of all imported goods that tourists buy (i.e. only include the local retail margins and possibly wholesale and transportation margins if these firms lie within the region).

Generally, only 60 to 70% of tourist spending appears as final demand in a local region. While all tourist purchases of services will accrue to the local region as final demand, only the margins on goods purchased at retail stores should be counted as local final demand. The ratio of local final demand to tourist spending is called the capture rate.

Capture rate = local final demand / tourism spending in local area. Capture rates, like multipliers, will vary with the size and nature of the region as well as the kind of tourist spending included. One must therefore be cautious in taking a multiplier or capture rate cited in one study and using it in another.

Another way of calculating a multiplier (generally the preferred approach among economists) is as a ratio of income or employment to sales. This kind of multiplier is sometimes called a Keynesian multiplier or response coefficient.

- Type III Income multiplier = Total direct, indirect, and induced income direct sales
- Type III Employment multiplier = Total direct, indirect, and induced employment direct sales

This income (employment) multiplier produces total income (employment) impacts when multiplied by the direct sales. One must still be careful in distinguishing between tourism spending/sales and direct sales effects. Some studies may embed the capture rate in the multiplier, expressing the ratio in terms of tourism spending rather than direct sales.

The economic impacts of tourism are typically estimated by some variation of the following simple formula:

*Economic Impact of Tourism = Number of Tourists * Average Spending per Visitor * Multiplier*

The formula suggests three distinct steps and corresponding measurements or models:

1. Estimate the change in the number and types of tourists to the region due to the proposed policy or action. Estimates or projections of tourist activity generally come from a demand model or some system for measuring levels of tourism activity in an area. Economic impact estimates will rest heavily on good estimates of the numbers and types of visitors. These must come from carefully designed measurements of tourist activity, a good demand model, or good judgement. This step is usually the weakest link in most tourism impact studies, as few regions have accurate counts of tourists, let alone good models for predicting changes in tourism activity or separating local visitors from visitors from outside the region.
2. Estimate average levels of spending (often within specific market segments) of tourists in the local area. Spending averages come from sample surveys or are sometimes borrowed or adapted from other studies. Spending estimates must be based on a representative sample of the population of tourists taking into account variations across seasons, types of tourists, and locations within the study area. As spending can vary widely across different kinds of tourists, we

recommend estimating average spending for a set of key tourist segments based on samples of at least 50-100 visitors within each tourism segment.

Segments should be defined to capture differences in spending between local residents vs. tourists, day users vs. overnight visitors, type of accommodation (motel, campground, seasonal home, with friends and relatives), and type of transportation (car, RV, air, rail, etc.). In broadly based tourism impact studies, it is useful to identify unique spending patterns of important activity segments such as downhill skiers, boaters, and convention & business travelers. Multiplying the number of tourists by the average spending per visitor (be careful the units are consistent) gives an estimate of total tourist spending in the area. Estimates of tourist spending will generally be more accurate if distinct spending profiles and use estimates are made for key tourism segments. The use and spending estimates are the two most important parts of an economic impact assessment. When combined, they capture the amount of money brought into the region by tourists. Multipliers are needed only if one is interested in the secondary effects of tourism spending.

3. Apply the change in spending to a regional economic model or set of multipliers to determine secondary effects.

   Secondary effects of tourism are estimated using multipliers or a model of the region's economy. Multipliers generally come from an economic base or input-output model of the region's economy. In many cases multipliers are borrowed (often improperly) or adjusted from published multipliers or other studies. One should not take a multiplier estimated for one region and apply it in a region with a quite different economic structure. Generally, multipliers are higher for larger regions with more diversified economies and lower for smaller regions with more limited economic development. A common error is to apply a statewide multiplier (since these are more widely published) to a local region. This will yield inflated estimates of local multiplier effects.

Multipliers can also be used to convert estimates of spending or sales to income and employment. Simple ratios can be used to capture how much income or jobs are generated per dollar of sales. These ratios will vary from region to region and across individual economic sectors due to the relative importance of labour inputs in each industry and different wage and salary rates in different regions of the country. Be aware that job estimates are generally not full time equivalents, making them difficult to compare across industries with different proportions of seasonal and part time jobs. Income or value added are generally the preferred measures of the contribution of tourism to a region's economy.

The Typical Approaches for an Economic Assessment

At the simple, "quick and dirty" end of the spectrum are highly aggregate approaches that rely mostly on judgement to determine tourism activity, spending and multipliers. Such estimates can be completed in a couple hours at little cost and rest largely on the expertise and judgement of the analyst. At the other extreme are studies that gather primary data from visitor spending studies and apply the spending estimates to formal regional economic models for the area in question. In between are a wide range of options that employ varying degrees of judgement, secondary data, primary data, and formal models.

Different levels of detail and corresponding expense (time and money) and accuracy are possible for each of the three steps — estimating tourist volume, spending, and multiplier effects. Four typical approaches illustrate the levels of detail that are possible and the associated methods to sales estimates.

With sound judgement in choosing the parameters, the MGM model can yield reasonable ballpark estimates of economic impacts at minimal cost. This approach, however, provides little detail on spending categories or which sectors of the economy benefit from either direct or secondary effects. The aggregate nature of the approach also makes it difficult to adjust recommended spending rates or multipliers to different applications.

The Bureau of Economic Analysis's (BEA) RIMS II user handbook illustrates how to apply published multipliers to estimate economic impacts. This approach starts with visitor spending (from survey or secondary sources) divided into a number of spending categories and makes use of sector specific multipliers to estimate the direct and total sales, income and employment effects. Multipliers from the BEA's RIMS II models are used to estimate secondary effects. Multipliers are reported for 39 sectors for each state in the second edition of their report (USDC 1992). This method uses margins to properly account for retail purchases of goods and makes use of disaggregate sector-specific multipliers for each state. Multipliers for sub-state regions are not as readily available, but can be acquired from BEA or other sources. Secondary effects cannot be disaggregated to individual sectors using the BEA approach.

The MI-REC/IMPLAN System: Stynes and Propst have developed a fairly complete micro-computer-based system for estimating economic impacts of recreation and tourism. The system combines spreadsheets for estimating spending with the IMPLAN input-output modeling system. IMPLAN uses county level data to estimate 528 sector input-output models for regions down to account level. IMPLAN generates a complete set of economic accounts for the region including multipliers and trade flows. MI-REC spreadsheets estimate visitor spending within up to 33categories based on the number and types of visitors attracted to an area. Spending is then bridged to the IMPLAN model sectors to estimate direct, indirect and induced effects in terms of sales, income and employment. Users may estimate spending via visitor surveys or use the MI-REC database of spending profiles, compiled from previous studies. The system also includes price indices to easily update spending data to a current year.

Two other systems for estimating economic impacts of tourism should be noted. The TEIM or Travel Economic Impact Model developed by the U.S. Travel Data Center (USTDC, 1997) has been widely used to estimate tourism and travel impacts at state and national levels. A more recent development is the satellite accounting approach developed by the World Travel and Tourism Council (WTTC 1996). Both of these systems are primarily designed for estimating the overall economic significance of tourism at national or state levels. They are not readily applied to estimate the impacts of particular policies and actions at the local level.

The TEIM relies on national travel surveys to estimate trip volume and spending on a state-by-state basis. Local estimates of impacts are obtained using simple allocation formulas to distribute statewide impacts to counties and cities within the state. These local estimates do not account very well for the distinct types of tourism activity or spending patterns in different sub-regions of a state. The WTTC effort also focuses on national and statewide accounting of tourism's economic significance. Their satellite tourism account identifies the contribution of travel and tourism to gross national product (GNP) or gross state product (GSP).

Using the standard national system of accounts, they identify the portion of sales, taxes and investment attributable directly to travel and tourism. The WTTC system does not use multipliers or attempt to estimate secondary effects. It does, however, capture a great deal of travel-related economic activity, not covered by visitor trip spending, such as durable goods purchases (boats and RV's), construction and investment in tourism, and government expenditures.

An economic impact study involves four basic:

1. Define the problem
2. Estimate the change in final demand (tourism spending).

3. Estimate the regional economic effects of this change
4. Interpret, apply, and communicate the results

The most important part of any study is the first step — clarifying the nature of the problem being addressed and intended uses of the results. Before launching an economic impact study, be sure this is the kind of study that is needed rather than one or more of the other kinds of economic analyses.

Stynes and Propst (1996) identify seven factors that should be specified as part of defining a problem for an economic impact assessment:

1. Define the action to be evaluated. Begin by clarifying the action or actions involved in the problem. Actions may include construction, government investment, changes in marketing, management, or policies, or changes in the quality or quantity of tourist facilities. If evaluating impacts of existing tourism activity, be sure to define what is to be included as "tourism".
2. Identify the change in the amount and kinds of recreation/tourism activity resulting from the action. The action must be defined precisely enough in step one to be able to estimate the changes in the number and types of visitors to the area and/or their spending patterns. As a general rule, the analysis should be with vs. without the action rather than simply before vs. after. Thus, if tourism has been growing by 5% per year and a new promotional programme increases this to 10% this year, only half of the 10% growth can likely be attributed to the promotional programme. Identifying the net changes in activity that are attributable to an action can be a complex and difficult task.

   Assessments of economic impact, however, rest firmly on such estimates, so attention to these details is very important. In situations of some uncertainty, we recommend evaluating impacts using a range of estimates in order to establish rough confidence intervals around your estimates. Evaluating a range of alternatives also helps to evaluate the sensitivity of the results to your initial estimates of changes in activity levels.

3. Identify the kinds of spending to be included. Tourism may impact the local economy through visitor trip spending, durable goods purchases, government spending, or investment and construction. Which to include in a given analysis depends on how the problem is defined, and again, on attributing given spending changes to the proposed action.
4. Identify the study region. Perhaps the most important, yet often neglected part of a recreation and tourism impact assessment is the definition of a study region. The region defines the area for which impacts are desired, as well as the portions of visitor spending that are relevant. An impact assessment evaluates the impacts on households, businesses, and organizations within the given region. Spending that visitors make outside of a study region either at home or en route are not included in assessing impacts of spending on the designated region. For an economic impact analysis, the study region should be large enough to constitute a viable economic region. Since little economic data exists below the county level, the county is generally the smallest region one should consider for a tourism impact assessment.
5. Identify key economic sectors and desired sectoral detail. The proposed action and anticipated uses/users of the results should suggest the key sectors that will be impacted. Recreation and tourism activity typically impact the lodging, restaurant, amusements, retail, transportation and government sectors most directly. In the problem definition stage consideration of impacted sectors helps to identify relevant

categories of spending. The desired sectoral detail plays an important role in structuring the presentation of results. In some cases only an aggregate measure of impacts may be desired. In other cases, clients may be interested in which particular sectors are most heavily affected and will want estimates of sales and jobs broken down by sector. If formal input-output models are used, impacts may be estimated in considerable sectoral detail. This is not possible if an aggregate spending estimate or multiplier is used.

6. Identify the most important measures of economic activity. Tourism impacts may be reported in terms of visitor spending, business receipts/sales/ production, wage and salary income, proprietors income and profits, value added, and employment. The direct effects are the most important and are captured well by estimates of visitor spending. Simple ratios can be used to convert direct spending or sales to the associated income and jobs. Input-output models and multipliers are needed only if one is interested in secondary effects.
7. Identify the tolerable levels of error in the results. Although confidence intervals and estimates of error are rare in economic impact studies, this doesn't mean they are not important. You should have at least a ballpark idea of how much error you can tolerate in the analysis, as this will dictate how much effort and expense you must put into it. The more accuracy you demand, the greater the requirements to gather up-to-date local data on visitation, spending and economic activity. These data allow you to fine tune the spending estimates and input-output models or multipliers. Such fine tuning will require time, knowledge, and money that must be weighed against the benefits of the improved estimates. Estimates of impacts are based on three components: visits, spending, and multipliers. You should try to balance the errors across these components.

9. What are some questions to ask when evaluating or interpreting a tourism economic impact study?

Evaluating, interpreting and applying an economic impact study requires a clear understanding of the findings and at least some knowledge of the underlying concepts and methods. Judging the accuracy or quality of a study can be based on the reputation of the author or the quality of presentation, although a careful evaluation of the methods that were used is the best approach. Here's some questions to ask when reading or evaluating a tourism economic impact study.

Impact of what? The report should identify the action being evaluated. An economic impact assessment is most useful when evaluating the effects of a particular action or policy. If so, the action and assumptions about alternatives should be spelled out in presenting a with vs. without scenario. If the study reports impacts of existing tourism activity, identify how tourism is defined (if at all). What kinds of tourism activity and spending are included? Which trip expenses are included? Does the study include all visitor spending or only spending of tourists who live outside the local region? Does the study address impacts of visitor trip spending, durable goods purchases, operational expenses of a programme, or construction and investment?

On what region? The study region should be defined (preferably with a map). It should be viable both economically and as a distinct tourism destination area. Spending that is included should be restricted to spending in this region and multipliers should represent the given region of interest. A short profile of tourism & economic activity in the region provides useful background for an economic impact study.

Sources and quality of the data: The report should identify the sources of the data for estimating visits, spending, and regional economic multipliers/models. The methods that were used to estimate impacts should be clear. Judgements of the quality of the estimates must be based largely on an understanding of the data and methods that were used. A more disaggregate analysis reporting spending within at least six categories, visitors for two or more distinct segments, and multipliers and results broken down by sector will generally be more accurate and meaningful than a study that only uses aggregate data. Disaggregation is particularly helpful when adjusting secondary data taken from government reports or other studies to a new situation. The fundamental question is whether the visit estimates, spending profiles and multipliers adequately represent the intended population and study area.

Quality of methods: There are a number of issues to watch for in evaluating methods.

Visits: Has the study clearly defined which visits/visitors will be affected by the proposed action, separated local visitors from tourists, and identified which visitors would be lost or gained due to the action (with vs. without the action)? Are secondary sources of visitation reliable? If models are used, how good are they and do the assumptions hold for the intended application? Has the study handled potential double counting problems in estimating visits?

Spending: How accurate are the spending estimates? Do the spending averages or totals seem reasonable? If spending averages are taken from a secondary source, evaluate the source, as well as how well these averages may apply to the intended application. What year does the spending represent? Has the data been price adjusted to the current (or model) year? If spending data come from a visitor survey, evaluate the survey methods - how was spending measured, what was the sample size, the response rate, soundness of the analysis? Are variances and confidence intervals reported for the spending estimates? Are visitors divided into distinct segments to reduce variances? Also make sure the units for which spending is reported match the units for visits, i.e., the study doesn't multiply a per party spending average times the number of person visits. If adjustments are made in units of analysis, evaluate the assumed or estimated average length of stay or party size assumptions.

Multipliers: If "off-the-shelf" or borrowed multipliers are used, investigate the source. Does the study clearly define what type of multiplier is being used (Type I, Type III, income, sales or employment, ratio or Keynesian) and use the multiplier appropriately? In particular, watch for studies that multiply tourism spending by a multiplier taken from an input-output model. They should adjust for the capture rate either by reducing spending, only using retail margins on goods purchased by tourists, or using a "tourist spending" multiplier that takes the capture rate into account. If an input-output model is used, the report should summarize where it came from, what year it represents, the levels of sectoral aggregation, and the basic assumptions of the model.

Communication and reporting of results: The study should communicate the study results in terms that are understandable to the intended audience. For most audiences, a summary and glossary of economic terms is helpful. Most readers will not fully understand terms like indirect and induced effects, Type I and Type III multipliers, and input-output models. Formal definitions of the measures of sales, income, and jobs that are reported are also needed to clarify what each of these terms include and the measurement units. For example, is income only wage and salary income or does it also include proprietors income, rents and profits? Study limitations and errors should be indicated.

Study Cost

The costs of a tourism economic impact study can range from $500 to $50,000 and more. Costs will depend largely on the size and scope of tourism activity to be covered, the size and complexity of the study region, how much primary data are to be gathered and the level of accuracy and detail desired. The greatest and perhaps most significant cost will be the technical expertise of the analysts involved. Tourism economic impact studies require considerable technical judgement of specialists and a mix of corresponding skills:

- Knowledge of tourism
- Expertise in conducting tourism surveys, particularly spending studies

- Regional economic modeling skills, including knowledge and access to economic data bases, multipliers and input-output modeling systems
- Communication skills

The cost of conducting economic impact studies has dropped substantially in the past ten years due to improvements in microcomputer programmes for estimating spending and regional economic models. The three principal components of an economic impact estimate (visits, spending, and multipliers) each involve different costs and somewhat different skills. The costs and needed skills will vary considerably depending on whether primary or existing data are to be used. If levels and types of tourism activity are known and spending averages and multipliers may be taken from secondary sources, a complete economic impact assessment can be conducted in less than a month and in many cases for under $5,000.

You are paying primarily for the time, judgement and skills of the analyst. A small visitor spending survey may add another $5,000. For a more complete analysis of secondary effects using a formal input- output model, figure another $2,000- $5,000. Increase the cost estimate if several distinct alternatives are to be evaluated or multiple regions are involved. There will generally be scale economies in these situations with additional impact analyses costing less than half of the initial one. Costs will increase significantly if the number and types of visitors must be estimated using a general visitor survey or a demand model. Large scale spending surveys and custom input-output models based on primary data will also increase costs considerably. In many cases, the tourism activity and visitor spending data needed for an economic impact analysis can be gathered in a general visitor survey or market study. Spending averages for particular tourist segments can be estimated by having a portion of the general survey respondents complete an extra page of spending questions. Armed with good estimates of the number and types of visitors and their spending patterns, one can complete an economic impact study at little additional cost.

The principal motivations for a business or region to serve tourists are generally economic. An individual business is interested primarily in its own revenues and costs, while a community or region is concerned with tourism's overall contribution to the economy, as well as its social, fiscal and environmental impacts. A good understanding of tourism's economic impacts is therefore important for the tourism industry, government officials, and the community as a whole.

Tourism economics is unfortunately a technical area, involving concepts, methods, and models that are unfamiliar to most non-economists. In this bulletin I've attempted to define the key concepts and explain the basic methods for estimating the economic impacts of tourism, hopefully in as "non-technical" a way as the subject allows. Understanding the concepts and methods is critical to interpreting, evaluating, and applying economic impact results. This bulletin should be read along with one or more economic impact reports that can be used as examples and opportunities to test your grasp of the issues.

At the risk of oversimplifying a complex topic, let me conclude with the five pieces of advice, most frequently give to people who ask about tourism economic impacts. First, tell them that the most important information for estimating tourism impacts is a good estimate of the number of tourists. This requires clearly defining what one wishes to include as "tourism" and the region of interest. Secondly, recommend that tourists be divided into distinct subgroups (segments) with distinct spending patterns and likely reacting differently to various policy and marketing actions. In particular, local customers should be distinguished from visitors from outside the region and day users from overnight visitors.

Thirdly, focus most of your effort on estimating the direct effects of tourism, usually as tourist spending in the area. Multiplier effects are not nearly as important in most cases, as their use in tourism would suggest and multipliers tend to introduce complexities that most users of the results do not fully understand. Even if multiplier effects are important to the study purpose, remember that any errors in estimates of the direct effects will also be multiplied by any multiplier. Fourth, if you must use multipliers be sure you understand them.

E-COMMERCE TOURISM

Tourism is growing fastest in the developing countries, where it is a major component of most economies. Tourism is one of the world's largest industries, and it is a natural partner for the Internet, where it is also the world's largest on-line industry. Community-based tourism (CBT) has been shown to foster local development in developing countries, particularly in the poorer rural areas. At the same time, Information and Communication Technologies are being deployed within poor communities in developing countries and are beginning to demonstrate their potential for inducing local development. This paper describes an action research initiative for introducing electronic commerce for community based tourism (e-CBT) in three Asian rural communities in order to reveal its potential for community development.

E-CBT targets an important and growing market segment in the developing world, consisting of individual travellers for whom travel is an essential component of their life-style and who seek new and authentic experiences that are not directed towards a mass market. The proposal describes strategic partnerships between a University in Hong Kong and three other Asian universities who will work with local communities and tourism authorities for the eventual propagation of the development benefits of e-CBT among wider rural populations in their countries.

The WTO forecasts that international arrivals are expected to reach over 1.56 billion by the year 2020. The total expected tourist arrivals by region shows that by 2020 the top three receiving regions will be Europe (717 million tourists), East

Asia and the Pacific (397 million) and Americas (282 million). East Asia and the Pacific, South Asia, the Middle East and Africa are forecasted to record growth at rates of over 5% per year, compared to the world average of 4.1 per cent. By 2010, WTO forecasts that the Americas will lose its number two position, behind Europe, to East Asia and the Pacific, which will receive 25 % of world arrivals.

Tourism offers huge opportunities for developing countries to increase incomes from the growing number of arrivals that land on their shores. However, it has been recognized that many tourism policies developed from central governments without local involvement fail to cater for the sensibilities and aspirations of the communities that tourists visit. The conference on Community Based Ecotourism in Southeast Asia agreed that local communities should have the right to self-determination and to decide whether to accept or not accept the policies that affect their livelihood. As tourism is essentially a micro- enterprise, tourism lends itself to local entrepreneurial activity, and community-based tourism has emerged as a mechanism for fostering locally based tourism operations, as opposed to those whose financial interests are often located away from the tourist destination.

Moreover, as Information and Communication Technologies (ICTs) are beginning to be deployed in rural communities for the purpose of fostering local development, communities are able to implement electronic commerce in support of their CBT operations, and engage in e-CBT. Furthermore, it will be shown that the Internet is not only a natural partner for tourism, it also a natural partner for the market segment that e-CBT should target. With more than 600 million people on-line by September 2002, and more than 60% of them residing in Europe or North America, even small and remote communities with an Internet connection can address huge global markets.

The purpose of this paper is to introduce the concept of electronic commerce for community based tourism, e-CBT, as a mechanism for local development. E-CBT involves the operation of local tourism activities which are promoted across the internet by a community using a community based telecentre, which provides community access to information and communication technologies. The concept is presented as a method for fostering rural development in developing countries.

Tourism is a principal export for developing countries and the least developed countries (LDCs). It is growing rapidly and is the most significant source of foreign exchange after petroleum (WTO, 2002). There is a general shift of tourism arrivals towards developing countries. Growth rates of international tourism receipts during the 1990s were, on average, 50% higher in the major developing country destinations than in comparison with the major developed country destinations. By far the largest single developing country international tourism destination is China.

The People's Republic accounted for US$10 billion in international tourism receipts in 1996, receiving 22.7 million international visitors, experiencing 19% annual growth rates of receipts since 1980. Together with earnings generated by the Hong Kong Special Administrative Region, China's 1996 receipts surpass US$20 billion. In 2001, China ranked fifth in the world's top tourism destinations, measured both by the number of international arrivals and by international tourism receipts. Yet in terms of Gross National Income per capita, China ranks 108 out of 173 countries in the World Bank's statistical indicators for 2001. China, Thailand and Indonesia together generated 40% of all international tourism receipts accruing to developing countries in 1996.

The World Tourism Organisation says there is a strong economic case for promoting tourism in developing countries, suggesting that affirmative action and pro-poor policies are able to go beyond trickle down and multiplier affects by unlocking opportunities for the poor within tourism (WTO 2002). Success in poverty alleviation through tourism depends, says the WTO, partly on effective community-public-private partnerships that serve to reduce financial leakages and increase economic linkages to the local economy. Financial leakages occur where a disproportionately low percentage of tourism revenues stays in the local market, and they reduce the development impact of tourism. Linkages with the local economy foster revenue retention from tourism activities, and they depend on quality, reliability and competitiveness of local products.

WTO suggest various steps that can be taken to increase the benefits to the local economy in tourist destination areas, by;

- Facilitating local community access to the tourism market,
- Minimising the financial leakages from the local economy,
- Maximising the linkages of tourism to the local economy,
- Building on and complimenting existing livelihood strategies through employment and small enterprise development,
- Ensuring that tourism products contribute to local economic development not just to national revenue generation.
- Tourism is a principal export for 83% of developing countries and it is the principal export for one third of them.
- Developing countries had 292.6 million arrivals in 2000, an increase since 1990 of nearly 95%. The 40 least developed countries had 5.1 million international arrivals in 2000; they achieved an increase of 75% in the decade.
- 80% of the world's poor, those living on less than US$1 per day, live in 12countries. In 11 of these countries, tourism is significant and growing
- The developing countries are attracting an increasing share of global international tourist arrivals up from 20% in 1973 to 42% in 2000.

The developing countries and particularly the LDCs secured a larger increase in the income per international arrival between 1990 and 2000 than did the OECD or the European Union countries. The LDCs secured an increase of 45% between1990 and 2000 and the developing countries nearly 20%. This compares with18% for the OECD countries and 7.8% for the EU.

In 2000, tourism ranked third among the major merchandise export sectors for both developing countries and LDCs. If petroleum industry exports are discounted (and they are significant in only three) tourism is the primary source of foreign exchange in the 49 LDCs.

COMMUNITY BASED TOURISM

Community-based tourism provides alternative economic opportunities, which are in essence in rural areas. Community-based tourism is regarded as a tool for natural and cultural resource conservation and community development and it is closely associated with ecotourism, sometimes referred to as community-based ecotourism. It is a community-based practice that provides contributions and incentives for natural and cultural conservation as well as providing opportunities for improved community livelihood. It has the potential to create jobs and generate entrepreneurial opportunities for people from a variety of backgrounds, skills and experiences, including rural communities and especially women. Community-based tourism has been implemented in many developing countries, often in support of wildlife management, environmental protection and/or development for indigenous peoples.

Community tourism should;

- Be run with the involvement and consent of local communities. (Local people should participate in planning and managing the tour.)
- Give a fair share of profits back to the local community. (Ideally this will include community projects (health, schools, etc).)

- Involve communities rather than individuals. (Working with individuals can disrupt social structures.)
- Be environmentally sustainable. (Local people must be involved if conservation projects are to succeed.)
- Respect traditional culture and social structures.
- Have mechanisms to help communities cope with the impact of western tourists.
- Keep groups small to minimise cultural / environmental impact.
- Brief tourists before the trip on appropriate behaviour.
- Not make local people perform inappropriate ceremonies, etc.
- Leave communities alone if they don't want tourism. (People should have the right to say 'no' to tourism.)

Community based tourism occurs when decisions about tourism activity and development are driven by the host community. It usually involves some form of cultural exchange where tourists meet with local communities and witness aspects of their lifestyle. Eco-tourism also emphasises observation and learning by the tourist, alongside economic and cultural conservation, and the delivery of benefits that ensure long-term sustainability of communities and natural resources. In Nepal, the Tourism for Rural Poverty Alleviation Programme began in 2001, jointly funded by the United Nations Development Programme (UNDP), the UK Department for International Development (DFID) with advisory services from SNV (Stichting Nederlandse Vrijwilligers) a Dutch development organisation.

Operating in six remote locations, the programme employed social mobilisation and tourist awareness programmes in villages to empower local communities to manage their own tourism development. In Vietnam, the International Union for Conservation of Nature and Natural Resources (IUCN) or World Conservation Union, is operating a community based tourism pilot in Sa Pa, a highly visited area with colourful ethnic minorities. Funded mainly by the Ford Foundation, the goal of the project is to assist local stakeholders to achieve an environmentally, culturally and socio-economically sustainable form of tourism, establishing mechanisms that support the active participation of the community in tourism decision-making and implementation.

The Nam Ha ecotourism project in Lao PDR uses community-based tourism as a vehicle to integrate environmental and cultural conservation with sustainable socio and economic development. Working closely with local villagers, limits were set on the number of trekking tourists allowed each year so as not to overwhelm the communities and to ensure that tourist incomes supplement rather than replace other economic activities.

Typically, with community-based tourism, the community runs all of the activities that a tourist engages in; lodging, food, guiding and craft sales. Benefits include; economic growth in rural regions; the distribution of tourism revenue, which can foster improved welfare and equity in the industry; improved resource conservation by local people; and diversification of the regional and national tourism product.

Intertwined with community-based tourism in developing countries is the concept of pro-poor tourism. In most counties with high levels of poverty, tourism is a significant and/or growing component of the economy. Governments and aid agencies acknowledge that whilst economic growth is essential for poverty reduction, of itself, it is insufficient to ensure a significant reduction. Growth that is specifically pro-poor is a pre-requisite for significant progress towards agreed targets for poverty reduction. Tourism has many characteristics that make it potentially pro-poor;

- It is a diverse industry, which increases the scope for wide participation,
- The customer comes to the product, providing important opportunities for linkages(e.g., souvenir sales),

- It is highly dependent on natural capital (wildlife, scenery) and culture, assets that some of the poor have in abundance, even if they have few financial resources,
- Tourism can be more labour intensive than manufacturing,
- A higher proportion of benefits (jobs, trade opportunities) go to women.

Pro-poor tourism is defined as tourism that generates net benefits for the poor. It maximises the potential for eradicating poverty by developing appropriate strategies in co-operation with all major groups, indigenous and local communities. Benefits may be economic, but they may also be social, environmental or cultural. Pro-poor tourism is not a specific product or sector of tourism, but an approach to the tourism industry. The core activity is to increase access of the poor to economic benefits. Pro-poor tourism strategies unlock opportunities for the poor; whether for economic gain, other livelihood benefits, or participation in decision- making.

Early experience shows that pro-poor tourism strategies do appear able to 'tilt' the industry at the margin, to expand opportunities for the poor and have potentially wide application across the industry. Poverty reduction through pro-poor tourism can therefore be significant at a local or district level. Moreover, the poverty impact may be greater in remote areas, though the tourism itself may be on a limited scale. Most examples of community-based in tourism in developing countries qualify as pro-poor tourism as they are designed to foster development at grassroots levels.

EFFECTS OF TOURISM TAXATION

The analysis reveals that, unlike the traditional outcome of a deadweight loss associated with higher taxes, increasing taxes on tourism can be welfare improving. Tourism is being targeted as a growing source of tax revenue by governments across the world. However, tourism taxation can have significant effects on welfare, which should be taken into account when taxes are levied. Little research has been undertaken on the welfare effects of tourism taxation and, given the special characteristics of tourism as an export sector, direct application of the literature on commodity taxation and export taxation to tourism taxation is not appropriate. This paper examines the welfare effects of tourism taxation on residents of a tourist destination country within a partial equilibrium framework, in the context of fixed and variable prices.

It is also found that the higher the proportion of tourism demand in total demand, and the more inelastic tourism demand is relative to domestic demand, the higher will be the welfare gain. Tourism's role as one of the fastest growing economic activities in the world makes it a key target for taxation. As a major source of foreign currency receipts, tourism appears to be the salvation for governments faced with budgetary constraints and pressures to decrease their reliance on income tax and tariffs as sources of revenue. On the other hand, taxes on tourism have proliferated and there are now calls from international bodies and tourism businesses and consumers for reductions in the range and levels of taxes on tourism.

Although the revenue gained from tourism taxation can be used to benefit the public by such means as increasing the provision of public services, it may also reduce welfare and act as a disincentive to tourism demand. Given the increasing importance of tourism taxation in both developed and developing countries, greater understanding of the economic underpinnings of tourism taxation and its effects is necessary, so that modeling of tourism taxation can be undertaken and appropriate policies for tourism taxation can be formulated. Tourism taxes thus have a direct effect on domestic consumption and hence domestic welfare.

Moreover, trade policies such as import tariffs aimed at the tradable sector also affect the tourism sector, with the tourists paying the domestic price instead of the world price.

Most importantly, the burden of a tax on the tourism sector falls on both domestic residents and foreigners (tourists). Therefore, the burden of a tourism tax is a combination of the burden of an export tax and a domestic tax. Formal analysis of the welfare effects of tourism taxation is undertaken in section 4, and the fifth section of the paper includes some parameter values in the equations for the welfare effects in order to determine the results of tourism taxation in alternative contexts

TAXING THE TOURISM SECTOR

In practice, the tourism sector can be taxed either by taxing the businesses in the tourism sector or by taxing the tourists directly. Both methods may be implemented either via the general tax system of the economy or through special tourism taxes. The World Tourism Organisation (WTO, 1998) has identified 40 different types of taxes applied to the tourism sector in both developed and developing countries. They are given in the tourism tax typology.

Additional taxes relating to tourists' use of the natural environment and general taxes that also fall on tourists have also been included. Of the 45 taxes, 30 are directly payable by the tourists and 15 are levied on tourism businesses. Five broad sectors involved in tourism taxation can be identified, namely airlines and airports, hotels and other accommodation, road transportation, food and beverages and provider of tourism services. The practicality of taxing each of these sectors is highlighted below.

Airlines and airports: In long haul destinations, international transport occupies a major part in the total cost of holiday packages and hence taxing this sector should, in principle, be lucrative. However, although this is an option for developed countries, this is beyond the reach of most developing countries because they normally do not own an airline company or if they do own one, it is often unprofitable. Revenue may, instead, be generated from airport-related taxes.

Hotels and other accommodation: This is normally the most important revenue generator of the tourism industry and is also easier to tax. However, the practicality of taxing the accommodation sector also varies between developed and developing countries and tends to be more problematic in the latter. The hotel sector is often highly subsidised or receives investment and tax incentives from the government in developing countries, with the aim of attracting foreign and domestic investment to the sector. The motivation is twofold, first to expand the sector as a part of a policy to expand the tourism industry and second, to protect the sector because it is a relatively unstable one due to its highly seasonal nature. The contradicting implication is that the easiest and major target for tourism taxation is most likely to be freed from taxation.

Taxis, food and beverages and tourism services: These sectors are relatively easy to tax in industrialised countries but form part of fragmented small business sectors and do not normally contribute a major proportion of tourism revenue. They include such sectors as entertainments, handicrafts, jewellery and other souvenirs. In most developing countries, these activities form part of the informal sector or of the hard-to-tax formal sector and it is difficult to raise much revenue from this source. Ecotourism tax is a relatively new form of taxation that destinations such as the Balearics levy in an attempt to counter the environmental damage caused by mass tourism. Carbon tax and landfill tax are more general environmental taxes on the level of carbon emissions and wastes respectively, but are borne by tourists as well.

Although gambling (in-shop and racing) is not legal in some countries mainly due to religious opposition, casinos are socially accepted in several countries. Tourists are involved in gambling and casinos, and hence bear the tax associated with those activities. The tax can be levied on the suppliers rather than tourists as in the case of the UK where the betting tax that was initially levied on the gamblers is now levied on the gross profit of bookmakers.

Taxing Tourists

Since taxing tourism businesses is not always a lucrative way of raising tax revenue, much tax revenue from tourism is generated from consumption taxes and special tourism taxes applied directly to tourists' consumption. Consumption taxes take the form of general sales taxes or value added tax (VAT). Sales tax/VAT is levied in almost all countries, regardless of the tourism taxation policies.

Therefore, in the presence of this type of sales tax, tourists are being taxed without any deliberate tourism tax policy on the part of the government. In the spirit of optimal taxation, some countries discriminate between domestic and tourism consumption, such that the latter is taxed at a higher rate or an additional tourism tax is applied to tourists' consumption. However, this entails administration problems in enforcing and monitoring such taxes. Special tourism taxes are generally levied directly on tourists and they can take several forms.

Common forms include taxes on hotels and restaurants, passenger services, tourist transport, entry/exit taxes and hotel accommodation taxes. The last tax is the most common and, as the name suggests, hotel accommodation tax is simply a tax on the tourists' expenditure on accommodation. The rate levied usually depends on hotel class and the season. It is relatively easy to collect, although discrimination across hotel classes sometimes creates administrative problems. In countries such as Jamaica, it is levied at a flat rate amounting to around $4-12 per night, and in other countries it is an ad valorem tax, which differs across countries: for example, 13% in South Africa, 12.5% in Senegal and 7.5% in Grenada. Entry/exit taxes include those on airport departures, which are fixed amounts that have to be paid when leaving the country, on airport embarkation, which is paid on entering the country, and the visa fee.

These taxes are usually levied at a flat rate and are relatively small in amount: for example, the airport departure tax has been within the range $1-6 in Singapore, Indonesia, Malaysia, Philippines, and Thailand, and was set at $10 in Malawi, Tanzania and Zambia.

CONTROVERSY

The WTO (1998) posits that the nature of the tourism sector makes it a target for tax revenue not only because tourism taxes are easy to collect and easy to administer but also because international tourists are rarely voters in the destination country they visit. Most of the arguments in favour of taxing the tourism sector are based on the fact that tourism products are consumed jointly with unpriced natural amenities and public goods.

Unpriced natural amenities include the sun, sea and wildlife, while public goods can include security and health services. As Gray (1982) argues, "the question of public goods, their supply and their pricing, is relatively more important in tourism than in many other industries, in part, because of the needed role of the government in asset preservation and, in part, because of the greater role of the government in the normal routine when foreigners reside temporarily within its own borders."

The main reasons for tourism taxation can be considered under the following categories. Besides providing law and order, under which contracts can be enforced and property rights protected, so ensuring that the private sector is operating efficiently, one of the main roles of the government is to provide 'public goods'. The technical definition of public goods comprises the following: indivisibility, ie. commodities are not divisible into units that can be sold individually; non-excludability, ie. no one can be excluded from benefiting from the product; the free-rider problem, where it is difficult to charge users an appropriate fee.

Common examples of public goods include national defence and street lighting. The distinctive characteristics of public goods makes it difficult to provide them via the private sector because there is no price mechanism that controls the market. They can be provided only by the government, which uses its right to tax to generate the resources necessary to supply them. Domestic taxpayers usually finance the provision of such goods. The influx of tourists imposes an extra cost on the government relating to the provision of items such as greater security and an improved environment. As non-residents, tourists do not pay to finance these extra costs.

A tourist tax will, therefore, serve to redress the balance and impose the burden on those who are responsible for them. There are often user charges for some attractions, such as parks and safaris, but in other cases, such as street lighting and public security, enforcing payment is difficult. In such circumstances, taxing the may be the only way of 'charging' them for the public goods they consume.

Higher government revenue can increase welfare by such means as financing improvements in public services. Furthermore, it may help to reduce the burden of income taxation on domestic residents, and it may also be an alternative policy for countries that want to reduce their dependency on trade taxes while, at the same time, not imposing an additional burden on domestic residents.

The WTO (1988) estimates that 'tourist countries' obtain around 10-25% of their tax revenue from the tourism sector. In some small specialised tourism countries such as the Bahamas, over 50% of government revenue is generated from the tourism sector. In Mauritius, about 12-15% of tax revenue is collected directly and indirectly from the tourism sector. The tourism sector is an unusual sector for revenue generation. Bird (1992) believes that developing countries tend to under tax their tourism sector, failing to exploiting fully the economic rent emerging from the sector.

Such rent results from less than perfectly elastic demand for their tourism products, due to the differentiated nature of their natural amenities. The degree of inelasticity of demand depends, in part, on the degree of differentiation of the destination and affects the ability to tax. The greater the degree of differentiation of the destination, the more inelastic demand will be and, hence, the greater the scope for taxation.

Tourism product differentiation generally occurs in terms of types and quality of attractions (endowments), types and quality of goods and services sold in the country, geographical location and distance. Examples of attractions with very inelastic demand are the pyramids of Egypt, the Taj Mahal and the Grand Canyon. Gray (1987) associates the demand for differentiated tourism products with 'wanderlust' tourism, involving seeing or doing something that is unique to the destination, as opposed to 'sunlust' tourism which refers to the sun, sea and sand destinations such as Mauritius and the Caribbean countries. 'Sunlust' destinations tend to have less inelastic demand because the tourism products tend to be less differentiated across countries.

Less than perfectly elastic demand implies that tourism gives rise to 'economic rents' which suppliers of tourism services may try to maximise and governments may attempt to tax. However, tourism is a composite product with multiple components, and each of the components can be taxed at a different rate. For example, Bonham et al. considered a room tax on hotel receipts in Hawaii and found that the tax resulted in an insignificant change in hotel revenue. Combs and Elledge found that a small ad-valorem tax room tax imposed on motels and other forms of tourist accommodation in the USA would have very little impact on the industry and would generate substantial revenue for the government.

However, an increase in taxation on one component of tourism can result in lower expenditure on another. In one of the first systematic tourism taxation studies, Mak and Nishimura investigated the effect of a hotel room tax on the length of stay of tourists in Hawaii. The results were that visitors' length of stay was insensitive to price changes and that an increase in the room tax would not reduce tourist arrivals in Hawaii significantly.

However, Mak and Nishimura also examined the effect of a hotel room tax on non-lodging consumption and find that tourists 'respond to marginal increases in price of lodging partly by reducing some of their non-lodging expenditures and partly by reducing their savings and/or spending at home'.

Exportability

Taxation on tourism may be exportable in the sense that tourists bear the major burden of the taxation. The issue of tax incidence is important in this respect, as discussed in the context of the UK by Durbarry and Sinclair. One of the first studies that examined the tax incidence of tourism taxes explicitly was by Fujii et al., who examined the incidence and the exportability of an ad valorem hotel room tax for Hawaii in a partial equilibrium framework.

Tax incidence refers to the distribution of the tax burden between the buyers and the hoteliers whereas tax exporting refers to the extent to which the burden of the tax is distributed between the residents and the non-residents. If the hotel industry is an enclave with a high proportion of foreign investment, then the distinction between tax incidence and tax exporting is minor because the incidence of the tax on the supplier is actually exported. Under a partial equilibrium framework, the incidence of a hotel room tax depends on the relative sizes of the elasticities of demand and of supply. Fujii et al. calculated the relative burden of the hotel tax on tourists and the tourism industry as the ratio of the supply and demand elasticities for accommodation.

They estimated the demand function for accommodation and found that the price elasticities of demand were negative and significant, and also found supply to be less than perfectly elastic. Their results suggested that one-third of the hotel room tax was borne by the tourism industry and the rest by the tourists. They also showed that the hotel room tax was more readily exported than similar taxes levied on meals, drinks and entertainment and the general sales tax. Hence the exportability of tourism taxes is liable to vary between different components of the tourism product.

Sustainability of the Environment

Many developing countries under balance of payments and foreign exchange pressure have targeted tourism as a means of development. In many cases, no proper management strategies have been formulated especially at the initial stage of the tourism development. Natural resources have been degraded to the point where environmental sustainability is threatened. Regulating the inflow of tourists and taxation are the two most popular tools used, or considered, to remedy the problem.

However, regulating the inflow of tourists may not be the ideal solution because it deliberately contracts the tourism sector and this may have negative repercussions on the economy. It should also be remembered that many countries are investing resources to expand the tourism sector, and therefore it would be contradictory to pursue these two policies simultaneously. Moreover, it is believed that unconstrained growth (not limiting tourist arrivals) is usually beneficial in the sense that it increases the level of per capita income, thus providing more funds for maintaining the environment and sustaining growth. On the other hand, regulation through taxation not only provides the government with revenue (if designed properly) but also targets only the activities and individuals involved in the environmental degradation process and is, therefore, an efficient way to tackle the problem.

Furthermore, with higher revenues, more resources will be available to sustain the development of the industry. The tourism sector does not only rely on the natural amenities in the country but also on public goods. A strong regulatory framework, such as maintaining high health and food preparation standards, is also important in the success of the tourism sector. Taxation can generate the necessary resources to provide these requirements. Of course, the tourism industry has no inherent right to have the taxes it pays ploughed back into the industry.

However, appropriate earmarking of tax revenue can help to sustain the tourism industry and also help to reduce and combat the associated degradation of the environment. The taxation issues involved in controlling environment degradation and sustaining tourism are similar. The basic method is to use the Pigouvian tax, whereby the tax rate should correct for the divergence between the market price and the social marginal cost. Such taxes should be applied to all users, including both domestic residents and tourists, and should as far as possible be directed to the goods and services that generate the externalities so as to avoid inefficiencies.

If resources are to be exploited only to the economically desirable limit, then the social marginal cost (hence tax rate) should be set sufficiently high to include not only the opportunity costs to local residents in terms of environmental damage and congestion costs, but also the maximum possible rent extractable. On the other hand the price, hence the tax rate, should not be set so high as to hinder consumption of the product and tourist arrivals in the country. Congestion is an important facet of sustainability. High congestion, often caused by tourists themselves, reduces the quality of tourism services, which can lead to a reduction in arrivals, especially of high class and high spending tourists. The presence of crowds may detract from the enjoyment of touri ts seeking solitude and privacy.

Discomfort in crowds, long queues at popular places, traffic congestion and an untidy environment will not only affect the quality of tourism services but also the quality of life of domestic residents. Tourism taxation may be used both to reduce the inflow of tourists and to compensate the local residents. However, many tourism activities are not priced, for example, sun, sea and sand, and if some are priced, the associated transaction costs relating to monitoring and enforcement are generally very high.

Thus, they are supplied at a zero fee to all users and the problem of free riders is difficult to avoid. In this context, regulatory processes such as parking fees near crowded beaches and taxes on car rental can be applied. An entry/exit tax, which is a fixed amount of money that tourists pay when they enter and leave the destination country, can also be used. An entry/exit tax is an easy way of extracting economic rents from the tourism services the destination country is selling because it is often a tax included in the airfare, unnoticed by many travellers. Sometimes countries discriminate between domestic residents and tourists, so that only tourists pay the tax. However, an entry/exit tax has some disadvantages.

First, by capturing rents from tourists, an entry/exit tax does not provide any incentive for tourism to reduce their demand for the specific good that is causing the externalities, as should optimally be the case. The tax will reduce the number of tourist arrivals. Hence not only the demand of the externality generating commodity will fall but demand for other tourism services will also fall because of the complementary nature of tourism demand. The economic benefits normally attached to expanding the tourism sector may then be constrained.

Second, a uniform entry/exit tax does not offer first degree price discrimination in the sense that both low and high income tourists or short and long stay tourists pay the same amount of tax. This may discourage short stay tourists. Third, since it is levied mainly on foreigners, or at a higher rate on foreigners, it may fail to take full account of the full contribution of residents to environmental degradation.

Despite the advantages of tourism taxation, governments have been cautious about the magnitude of the taxes levied on the tourism sector because there are also negative effects associated with tourism taxation. A range of arguments has been levelled against tourism taxation, and some of the key arguments can be included under the following headings.

Costs of Compliance

Taxes levied directly on the tourism sector are sometimes difficult to justify. The amount of tax collected may be small but the tax can still have a substantial negative impact on the tourism sector, with repercussions on the overall economy. This happens especially with taxes levied directly on tourists, such as visa fees. It is not only the high fees required; there is often unnecessary bureaucracy (indeed discrimination between tourists of different nationalities) that can greatly raise the compliance costs for the tax payer and act as a deterrent to visiting the country.

This may contract tourist arrivals and affect other sectors related to the tourism sector. For countries where tourism comprises a major part of the economy, this can adversely affect the employment level and the balance of payments resulting in an overall contraction of the level of economic activity of the economy. The fiscal effects are likely to differ from country to country and from time to time, for three main reasons.

First, the effects depend on the policy of the government. If the government wants to maximise revenue, the tax rates will tend to be high. On the other hand, if the government wants to promote the sector, tax rates can be very low. In some case the government goes further by providing subsidies, such as subsidies for airport and parking infrastructure, and investment incentives to businesses. Second, the effects also depend on how important tourism is to the economy. Obviously, the higher the contribution of tourism in the economy, the higher will be the effects of tourism taxes on the government budget.

Thirdly, the number and types of linkages with other sectors in the economy and leakages from the economy that the tourism sector brings about are also important. As a general rule, linkages tend to increase government revenue and leakages lead to a reduction in revenue. The amount of revenue that is obtained from tourism taxation depends, in part, upon the value of the price elasticity of demand for tourism. If the price elasticity of demand is high, the effect of an increase in tax may be to decrease revenue.

In the case of tourist accommodation, all obtained demand elasticities for accommodation that were significantly different from zero. Hiemstra and Ismail reported a significant price elasticity of demand for the lodging industry based on a survey of the properties owned and managed by the American Hotel and Motel Association.

Retaliation

Taxation generates revenue but, as in the case of trade taxes, it invites retaliation by other countries if they feel that the other government is unfairly treating their citizens. For example, Kenya and Tanzania introduced visa charges for UK citizens in retaliation to the application of visa fees by the UK on their citizens. Retaliation is always a threat and in most cases the eventual outcome is lower welfare for both countries. Tisdell (1983) showed how retaliation in the case of tourism taxes can lead to a lower economic surplus for both countries.

This is because the consumer surplus that the tourists from the leader country were enjoying in the retaliating country will disappear after the tax. The country with a more inelastic demand for tourism will lose less but, compared with the case without retaliation, both countries lose. However, if a developing country imposes, say, an entry tax on tourists who are mainly from developed countries, then retaliation will tend to affect the developing country to a lesser extent. This is because the number of tourists from the developing country visiting the developed is fewer than the number of tourists from the developed countries who visit developing country.

WELFARE IMPLICATIONS OF TOURISM TAXATION

It is widely accepted in the literature that taxation should comply with three main principles: efficiency, equity and having a low disincentive to work effect. Tourism taxation may meet all three criteria or only some of them. The efficiency principle can be achieved because, unlike other taxes, tourism taxes can lead to an increase in welfare, thereby rendering tourism taxation more efficient than taxing other sectors. The main reason why this occurs is that the presence of tourists increases the tax base for commodity taxation and hence higher tax revenue is generated. However, the welfare loss corresponding to a tax increase is not reflected in domestic welfare since utility of tourists is not included in the social welfare function. This is explained in more detail below.

The equity principle can also be achieved as some tourism products are classified as luxuries. Following the redistributive effect of taxation literature, taxing such products entails positive equity effects because they are consumed mainly by individuals from the higher income brackets. The disincentive to work effect of taxation is also considered to be an important criterion for good taxation principles. It is believed that taxation leads to a disincentive to work because the more a person works, the more tax the person pays, so that to avoid paying high taxes, people work less and take more leisure. This effect is more notable with direct income taxation, but Corlette and Hague demonstrate how commodity taxation can be used to circumvent the problem. They argue that goods that complement leisure more can be taxed at a higher rate. The intuition is that by taxing goods that are complementary to leisure, the price of leisure will increase.

Hence, people will be less willing to undertake leisure activities, thereby reducing the disincentive to work effect of taxation. Taxing tourism products reinforces the above proposition because taxing tourism is equivalent to taxing commodities that are complementary to leisure, thereby not only reducing the disincentive effects inflicted by the commodity tax but also reducing those introduced by income taxation, hence making the overall taxation system more efficient. The latter two principles will not be considered further here but the focus of the analysis will be on the first principle and will concern the welfare implications of tourism taxation, based on the normative analysis of the taxation literature using demand and supply analysis.

A practical and common method of taxing the tourism sector is through consumption taxes. Consumption taxes can either take the form of special taxes designed specifically to tax the tourism sector, such as a hotel room tax, or can be levied through the general sales tax system. Tourism may be the only export sector that can be taxed using the domestic sales tax. This is because of the special nature of the tourism product as an exported commodity. In contrast to conventional commodity exports, foreign tourists who want to consume tourism travel to the exporting country; ie. rather than sending goods across boundaries, consumers move across boundaries to consume the product. Consumption of goods and services will thus have a non-tourism consumption and a tourism consumption component.

Therefore, in an economy where a sales tax already exists, the tourism sector is taxed even without any deliberate actions from the government. This is, of course, true unless there is price discrimination between local consumers and tourists in the sense that tourists are exempted from sales tax. However, this happens rarely, especially in developing countries, and if price discrimination is present, it is generally in favour of the domestic residents rather than the tourists. It is widely accepted in economics that there is a deadweight loss (a reduction in social welfare) attached to almost all taxes.

Sales tax may not always be welfare diminishing in the presence of tourists. Taxing tourists using the existing sales tax can be welfare improving. The presence of tourists means higher demand and, thus, a higher tax base that will generate more tax revenue. On the other hand, part of the burden of this additional tax revenue is borne by the tourists and is not accounted for in domestic welfare.

Therefore with higher tax revenue and a relatively lower reduction in domestic consumer surplus, the increase in the tax rate in the presence of tourists will have a lower deadweight loss, and in some cases a windfall gain may emerge. In this section, we examine this issue within a one commodity partial equilibrium framework. Although, the latter does not take account of general equilibrium effects, it provides a range of interesting insights about the possible sources and directions of welfare gains or losses. We consider two cases, the fixed producer price and the variable producer price case.

Fixed Producer Price

In the fixed producer price case, prices are sticky over the short run, for example owing to contractual arrangements or costs of changing prices in the form of loss of goodwill or prohibitive marketing. In this case, the supply curve is perfectly elastic. The presence of tourists shifts the demand curve outwards and, with a perfectly elastic supply curve, price does not increase. DH is the domestic demand curve without the presence of tourists and DT is the tourism demand curve such that the post-tourism aggregate demand curve is DA, which is the horizontal aggregation of DH and DT. It is assumed that DH exceeds DT at any common price, and that DH is more elastic than DT. The latter assumption is realistic as, being foreigners in the destination country for a relatively short period of time, tourists have limited knowledge about the ways of bypassing taxes in terms of finding substitutes.

Without Tax Case

When there are tourists but no tax in the economy, the analysis of the introduction of tax is analogous to the analysis for the case where a country increases tax on tourism products when tourists were already present. These practices have been common in countries that are attempting to extract the maximum possible rent from the tourism sector to ease their budget deficit. The scenario is upward sloping to denote that increasing output is supplied at higher prices (the variable producer price case). The base position of the economy, with tourists and without tax, is illustrated by the initial price and quantity, given by p0 and Aq 0 respectively.

The introduction of the tax increases the price paid by consumers to pD and decreases the price received by producers to pS. Hence, the burden of the tax is borne by both consumers (domestic residents and tourists) and producers. Consequently, there is a decrease in the consumer surplus of domestic consumers given by area (since we are concerned with the welfare of domestic consumers), and also a decrease in producer surplus given by the shaded area [B+F]. The increase in government tax revenue is given by the square [F], which is equal to area [A+B+C]. Therefore, the change in domestic welfare is given by the area.

With Tax Case

In the case where tourists arrive at a destination in the context of an existing tourism tax, the analysis is similar to analysing the effect of an expansion in the tourism sector in the presence of tax in the domestic economy. Copeland (1991) has also investigated this issue using the duality framework of trade theory, and found that tourism expansion is welfare improving when tax is already in place. 'Back-to-back' demand and supply diagrams are a convenient way of representing the problem.

Tourism taxes have proliferated around the world as governments have viewed the expanding tourism sector as a ready source of tax revenue. The taxes are levied on both tourists and tourism businesses at rates that vary considerably from country to country and have often been introduced in an ad hoc fashion, without serious consideration of their economic and social effects. This is a serious limitation as the effects can be advantageous or adverse.

On the one hand, tourism taxes can help to generate revenue to finance the provision of public goods, to contribute towards the costs of using environmental assets and to decrease negative externalities such as congestion. Moreover, much or all or much of the tax burden can be paid by tourists who are not resident in the country in which the taxes are levied. On the other hand, the imposition of tourism taxes may generate retaliatory measures by other governments, significant costs may be involved in the collection of the taxes and an increase in the tax rate may even result in lower tax revenue. Thus, the case for or against imposing or changing tourism taxes is complex and each of the above issues requires further empirical investigation.

The major focus of attention in the paper concerned the effects of tourism taxation on the welfare of the residents of tourism destinations - an issue which has previously lacked attention in research, although it has often been assumed that taxation has the effect of decreasing welfare. This issue was considered in the context of fixed and variable prices, to illustrate the outcomes that would occur in different empirical contexts. The analysis showed that the excess burden associated with commodity taxation is reduced and can even be negative (welfare gain) in the presence of tourists. Welfare will increase more, the more inelastic tourism demand is relative to domestic demand. Welfare also increases more, the higher the share of tourism demand relative to total demand. In the case of variable prices, the value of the supply elasticity is also relevant.

The results of changes in the values of the demand and supply elasticities differ between the cases of fixed and variable prices and also according to the sequence in which the tax is introduced; i.e. before or after the presence of tourists in the economy. An increase in the price elasticity of tourism demand decreases welfare because foreign tourists bear a lower proportion of the tax burden. In contrast, an increase in the elasticity of domestic demand increases welfare as the proportion of the tax burden that is borne by domestic residents relative to foreign tourists decreases.

In the case of variable prices, an increase in the elasticity of supply increases welfare relative to the initial values of the parameters and an increase in the tourism ratio increases welfare in all cases. Changes in the rate of taxation on tourism give rise to different effects on welfare in the different contexts of fixed and variable producer prices. In the former case, the change in welfare peaks at a specific tax rate and the value of the total change in welfare is maximised at a higher tax rate, decreasing thereafter. In the latter case, the optimal tax rate can be indeterminate.

The implications of the preceding results are that before introducing or changing tourism taxes, policy makers should pay explicit attention to the welfare effects that are likely to arise from them. Increases in taxes can give rise to adverse effects if the demand for tourism from non-residents is price elastic relative to domestic demand and/or if supply is inelastic. Under these circumstances, policy makers may wish to consider the alternative strategy of reducing taxes.

Conversely, an increase in tourism taxes in the context of inelastic demand for tourism by non-residents relative to domestic demand, in conjunction with elastic supply, can give rise to gains in domestic welfare. If policy makers wish to increase tourism taxes, they can also consider the longer term strategy of attempting to make tourism demand by non-residents more price inelastic, for example, by increasing the quality of the tourism product and/or differentiating the product such that it gains some type of monopolistic advantage.

Chapter 7

Need for Tourism Modelling

The TPF model consists of an innovative integration of tourism and travel analysis within a computable general equilibrium (CGE) modelling framework, to assist the formation of government policies relating to tourism and travel. The current research with Tourism Satellite Accounts (TSAs) can be complemented and extended by the use for analysing tourism and travel. These models are formal economic models that extend, rather than replace, tourism satellite accounts (TSAs). Indeed, the increasing implementation of TSAs is a stimulus to the use of TPF models because they provide data that is ideal for implementing a TPF model.

These models allow the full potential of the detailed data contained within TSAs to be realised and facilitate:

- The assessment of tourism's overall economic impact,
- The analysis of tourism policy,
- Tourism forecasting, predicting long-term trends in tourist numbers and expenditures.

TOURISM SATELLITE ACCOUNTS AND TPF MODELS

Tourism satellite accounts are being formulated by countries across the world, in order to provide accurate measures of the size of tourism sectors, the nature of demand for tourism, the nature of supply in tourism sectors, and the direct contribution of tourism to GDP and employment. This makes an invaluable contribution to our knowledge of the tourism sector. When measuring the economic impact of tourism, input-output (IO) models have often been used in the past. While these models successfully capture some of the economic impact of tourism, they do not capture all of the economic impact, leading to estimates of the economic impact of tourism that are not only unreliable but heavily biased.

Computable general equilibrium (CGE) models have their historical origins in input-output methodology, but were developed to overcome the many shortcomings of IO models. In particular, CGE models allow prices to vary and resources to be reallocated between production sectors. Tourism Policy and Forecasting (TPF) models build upon this framework by including tourism data from TSAs to provide a consistent means of modelling tourism in the entire economy.

Computable general equilibrium modelling is one of the most flexible and innovative economic techniques developed in recent decades. It has been used extensively by such international organisations as the World Bank, the World Trade Organisation and the OECD as well as in academia. It has been used in the fields of international trade, economic development, agricultural economics and environmental economics. Tourism impact models have traditionally relied on input-output (IO) modelling.

More recently, there have been initial applications of CGE models in the tourism field. The use of CGE models uses the latest methodology and gives more accurate predictions than techniques such as IO modelling. CGE models are formulated in a way that is radically different from input-output modelling, macroeconomic modelling, partial equilibrium modelling or, indeed, any other form of numerical simulation. Whereas the other modelling techniques rely on an initial stimulus which is then traced through the economic system in a systematic and deterministic manner, CGE models are formulated by specifying how economic agents react to changes in the economy. A CGE model is then solved simultaneously for all markets, production sectors and economic agents.

This gives CGE models a significant advantage in flexibility over other forms of modelling, because other forms of modelling can only trace the effects of specific initial stimuli, and do so in a one-way deterministic system. In a CGE model, the initial stimulus can originate anywhere in the economy, and can be literally anything that can occur in an economic framework, ranging from changes in taxes and subsidies, to technological change, population growth, shifts in demand and regulatory changes. CGE models are not deterministic in the same way that other simulation approaches are.

The initial stimulus affects markets, production sectors and economic agents who react to the stimulus and provide further changes to the economy. These changes do not work in a one-way direction, so effects can feed back to where the stimulus started. Broadly speaking, the construction of a CGE model is a process of setting up a series of markets (for goods, services and factors of production), production sectors and demand groups (households). Each market, sector and household has its own set of economic rules that determine how it reacts to external changes.

Typically, markets for goods and services are market clearing, so that if demand exceeds supply, the price of the good or service will increase until the market clears. If the price of the good that a production sector produces increases, the output of the sector will increase. Consequently its use of factors of production will increase and the supply of the good will increase. Eventually these demand and supply changes will (due to the demand-supply correcting behaviour of prices in markets) increase the price of factors of production and decrease the price of the output good, until it is no longer profitable to increase output any further.

By setting up the economic conditions whereby each market, sector and household reacts to changes in the economy, a CGE model can then model a variety of possible scenarios. In other forms of numerical simulation, models are set up whereby the simulation follows a direct causal relationship from one effect to the next. CGE models by their very nature allow interactions between markets, and between sectors, that may be very complex. IO models rely on an input-output table for data, and trace the intermediate demands for goods and services that are needed to satisfy final demands by consumers, the government, investment and exports.

Hence, they calculate the indirect effects of final demand. The earnings of income (by private consumers and the government) can also be included to calculate the induced effects, which are similar to Keynesian multipliers. CGE models include other effects through factor markets and foreign currency. In doing so, the CGE models include not only the indirect effects but also the induced effects. Tourism Policy and Forecasting models extend the CGE framework to incorporate tourism and travel, with data on tourism demand and the supply of tourism industries, and frameworks for modelling tourism and travel.

Four basic characteristics differentiate Nottingham TPF models from IO models of tourism and travel.

- A TPF model includes flexible prices and wages. This enables factors of production, such as labour and capital, and foreign exchange markets to be modelled.
- Income-expenditure consistency must be maintained for all private households, the government, firms and any other economic agents that are modelled.
- Consumers' responses to changes in prices and income levels are taken into account by behavioural assumptions.
- Substitution between intermediate inputs and factors of production, as prices and wages change, is taken into account by production assumptions.

A TPF model contains four types of equation:

- Equilibrium conditions for each market ensure that supply is equal to demand for each good, service, factor of production and for foreign exchange.

- Income-expenditure identities ensure that the economic model is a closed system. All earnings must be accounted for through expenditure or savings. These conditions apply to all private house holds, the government, firms and any other economic agents that are modelled.
- Behavioural relationships state how economic agents react to changing prices and income levels. These then determine consumers' demand levels for each good and service.
- Production functions determine how much is produced for any given level of factor employment. With assumptions regarding market structure, these determine what levels of labour employment, capital usage and intermediate input usage are required to satisfy a given level of output for a set of prices.

One of the strengths of the TPF models is their flexibility. As demonstrated in figure 3, the TPF models usually contain certain core components of the model structure, and can be expanded by extending the scope of the model to suit the circumstances of the tourist origin/destination country or region. Model structure components include:

- Market competition. Various forms of market competition can be included, from perfect competition to monopoly.
- Labour markets can be modelled in various forms, with the possibility of allowing for unemployment.
- Foreign trade can be treated in several different ways, to enable the modelling of small and large countries.
- Dynamics can be incorporated to show how the economy moves through time, with economic agents' expectations about future events incorporated into their decision-making processes.

In addition, extensions to the model scope can be made, such as:

- Income distribution can be modelled by incorporating many household groups. The distributional effects of tourism or tourism policies could then be examined.
- Inter-regional effects could be modelled by modelling distinct regions within a country.
- International effects can show how tourism's effects are spread between countries.
- The environment can be incorporated to show the effects of tourism and tourism policy on environmental issues.

Impact Modelling

TSAs represent a major step forward in the measurement of the economic size of tourism, but do not assess the total impact of tourism. Estimating the impact of tourism has the advantage of showing the desirability of tourism, in addition to measurement of size. It can also show what impact tourism has on different sectors, regions or on income distribution, depending on the specification of the model.

One problem with any attempt to measure the size of a sector such as tourism is that it is usually measured from the demand-side and it is difficult to compare results with sectors such as mining, agriculture or manufacturing that are usually measured from the supply- side. The direct impact of tourism is, on the surface, the most comparable with supply-side sectors, but falls into definitional problems. If an aircraft is owned by an airline, for example, a proportion (corresponding to the proportion of airline services consumed by tourists) of the aircraft will be included in the direct measurement of tourism.

If, however, the airline rents the aircraft from another company, the value of the rental service will be attributed as an intermediate input into tourism, and the corresponding returns to investment will not be included in tourism value added. In an attempt to rectify this situation, various countries have included indirect effects through input-output (IO) models as an alternative in their TSAs.

While this solves problems relating to definitions of intermediates, it goes beyond the measurement of the size of tourism in an accounting sense and loses direct comparability with supply-side sectors. IO models include some intermediate purchases (such as food and fuel, for example) that should clearly be thought of as intermediate purchases and not as being within the tourism sector itself. In short, the IO models go some way beyond measuring the size of the sector to measuring its economic impact. IO models do not, however, measure the full impact of tourism.

These models make various assumptions that evidently exclude some of the economic effects that a sector has. Therefore the measurement of indirect impacts through IO models gives only a partial picture of the full impact of tourism. In fact, the TPF results are more comprehensive and IO results more misleading because they incorporate only some of the impact of tourism.

Tourism Policy Analysis

The TPF models can be readily utilised to provide other forms of economic analysis. Policy analysis is an important way in which the potential of TPF models can be further demonstrated. The TPF models offer the ability to perform "what-if" simulations.

- Examine the economic effects of existing policies on tourism or of proposed alternatives. For example, they can show the net effective taxation of tourism that exists or provide a quantitative assessment of policy alternatives.
- Provide a theoretical viewpoint or an applied quantitative estimate.
- Examine purely taxation issues, or other policy instruments such as investment incentives and planning regulations.
- Examine the effects of tourism policy, or the effects that other policies have on tourism.

These examples demonstrate that the scope for tourism policy analysis with the TPF models is large.

Cases of particular relevance include:

- Examination of the current levels of tourism taxation, i.e. whether tourism is taxed at too low or too high rates relative to the rest of the economy.
- Quantitative estimates of tourism policy alternatives, such as planned tax changes or tourism development plans.
- Quantitative estimates of the effects of other policies on tourism, such as trade liberalisation or general taxation changes.

Forecasting

TPF models can be used to forecast future trends in the tourism industry. Such forecasting models show how changes in the world economy will feed through to tourism.

Three main causes of change are highlighted here:

- Factor accumulation, including capital accumulation through investment, labour growth through population growth, and changes to the skills of labour through education and training.
- Technological change, through technical progress.
- Policy changes, which may be foreseeable.

These factors influence both income growth on the demand side and production costs on the supply side. As each factor may be changing at different rates in different sectors and in different countries, forecasting their total effect requires a TPF model. Relative prices balance the demand and supply side factors to achieve equilibrium in each market. Continuing increases in overall skill and education levels will, for example, lead to high growth rates in sectors that use highly skilled and highly educated labour.

How this affects tourism depends very much on the skill and education levels in tourism characteristic sectors, and on the intermediate relationships between tourism characteristic sectors and the rest of the economy. Differential growth rates between tourist source countries will affect international tourism growth rates in different destination markets. Tourism growth will, in general, be highly responsive to increases in income levels in source countries, and will depend on the relative prices for tourism and other goods and services. The TPF models provide the opportunity to assess the potential long-term growth of tourism in response to changes in the economy (such as population growth and changing education levels) that are highly predictable, as well as the short-term impact of macroeconomic changes such as currency market crises and natural disasters.

TSAs and a TPF Model of the USA

Tourism satellite accounts provide detailed data on tourism activities that are not otherwise available in national accounts because national accounts provide data classified according to production activities and commodities, and tourism spans many of these standard classifications. The U.S. TSA used here specifies 18 industries and 23 commodities. The tables that it provides are:

1. Production Account of Tourism Industries and All Other Industries.

   This table provides a "make" matrix showing the output of each commodity in each industry and a breakdown of costs by industry into three categories: intermediate inputs, compensation of employees, and other value added.

2. Supply and Consumption of Tourism and All Other Commodities.

   This table shows (i)a breakdown of total supply of each commodity into various categories - such as domestic production, imports government sales; and

   (ii) A breakdown of demand into categories - intermediate, personal consumption, investment, exports and government expenditures.

3. Tourism Demand by Type of Visitor.

   This provides expenditures on each category by visitors, broken down into the following categories: business, government, resident and non-resident.

4. Tourism GDP of Tourism Industries and Other Industries.

   Using a tourism industry ratio derived as tourism output divided by industry output, this table provides details of how much GDP is generated by tourism in each industry.

5. Tourism Employment and Compensation of Employees.

   Using the tourism industry ratio, this table derives tourism employment and compensation of employees by industry. The ability to define different categories of tourism expenditure and trace the effects of this expenditure through the economy is an important and substantial step in tourism research. The data provided by such tables are invaluable for economists when modelling tourism.

The data requirements of tourism policy and forecasting models are that input-output tables and tourism demand data are available for a consistent classification of industries and commodities. Therefore, where published input-output tables adequately classify tourism and travel sectors, only the demand data is required from TSAs. Where published input-output tables do not adequately define tourism industries, data from the TSAs on the structure of supply may also be necessary. The U.S. TPF model combines the tourism demand data for 1997 with the published 1997 benchmark input-output table containing data for 494 sectors and 37 categories of final demand, in addition to other sources of data.

We present illustrative results here of an aggregated version of the Tourism Policy and Forecasting Model for the USA. It has 18 sectors and commodities that correspond as closely as possible, given the necessary matching of TSA data, IO data and data from other sources, to the published TSA.

The Effect of a 10% Increase in Foreign Tourist Expenditures

In order to measure the impact of foreign tourism, we simulate a 10% increase in foreign tourist expenditures. This 10% increase is $9.6bn. Economic welfare, as measured by equivalent variation rises by $5.8bn, just under 0.1% of GDP. These comparative illustrate that just over half of the expenditure is captured as an increase in welfare, as markets adjust to reallocate resources, imports increase, and other exports are crowded out.

The impact of this expenditure is captured by GDP, in terms of

(i) Direct expenditure impact,

(ii) Input-output estimates, and

(iii) General equilibrium estimates with the TPF model. While the direct impact of the $9.6bn extra expenditures is $4.5bn and the input-output estimate is $9.4bn, the TPF estimate is $6.0bn. This indicates that:

- A large proportion of the expenditures leads directly to purchases of intermediate inputs, hence the low figure for the direct expenditure impact.
- Almost all of the expenditure leads to increased GDP in the input-output estimate. The IO estimate has no crowding-out, and there is very little import leakage.
- The TPF estimate includes significant levels of crowding-out and resource reallocation.
- Some tourism and travel sectors have significantly higher increases in GDP in the TPF model than the IO model suggests. Here, the initial stimulus of foreign tourism expenditures is reinforced by domestic expenditures as firms benefiting from the initial expenditures increase there own expenditures on business tourism, and

private households which have increases in income spend more on domestic tourism.

- Others tourism and travel sectors, such as water and rail transport, have a lower GDP increase than the IO model suggests. These are sectors that sell products that are relatively small proportions of the foreign tourist's expenditures. Resources are reallocated to other sectors that are able to pay higher wages. These reallocation effects outweigh the induced effects that these sectors experience from higher incomes.
- Non-tourism industries (here, 'all other commodities') have a decline in sector GDP that the IO model completely misses, because it does not include price crowding-out effects and resource allocation. Here, there is no direct stimulus from the foreign tourism expenditures. Indirect (intermediate demands, as captured through the IO model) and induced effects are positive, but are outweighed by resource allocation effects.

Indirect Taxation

The overall effect of indirect taxation exposes the levels of effective protection that the structure of taxation gives to industries, and shows how distortions that indirect taxes introduce lead to economic loses. As such, it is an important indicator as to how economically efficient taxes are in each sector. The results therefore remove arguments about the motives for taxation because the total level of taxation is maintained. The changes to the GDP contribution of labour and capital are given in the first column.

Changes to the GDP contribution of taxation are given in the second column. Changes to the total GDP contribution by sector, and in total, are given in the third column, and in the fourth column as a percentage of the 1997 GDP contribution. Overall, removing all indirect taxes and replacing them with non-distorting direct taxes leads to an improvement to GDP of $528.4bn, which is 2.1% of GDP in 1997. This therefore is the measure of the total distortionary impact of the indirect taxation system.

This improvement to GDP comes about through an increase in the GDP contribution of labour and capital ($1,033.8bn) outweighing the loss in indirect taxation revenue ($-505.4bn). With some exceptions, tourism and travel sectors have a lower GDP increase than the national average of 2.1%. Non-tourism sectors ('all other commodities' is a much larger sector than 'gasoline and oil' or the wholesale sector) have a larger GDP effect than the national average. This implies, since tourism sectors do not expand by the national average when indirect taxation is removed, that the tourism sectors have levels of effective taxation that are higher than the national average. The results of these 17 separate simulations are summarised as the welfare effect of removing the individual taxes.

Taxes in a range of sectors such as auto and truck rental, recreation and entertainment and retail margins, impose distortions on the economy that lead to a higher welfare loss than the tax revenue that they raise. Some sectors, such as water transport, air transport and hotels and lodging places, have much lower distortionary impact when compared to the tax revenue.

There are many reasons why sectors have different distortionary impacts, including:

- The distortionary impact of tax rates are often more than proportional to the tax revenue raised, so that higher tax rates lead to a higher distortion/revenue ratio.
- The distortionary impacts are related to other sectors through intermediate demands, and substitution in final demand. Sectors that have high distortions can effectively pass some of these distortions to related sectors.

- The distortionary impacts are related to how readily supply and demand change in response to price changes, in other words to the elasticities of supply and demand. Sectors with inelastic supply and demand (i.e. low levels of supply and demand response to prices) tend to have lower distortionary impacts from taxation. In a general equilibrium framework, the responsiveness of supply and demand depends on many factors, such as who purchases the product (a product mainly purchased by firms will often have a lower demand elasticity than one purchased by households) and the structure of production (an industry that relies heavily on one type of input will tend to have a lower supply elasticity than other industries).

What-if' scenarios can simulate the effects of anything from productivity growth, changes to competition (anti-trust) legislation and environmental controls. The total general equilibrium effects of such diverse issues can be a complex product of many different changes. Here, we show the results of a productivity improvement in air transport. The $20.6bn increase in GDP that results is spread across industries, with air transport itself increasing in size to account for an extra $2bn in GDP, industries that use air transport such as 'all other commodities' also increasing.

Most sectors that have a reduced GDP contribution are other transport industries, which compete with air transport. The Nottingham Tourism, Policy and Forecasting models apply tourism within a general equilibrium setting. They are an innovative and significant means of combining tourism satellite accounts, input-output tables and economic modelling. They expand on the TSA's measurement of tourism's economic size to provide estimates of tourism's economic impact, including many effects that are not captured in input-output models. TPF models also provide an important tool for policy analysis, enabling the complex interactions in the economy that result from policy actions to be traced through a general equilibrium framework and assessed. The ability to have quantitative estimates of the effects of policy is of vital importance to policy makers.

TPF models can also be used as a basis for forecasting the levels and expenditures of tourists, taking relatively stable and predictable long-term trends in tourism source and destination countries to provide a method of robust long-term forecasting. The results presented here for the USA Tourism, Policy and Forecasting model provide an example of the TPF model's capabilities. The impact of tourism when including induced income effects and resource reallocation effects is dramatically different to the standard input-output results. In particular, the IO models overestimate the total GDP effect, underestimate the total effect on tourism sectors and completely miss the negative effects on non-tourism sectors. The results of the policy analysis using the TPF model are that most tourism sectors are effectively taxed at higher than the national average level.

In sectors such as hotels and transport sectors indirect taxation imposes lower welfare losses on the economy than in other sectors. This implies that the most urgent sectors for tax reductions (i.e. those where welfare distortions are disproportionately high relative to tax revenues) are auto and truck rental, retail, eating and drinking, recreation and entertainment, participant sports, and parking, automotive repair and highway tolls. We also report the results of a 'what-if' scenario that shows the effect of improved productivity in the air transport sector. The results show that increases in GDP are spread across the economy in sectors that use air transport. Competing transport sectors may contract as a result. The USA TPF model is intended to give an indication of the potential applications that TPF modelling has.

While the sector classification for this model is small to match the U.S. TSA as closely as possible, a full 494-sector model is also in operation. For the U.S., the model can be extended in various directions: tourism demand data on domestic tourism by state would enable the TPF model to include state effects. Otherwise, the model can be expanded to include different skill categories of labour and different households groups according to geographical location, income category, or other classification. This would be able to show how these different household groups are affected by both an expansion in tourism and by policies. Other possible ways of expanding this model are to incorporate similar data from other countries: a model of North America would, for example, include Canada and Mexico.

This would incorporate cross-border effects, to assess the effects that a tax on a tourism sector in the U.S. has on the economies of Canada and Mexico. As well as these extensions the U.S. TPF model, it is of course possible to build similar models for any country where a TSA and input-output table exist, and these can also incorporate regional differences, household distributions and different types of labour as well as incorporating more than one country. The underlying methodology of TPF models is well suited to developing countries, for which computable general equilibrium modelling has long been used.

THE IMPORTANCE OF TOURISM

Tourism can also be one of the most effective drivers for the development of regional economies. These patterns apply to both developed and emerging economies. Travel & Tourism is the world's largest industry and creator of jobs across national and regional economies. WTTC/WEFA research show that in 2000, Travel & Tourism will generate, directly and indirectly, 11.7% of GDP and nearly 200 million jobs in the world-wide economy. These figures are forecasted to total 11.7% and 255 million respectively in 2010. Jobs generated by Travel & Tourism are spread across the economy - in retail, construction, manufacturing and telecommunications, as well as directly in Travel & Tourism companies. These jobs employ a large proportion of women, minorities and young people; are predominantly in small and medium sized companies; and offer good training and transferability.

Contributing to sustainable development

The 1992 United Nations Conference on Environment and Development (UNCED), the Rio Earth Summit, identified Travel & Tourism as one of the key sectors of the economy which could make a positive contribution to achieving sustainable development. The Earth Summit lead to the adoption of Agenda 21, a comprehensive programme of action adopted by 182 governments to provide a global blueprint for achieving sustainable development. Travel & Tourism is the first industry sector to have launched an industry-specific action plan based on Agenda 21.

Travel & Tourism is able to contribute to development which is economically, ecologically and socially sustainable, because it:

- Has less impact on natural resources and the environment than most other industries;
- Is based on enjoyment and appreciation of local culture, built heritage, and natural environment, as such that the industry has a direct and powerful motivation to protect these assets;
- Can play a positive part in increasing consumer commitment to sustainable development principles through its unparalleled consumer distribution channels; and
- Provides an economic incentive to conserve natural environments and habitats which might otherwise be allocated to more environmentally damaging land uses, thereby, helping to maintain bio-diversity.

There are numerous good examples of where Travel & Tourism is acting as a catalyst for conservation and improvement of the environment and maintenance of local diversity and culture. (Some of these are set out in Section B of this paper and a fuller illustration of the range of industry action can be found on the World Travel & Tourism Council's. Of course, there are also examples where development has not been sustainable.

Providing Infrastructure

To a greater degree than most activities, Travel & Tourism depends on a wide range of infrastructure services - airports, air navigation, roads, railheads and ports, as well as basic infrastructure services required by hotels, restaurants, shops, and recreation facilities (e.g. telecommunications and utilities).

It is the combination of tourism and good infrastructure that underpins the economic, environmental and social benefits. It is important to balance any decision to develop an area for tourism against the need to preserve fragile or threatened environments and cultures. However, once a decision has been taken where an area is appropriate for new tourism development, or that an existing tourist site should be developed further, then good infrastructure will be essential to sustain the quality, economic viability and growth of Travel & Tourism. Good infrastructure will also be a key factor in the industry's ability to manage visitor flows in ways that do not affect the natural or built heritage, nor counteract against local interests.

Challenge for the Future

Travel & Tourism creates jobs and wealth and has tremendous potential to contribute to economically, environmentally and socially sustainable development in both developed countries and emerging nations. It has a comparative advantage in that its start up and running costs can be low compared to many other forms of industry development. It is also often one of the few realistic options for development in many areas. Therefore, there is a strong likelihood that the Travel & Tourism industry will continue to grow globally over the short to medium term.

Of course, if Travel & Tourism is managed badly, it can have a detrimental effect - it can damage fragile environments and destroy local cultures. The challenge is to manage the future growth of the industry so as to minimise its negative impacts on the environment and host communities whilst maximising the benefits it brings in terms of jobs, wealth and support for local culture and industry, and protection of the built and natural environment.

Industry Initiatives

Travel & Tourism takes many different forms - from a trip only a few hours away from home to long distance travel overseas. A common belief is that most Travel & Tourism involves large numbers of visitors from developed countries travelling by air to destinations in emerging countries. In fact, in most countries, the domestic tourism market is larger than the inbound market. Of course, the social and cultural impact of inbound visitors is often greater than that of domestic tourists. Whether tourism is domestic or international, it involves visiting a destination away from the area in which one lives and using the services available in that destination. Therefore, tourists' requirements are for travel services to reach their destinations and once there, for services such as shelter, water, food, sanitation and entertainment.

What makes tourism special is that, many of these different products and services are often supplied by different operators: usually small or medium sized businesses in local ownership. This makes tourism a highly fragmented and diverse industry and so co-ordinated, industry-wide action is difficult to achieve. The influence of Travel & Tourism's demand also extends far beyond traditional tourism companies, into upstream suppliers like aircraft manufacturers or food producers and into the downstream service providers for travellers, like retail shops.

Despite the difficulties caused by fragmentation and lengthy supply chains, there has been a steady growth in environmental good practice across the industry in recent years. There are examples of airlines and airports reducing pollution and noise impacts; cruise liners practising marine conservation; hotels implementing energy consumption and waste disposal programmes; car rental companies investing in increasingly fuel efficient fleets and railways sound proofing to dampen noise. The result is that there are a number of excellent initiatives in place designed to improve the environmental management of Travel & Tourism businesses. Of course, more needs to be done.

WTTC with 105 members is the global business leaders' forum for the Travel & Tourism industry. The WTTC have set in place an extensive strategy to promote a culture of sustainable development and have put in place a three-tiered structure for its achievement. This involves:

In 1996 the WTTC, the World Tourism Organization and the Earth Council, joined together to launch an action plan entitled "Agenda 21 for the Travel & Tourism Industry: Towards Environmentally Sustainable Development" - a sectional sustainable development programme based on the results of the Rio Earth Summit in 1992. Since the launch of the document, the three organisations have begun a series of regional seminars to increase awareness of the conclusions, and to adapt the programme for local implementation. The programme has held regional seminars in London and Jakarta in 1997 and Victoria Falls and Dominica in 1998.

WTTC has recently introduced a major addition to the programme - the "Alliance for Sustainable Tourism", which invites public and private sector Travel & Tourism organisations to record their Agenda 21 based activities on a central web site and commit to co-operation with all other partners. In order to develop the programme from global principles to community based action, WTTC is also discussing with the International Council for Local Environment Initiatives (ICLEI) on how the principles of "Agenda 21 for Travel & Tourism" can be built into Local Agenda 21 programmes. Furthermore, WTTC is considering pilot projects in 5 cities around the world to serve as models for other destinations.

In 1994, WTTC initiated the "GREEN GLOBE", an Agenda 21 based industry improvement programme, which provides guidance material and a certification process linked to both ISO standards and Agenda 21 principles. There are now 500 "GREEN GLOBE "members in 100 countries dedicated to improving environmental practice. The first certification has commenced with hotels groups in Jamaica and Manchester (UK). "GREEN GLOBE" has also developed a specific Destination Programme, which provides a methodology for Travel & Tourism destinations to implement sustainable development.

The ultimate aim is that "GREEN GLOBE" will become the primary global standard of environmental commitment by the global Travel & Tourism industry and will be recognised by the public as such. Currently, "GREEN GLOBE" has the support of over 20 international industry organisations representing thousands of businesses world-wide and the support of the World Tourism Organization, the United Nations Environment Programme and the Earth Council.

WTTC have also developed "ECoNETT", a web-site containing advice and data on good practice and sources of help and advice. "ECoNETT" is increasingly recognised as a focal point for environmental information, good practice, new techniques and technologies. The International Hotel & Restaurant Association (IH&RA), based in Paris, represents over 700,000 establishments in more than 150 countries. Its membership comprises some 50 national and international hotel and restaurant chains, over 110 national hotel and restaurant associations, independent hotel operators and restaurateurs, industry suppliers and 130 hotel schools. The IH&RA has offices in Asia-Pacific and Latin America. It is also the voice of the world's hotels and restaurants and plays a global role in representing, protecting, promoting and informing the industry to enable its members to achieve their business objectives.

The IH&RA has:

- Raised environmental awareness and developed programmes through joint workshops with national hotel associations and regularly encourages them to develop their own environmental awareness programmes;
- Established an annual Environmental Award sponsored by American Express and judged by the

United Nations Environment Programme (UNEP) that recognises efforts by independent and chain hotels to "green" the industry;

- Published advice including practical publications such as the "Environmental Action Pack for Hotels" with the International Hotel Environment Initiative and UNEP and "Environmental Good Practice in Hotels" with UNEP;
- Supported regional initiatives such as the Caribbean Action for Sustainable Tourism; and
- Joined forces with UNEP and the International Hotel School Directors' Association to develop an "Environmental Teaching Resource Package for Hospitality Educational Institutes".

Corporate Initiatives

The International Hotel Environment Initiative (IHEI), based in London, England, is a programme of The Prince of Wales Business Leaders Forum. Founded in 1992 by a consortium of chief executives from 10 multinational hotel groups, IHEI is an educational charity designed to encourage continuous improvement in the environmental performance of the global hotel industry. It does this through:

- Raising environmental awareness in the hotel industry by promoting good practiceinternationally;
- Developing hotel-specific guidance, enabling hotels of all sizes to implement environmentalprogrammes; and
- Multiplying the reach and impact of IHEI by working with partners, including hotelassociations, governments, NGOs, tourism bodies and businesses.

IHEI is a catalyst and conduit for hotels to pool their resources and to share experience via a non- competitive platform. In 5 years it has evolved into an organisation with global impact. IHEI has worked in 111 countries, stimulating and assisting with the establishment of local initiatives such as New Zealand's "Environmental Hotels of Auckland, the

Asia Pacific Hotel Environment Initiative" and the Caribbean Action for Sustainable Tourism.

Member hotels now represent over 1 million guest rooms and more than 8,000 hotels on 5 continents. The Co-operative Research Centre for Sustainable Tourism, based in Australia, was established in 1997 to enhance the strategic knowledge available to the Travel & Tourism industry through:

- Long-term high-quality scientific and technological research which contributes to the development of an internationally competitive tourism industry;
- Strengthening the links between research and its commercial and other applications;
- Promoting co-operative research; and
- Stimulating education and training, particularly in graduate programmes, through active involvement of researchers from outside the higher education system in educational activities, and of graduate students in major research programmes.

Company initiatives

The number of initiatives undertaken by individual companies is large. Just two examples from this are as follows:

The Kandalama hotel in Sri Lanka has been a recipient of the "GREEN GLOBE" award, 3 years in a row, for its commitment to environmental excellence. The hotel has undertaken measures in the following areas to ensure that its operations are more sustainable:

- Cultural and social - hotel employment, providing community infrastructure and development;
- Natural environment - soil erosion measures and planting forests;
- Pollution - sewage, solid waste and noise pollution reduction programmes; and
- Environmental communication - construction of an Eco Park where all waste is treated within the park, a

dry debris sorting centre, a lecture room to promote environmental awareness and a sustainable development library.

Canadian Pacific Hotels, the largest hotel conglomerate in Canada, has developed an environmental programme which is recognised as the most comprehensive in the North American hotel industry. Based on the results of a survey, employee suggestions and the recommendations of a professional environmental consultant, Canadian Pacific Hotels developed a list of 16 goals to be attained by all hotels. In addition to individual projects implemented at each of the 26 hotels, the goals set for the chain as a whole were ambitious:

(I) To reduce the amount of waste sent to landfill by 50% across the chain, by launching an extensive recycling programme;

(ii) To redesign purchasing policies to ensure that waste is reduced at source, and supplies used in the hotels are nature friendly.

Inter-regional Level

The Caribbean Action for Sustainable Tourism (CAST) is an alliance for sustainable growth developed by the Caribbean Hoteliers Association with the support of the WTTC, the IHEI and the Caribbean Tourism Organisation. CAST has developed workshops, training courses and guidance material for its members on a wide range of environmental issues, including:

- Setting up environmental management systems;
- Energy efficiency;
- Renewable energy; and
- Waste water management.

Agents and Partnerships for Change

The public sectors, particularly national and local government, have an important role to play by setting the agenda and providing the framework in which action should take place. The regulatory environment also plays an important role in creating the conditions suitable for sustainable tourism. Self-regulation involving the agreement and co-operation of industry is always likely to be the most effective solution. Therefore, the role of trade associations and industry organisations in distributing information among their members and encouraging participation is essential.

The major partnerships to be formed are between:

- Industry and the public sector - to ensure consistency with the framework;
- Industry and the voluntary sector - to tap into the enormous resources of expertise and goodwill that this sector is able to generate; and
- Industry and the public - both travellers themselves and the people who live in the places they visit to develop more sustainable forms of tourism.

Areas for further Action

The industry is already doing much to improve its performance in terms of sustainable development. The challenge for the new millennium is to move from the existing ad hoc approach to a more systematic one. To do this will involve a partnership between industry and national governments to deliver the following:

(i) Governments:

- Integration of travel and tourism policy into broader government policies, especially the environment;
- Incentives for the Travel & Tourism industry, backed up where necessary by effective regulation.

(ii) Public/Private partnership:

- Infrastructure planned and developed with a long-term view and within a reference framework based on Agenda 21;
- Indicators and environmental impact assessment tools to enable effective local management and appropriate development.

(iii) International bodies:

- Co-ordination at an international level of environmental action undertaken by all sectors of the Travel & Tourism industry;
- Review of existing voluntary initiatives to improve the quality of reporting, their transparency and credibility, and the assessment of their contribution to sustainability.

(iv) Companies:

- Commitment to place sustainable development issues at the core of the management structure;
- Innovation of process and application through new technology;
- Commitment to education and environmental training of staff.

Influencing Consumer Behaviour to Promote Sustainable Tourism

Problems

At the 1998 World Travel Market, WTTC hosted, as a part of its Environmental Awareness Day, a seminar entitled "Does the Consumer Care?" At this event, MORI presented the latest findings from their Business and the Environment survey - an annual UK survey devoted to public attitudes to the environment. The survey is now in its tenth year and illustrates the challenge facing the Travel & Tourism industry in influencing consumer behaviour to promote sustainable tourism. According to this survey, Travel & Tourism is now more associated with environmental damage than it has been in the past.

Despite this decline in perception, the industry's economic success is not dependent on its green record - public sensitivity to environmental problems on holiday/business trips has not increased and is no more of a deterrent to repeat travel than it was previously. There is a downward trend in the public's willingness to pay extra for environmental protection and environmentally friendly products, including "green" Travel

& Tourism. Awareness of companies making environmental commitments is only marginally up.

Therefore, the challenge is to persuade the consumer that it is in their interests to adopt and promote a sustainable approach in their activities and purchasing decisions. Education programmes and the development and widespread acceptance of codes of conduct are useful tools in achieving this step. Once this message has been conveyed, it is then important to back this up with the necessary information to enable consumers to make informed choices. It is here that "ecolabels" and award programmes have value.

Education Programmes

The Foundation for Environmental Education in Europe (FEEE) seeks to promote environmental education by carrying out campaigns and improving awareness of the importance of environmental education. It is composed of a network of international organisations. The FEEE (headquarters in Denmark) runs three major campaigns in Europe for providing safe and clean beaches and marinas. The award itself is given annually to beaches and marinas that satisfy a number of essential criteria in three separate areas: water quality; beach management and safety; and environmental information and education.

"GREEN GLOBE"'s Dodo Campaign, is based on a cartoon character, who features in 65 Travel & Tourism videos. Dodo explains and promotes the actions that visitors can take to reduce the impacts of their travels. The videos are aimed at children and are designed to be fun, whilst conveying important messages about sustainable Travel & Tourism. The aim is to have these videos shown on in flight and in-room television channels to raise awareness and influence consumer behaviour.

Codes of conduct

Codes of conduct are also used to try and influence consumer behaviour. For example, "Guidelines for Responsible Environmental Tourism" are prepared and distributed by the American Society of Travel Agents to all customers who book holidays through their members' branches. The Guidelines aim to "encourage the growth of peaceful tourism and environmentally responsible travel" and include 10 recommendations to encourage tourists to act responsibly and show respect for their hosts and the environment of their destinations.

The Pacific Asia Tourism Association (PATA) is an industrial association, which promotes the Pacific Asia area's Travel & Tourism destinations, products and services. PATA also serves as a central resource of information and research, travel industry education and training, as well as quality product development with sensitivity for culture, heritage and environment. In 1992, PATA introduced its "Code for Environmentally Responsible Tourism" to strengthen the principles of preservation in the region.

Businesses, organisations and individuals wishing to affirm their support for the PATA Code are encouraged to participate in the PATA Green Leaf programme. The Africa Travel Association has produced "Responsible Traveller Guidelines"; the Japanese Association of Travel Agents has produced the "Declaration of Earth Friendly Travellers" and there are many more examples of industry codes aimed at educating and influencing their customers.

Eco Labelling

There are numerous examples of industry sponsored labelling schemes, whose aim is to recognise good industry practice and influence consumer behaviour into purchasing the labelled products. For example, the "Green Key, Denmark" certificate operated by the Hotel, Restaurant and Leisure Industry Association (HORESTA) has 56 criteria that includes environmental information, water & energy consumption and waste management. Special features also include ecological food products, outdoor areas, non-smoking rooms, and adaptations for access by disabled persons. There are a number of industries that runs and sponsors award programmes to highlight and promote examples of good practice.

For example, British Airways has run the "Tourism for Tomorrow" awards since 1992 to encourage action to protect the environment. The awards are directed at tour operators, hotels, national parks and heritage sites, and other activities associated with tourism. By selecting projects showing best practice in their field as role models, others are encouraged to follow suit and consider the environment in the everyday running of their tourism business. The awards are run annually, with a winner selected from each of five regions and an overall winner. In addition, two special awards are made for mass tourism destinations. The awards are run in association with the British Tourist Authority, the Association of British Travel Agents, the Pacific Asia Travel Association and the American Society of Travel Agents. Entries to the awards have been increases every year. American Express also sponsors a variety of environmental awards for international tourism organisations.

Agents and Partnerships for Change

- A broad based approach is called for which requires Travel & Tourism to work with: national governments to raise the profile of environmental and social issues within the education system;
- NGOs to raise awareness of tourism issues in their work and activities and provide feedback to the Travel & Tourism industry;
- Development organisations to communicate with host communities to understand their needs and requirements;
- Local authorities to engage local people through the inclusion of tourism issues in Local Agenda21 plans;
- National and international trade associations, labour representative organisations and training providers to increase awareness and training of staff in environmental and social issues;
- Travel & Tourism publications (such as travel guides);

- Travel & Tourism journalists to raise the profile of reporting environmental and social impacts of tourism among consumers and tourism businesses; and
- The Internet as a source of information for potential travellers.

Areas for further Action

The WTTC/MORI data shows the scale of the task still remaining. The industry has developed a number of initiatives to influence consumer behaviour. However, if consumers do not understand or are not aware of the issues involved and do not demand more sustainable products then, in the long term, it will not be in the industry's interests to move in that direction. The priority for future action, therefore, should be to raise awareness among travellers of the issues associated with tourism and the impact their activities can have on local destinations and cultures.

Broad-based Sustainable Development through Tourism

The Travel & Tourism industry has a vested interest in protecting the natural and cultural resources that are the core of its business. Travel & Tourism has less impacts on natural resources and the environment than other sectors and it has already done much to address the issues arising from its activities.

There are examples, however, from around the world where the impact of Travel & Tourism has been damaging to the local environment and people. Some of the factors which contributes to the harmful impact of tourism are:

- A lack of awareness on the part of those making decisions about tourism development of the social, economic and environmental balance to be pursued in achieving sustainable development;
- A lack of commitment by tourism operators and travellers to contribute to the maintenance of the local environment and culture of the host destination;

- A weak institutional framework with inadequate controls can lead to tourism development which is both inappropriate and intrusive;
- Unfairly traded tourism, whereby local communities are unable to share in its benefits;
- Large flows of visitors in remote or sensitive locations can place considerable strains on local resources (particularly water) and supply systems. Travellers' expectations of the goods and services, which should be available, can lead to these items or services, being imported from outside or local supply chains, being distorted to meet demands; and
- Tourism can change a destination's cultural make-up and, if poorly developed, can increase crime, prostitution and other social problems.

In order for tourism to realise its potential to achieve broad-based sustainable development, an effective partnership between Government and all sectors of the industry will be required. The following illustrates what is being done:

International Co-operation

IH&RA and the United Nations Organisation for Education, Science and Culture (UNESCO) have signed a co-operation agreement to encourage world-wide hotel chains to sponsor UNESCO cultural heritage sites and attract tourism to them via their marketing campaigns.

National Governments

In India, the government is pump priming local "eco-tourism" activities, which are primarily driven by local women. In Mexico, the government is kick starting village development for "eco-tourism" lodges in the Chiapas region involving the whole community. In England, the government has recently held a national consultation on sustainable tourism and, as a result, is developing a new strategy for tourism, which incorporates the principles of sustainable development as a core component. The Caribbean Tourism

Organisation has developed a comprehensive strategy to develop "eco-tourism" in the Caribbean region. This strategy is closely integrated with the goals of the Association for Caribbean States (ACE) for a green Caribbean.

"GREEN GLOBE" has developed a specific "Destinations" programme to recognise those tourist destinations where there is a concerted effort by all those involved in the local tourism industry to improve the quality of the environment. The Destinations process provides a framework to guide tourist locations towards achieving sustainable development based on the principles of Agenda 21. The Destinations programmes are tailor made to reflect local circumstances, such as the level of environmental awareness, action taken to date and available resources. Each programme is based on achieving progressive environmental improvements.

Targets are set within a realistic timetable and are developed by a steering group made up of key partners. The island of Jersey has become the first "GREEN GLOBE" Destination. Vilamoura in Portugal, Dominica in the Caribbean and 3 destinations in the Philippines have also entered the Destination programme.

For example, in 1996 Luso tour SA, a tourism development company, enacted a management plan for Vilamoura whereby employees are given responsibility for individual environmental tasks. The company has invested money into rehabilitating the surrounding natural environment, which includes pine forests and a lake that has significance to local wetland areas. Guests are provided with a copy of the environmental policy and are encouraged to participate in the scheme through specialised brochures.

The campaign includes recycling; treating diseased pine areas; regular cleaning of the beaches and marinas; development of a sewage treatment plant and new buildings in the resort are designed to minimise visual and environmental impacts. For its work in Vilamoura, Lusotour SA is also a winner of the British Airways Tourism for Tomorrow Awards.

The "Africa tourism" brand has been developed by the Open Africa Foundation to encourage products, which embraces sustainable ecological, economic and social development based on Africa's unique cultural, natural and wildlife heritage. "Open Africa" is also developing a continuous network of "Africa tourism" routes from the Cape to Cairo, known as the "African Dream". The Dream helps to create awareness of the many rural and environmental projects, which exist throughout Africa. "Team Africa", a transcontinental alliance of governments, corporations, institutions, professionals and individuals, provides leadership and motivation in the development of the "African Dream".

Host Communities

"Whale Watch Kaikoura" is an initiative of local Maori people from a small town on the East Coast of New Zealand's South Island. Within a kilometre of the Kaikoura shore is an area ideal for whales, where visitors are guaranteed to see them all year round. The Whale Watch began 11 years ago and is now a booming tourist destination, run by indigenous people with a strong sense of heritage and a view of the future based on strong principles of sustainability.

Jordan Tourism Investments, has revitalised the traditional village of Taybeh, in Jordan, into a cultural tourist resort, with the help and agreement of villagers. With many of the younger generation moving to the cities, the village was losing its character. By restoring its 19th century buildings and reviving old crafts, the village is now thriving again. The village lies 9km south east of the historic city of Petra. Opened in July 1994, the village now accommodates around 60,000 guests each year.

Uluru and Kakadu National Parks are both owned by indigenous Australians, the local Aboriginal communities, and jointly run with the National Parks and Wildlife Service. They are both major tourism destinations and involve indigenous participation in planning, management, and ownership of tourism infrastructure, as well as interpretation for visitors.

They bring significant economic, social and cultural benefits to the local indigenous communities. The Conservation Corporation in Africa has established a series of high quality game parks in which local communities are major stakeholders and beneficiaries of tourism. This initiative is also helping to re-invigorate local crafts.

Agents and Partnerships

The challenge facing the tourism industry in moving towards a more sustainable future is set out in "Agenda 21 for the Travel & Tourism Industry". To achieve the goals set out in this document will require a partnership between government departments, national tourism authorities, international and national trade organisations and Travel & Tourism companies. Working together in close co-operation such partnerships should aim to deliver the following:

- Close co-operation between the public and private sectors to deliver a regulatory regime, which encourages voluntary action but supplement, where necessary, with regulation in areas such as land-use and waste management.
- Agreed common standards and tools to enable the measurement of progress towards achieving sustainable development.
- Certification criteria developed and more widely applied to industry initiatives.
- A commitment to the controlled expansion, where appropriate, of infrastructure.
- Environmental taxes, where applied, should be fair and non-discriminatory. They should be carefully thought out to minimise their impact on economic development, and revenues should be allocated to Travel & Tourism associated environment improvement programmes.
- International, national and local funding bodies should include sustainable development as apart of

their criteria, so that in time, all funding would be dependent on sound environmental practice.

- Contemporary research into sustainable tourism needs to be funded and developed. Issues requiring attention include design, carrying capacity, tour operator activities, environmental reporting, auditing and environmental impact assessments.
- Environmental education and training should be increased, particularly in schools, for future hotel and tourism staff.
- Greater investment and commitment to the use of new technology.

COASTAL IMPACT OF TOURISM

Tourism provides an essential lifeline for many coastal communities. Faced with the prospect of increasing financial hardship, more and more coastal communities have turned to tourism as a means of generating income and survival. Tourism's impact on the coastal zone has, therefore, been largely positive. Of course, as in any area, if Tourism is not properly managed and developed, it can be harmful.

Impacts arise from the construction of infrastructure (hotels, marinas, transport, waste treatment facilities, groynes etc.) and from recreation (golf courses, water sports, theme parks etc). Coastal communities are now faced with tourism on a considerable scale, and the host to guest ratio can be very high in such areas. At the same time, coastal communities must try to maintain the resort's attraction as tourist demands change, sometimes quite rapidly.

With coastal regions being primary tourist destinations, sensitive marine and coastal environments can suffer dramatically. For example, as a result of large-scale sea-front tourist development, considerable beach and dune erosion can occur.

Tourism also impacts on environmental quality in the following ways:

- Ribbon development, infrastructure requirements, particularly transport links;
- The treatment and disposal of solid and/or liquid wastes, particularly during peak tourist seasons, may be inadequate or at worst non-existent; and
- Water is often consumed excessively, not only for drinking but for showers, laundry, swimming pools, maintenance of golf courses etc. This can affect the quantity and quality of fresh water available to indigenous coastal populations.

Recreational activities can also have a significant impact on the coastal zone:

- Golf course's impact can be considerable, with those situated directly on coastal habitats(especially sand dunes) in particular;
- Erosion of reefs and coral from divers and swimmers;
- Pollution from boats and jets skis; and
- Noise from motor boats and jet skis, cars and buses, nightlife and other activities.

The development of a sustainable tourism industry in the coastal zone offers numerous opportunities. Opportunities includes, those for nature conservation - which, given the increasing interest in high quality natural and cultural experiences, can help to reverse the decline in market share of many coastal destinations. Tourism also provides important opportunities for strengthening local industries. Where industries are in decline, tourism ventures can help supplement declining income.

The following examples illustrate what can be done to make the most of the opportunities offered by tourism in the coastal zone:

Calvia is a Municipality on the Mediterranean coast that has undertaken an Agenda 21 project to assist the sustainable development of its tourism sector, in order to counter the negative impact of short-term tourism development since the

1960s. The local council has now implemented a transferable policy aimed at modernising, improving and diversifying the local tourist industry, involving all stakeholders, including the local population.

A Project Plan was enacted, and achievements so far include:

- Indigenous development, based on the sustainable use of available resources;
- High quality services and an appropriate bed night capacity;
- A ban on new development on 1,700 acres;
- Active participation of the residents in community life; and
- Environmental management of municipality buildings, waste recycling, reduction in spending on electricity, and use of environmentally friendly materials for office use.

Quicksilver Tours, Queensland, Australia, is owned by one of the largest tourism operators to the Great Barrier Reef. Quicksilver have five large catamarans, which take about 1,000 tourists a day to dive on the reef. They have their own reef site with fixed diving platforms. They employ a team of biologists, both for environmental management and assessment as well as widespread environmental interpretation. Recent assessment of the reef, in the vicinity of the operation, shows that it is being maintained in pristine condition.

Kingfisher Bay Resort is found at Fraser Island, Queensland. It is a large five star "ecotourism" resort built in a beautiful, but fragile environment off the Queensland coast. Its concept, design, construction and management were conceived using the latest ecologically sustainable principles. It is a state-of-the-art "ecotourism" resort, which has won Australia's top tourism awards, and its economic and environmental success has influenced new coastal tourism developments.

Maho Bay's camps and studios in the US Virgin Islands have based their product on a commitment to minimise impact on the environment, conserve natural resources, engage in active and passive environmental education of their guests, and contribute to the local economy. Specific initiatives introduced at Maho Bay include the following: use of new technology; purchasing policies; waste management; environmental education; energy and water conservation; and support for local communities and culture.

These initiatives show an appreciation of the need for alternative solutions to issues such as packaging and waste disposal through landfill. These are issues, which as the industry grows, will be increasingly important for the Travel & Tourism industry as a whole to address.

The agents, partnerships for change and areas for further action in relation to tourism in the coastal zone are similar to the development of broad based sustainable tourism in general. A number of issues do, of course, have particular importance for the coastal zone. Above all, the key to success is better participation at destination level among all the stakeholders concerned. In the case of the coastal zone, there are a number of additional organisations with an interest in coastal policy, marine conservation, shipping etc., which needs to be identified and included in partnerships for the coastal zone.

Successful planning for tourism is very important for the future of the industry in coastal regions, because a significant percentage of tourism occurs within the geographical parameters of the definition of a coastal zone. Concerted support from all countries involved (and the industries within them) is vital to protect the shared natural resources that coastal zones represent.

Historically, the influence most hoteliers have on the environmental impact of their business is limited to working within existing buildings, or after a new site has been completed. In April 1998, the IHEI convened a group of hoteliers, tour operators, architectural firms and sustainable development specialists with the goal of creating a partnership to be called the "Sitting and Design Programme". The new initiative's mission will be to define responsible planning and design specifications that will cause minimal environmental damage at new sites. Particular attention will be paid to sites located within ecologically sensitive areas and upon waterfronts.

The "Siting and Design Programme" will strive to reach hotel owners, investors and developers to bring these issues to the attention of the entire industry. Linkages with government authorities that uphold responsible development standards would complete the partnership.

Travel & Tourism has a number of advantages over other industry sectors:

- It creates jobs and wealth whilst;
- At the same time, it can contribute to sustainable development;
- It tends to have low start-up costs;
- Is a viable option in a wide range of areas and regions;
- Is likely to continue to grow for the foreseeable future; and
- The industry is, in a large part, aware of the need to protect the resource on which it is based - local culture and built and natural environment - and it is committed to these resources' preservation and enhancement.

The industry is, therefore, making a concerted effort to build up programmes for sustainable development. However, it cannot do this alone. If Travel & Tourism is to continue to flourish and to contribute to sustainable development, it needs help from national Governments. This assistance is needed in two forms: - both positive encouragement for sustainable tourism initiatives and an understanding that policy decisions in other areas can effect Travel & Tourism. In practical terms, what this means is the following:

The first point of action needed from Governments is to incorporate Agenda 21 principles into tourism policies at international and national level, and to promote their inclusion in regional and local tourism strategies. By providing such a lead and establishing a coherent global framework based on Agenda 21, national governments will make a vital contribution to developing a more sustainable tourism industry.

Governments should also recognise that Travel & Tourism is a core service sector which should always be considered when looking at policies to expand trade, increase employment, modernise infrastructure and encourage investment - at both domestic and international level. It should also be included in national statistics with its economic impact calculated by means of a national tourism satellite account.

Governments should also consider helping Travel & Tourism by seeking to minimise regulatory impediments and by offering appropriate investment incentives. By supporting tourism and allowing it to compete in open and fair markets, tourism's benefits can be more easily secured. Finally, governments can address some of the fundamental barriers to tourism growth by looking at how to expand and modernise infrastructure, to apply taxes fairly and to invest in human resource development. If the programme of action outlined above can be undertaken by national governments in co-operation with continued industry commitments and initiatives for sustainable tourism then we can look to a brighter future.

Index

Y

Z